"A superb book that stands out from books with comparable concepts. This is a book that is veteran focused, superbly organized, and void of any covert or overt agendas. These qualities combine to offer a volume that will be eye-opening to those not particularly familiar with the wars of Iraq and Afghanistan and the veterans who served in them. Eide and Gibler have crafted a book that will unquestionably benefit and educate the general public."
—Rick Baillergeon, *Military Review*

"Marian Eide and Michael Gibler seek to construct one big narrative from interviews with thirty veterans about their experiences [in Iraq and Afghanistan]. Does this approach work? Yes, and far better than I expected. I finished this book wishing that there were companion volumes for the American Revolution and the Civil War."
—Thomas E. Ricks, *New York Times Book Review*

"The greatest value of *After Combat* is in the authors' achievement of their aims: to create a book that bridges the gap between what Hollywood and the media has presented to the public about the realities of war and the actual realities of war and combat. Without the filters of professional writers and reporters creating a narrative they can use to promote a product, including the product of war, Eide and Gibler have given the veterans' ownership of their stories to create their book. . . . *After Combat* should be read by anyone who wants to gain a greater understanding of what life in and after combat is really like."
—Sarah E. Minnis, *Journal of Veterans Studies*

"*After Combat* paints a picture of the messy aspects of war and their aftermath on veterans, their families, their friends, and their personal and professional lives. There are no ordinary stories of the men and women who are deployed to fight our nation's wars. America is fortunate to have those who volunteer to wear the cloth of our country. A must-read if you care about America and its military men and women."

—Lt. Gen. Frank Helmick, U.S Army (Ret.)

"In *After Combat* Marian Eide and Michael Gibler capture the true essence of our generation's defenders of freedom. From the warrior perspective *After Combat* highlights the emotion, the sacrifice, the anguish, and, most important, the heart of what it means to serve in combat. Once again we witness the selfless sacrifice of our nation's greatest treasure: her sons and daughters, as they tell their stories of their time in the 'crucible of fire.' Where do we find men and women of such courage, patriotism, and selflessness?"

—Lt. Gen. Frank Wiercinski, U.S Army (Ret.)

AFTER COMBAT

After Combat

True War Stories from Iraq and Afghanistan

MARIAN EIDE & MICHAEL GIBLER

Potomac Books
An imprint of the University of Nebraska Press

To those who served
and
for Tor and Dorothy

CONTENTS

ACKNOWLEDGMENTS

OUR THANKS TO THE Glasscock Center for Humanities Research at Texas A&M University for the support that allowed us to launch this initiative. Over the course of several years we were fortunate to work with a group of talented research assistants, including our project coordinator, Matthew Bizzell, as well as Charles Alexander Blanks, Jacob Cotton, Catherine Crozier, Neddie-Anne French, Clayton Hensley, Marissa Madsen, Olivia Oliver, Stephen O'Shea, Laura Reid, and Peyton Richie.

View from a helicopter on Alexander the Great's castle in Qalat,
Afghanistan. Photo by David Eisler.

INTRODUCTION

APPROXIMATELY 2.5 MILLION MEN and women have deployed to Iraq and Afghanistan. Yet because the military is an all-volunteer organization, it is also a relatively isolated sector of the U.S. population. As a result, comparatively few Americans have direct connections to military veterans or to the daily conduct of the wars in those countries. Veterans may decline to discuss their experiences of deployment for years following the events. Others wish only to talk among themselves, suspicious of civilian agendas or ignorance. A few will never talk about deployment, though they might think of it often.

Most Americans have access to combat experience through various news media. However, it isn't *news* if it isn't unprecedented, extreme, unusual, or pivotal, so even responsible journalism can be or seem to be sensational. For veterans returning from nine, twelve, or even fifteen months of ordinary days in Fallujah or Kandahar, such media representations can be alienating or dispiriting.

In this book, we introduce readers to contemporary war from the perspective of combatants. For four years we interviewed men and women deployed to Iraq and Afghanistan, as well as other locations in the global "war on terror" such as Yemen, the Philippines, and the Horn of Africa. We met veterans who served during the first invasions and others who closed down bases or transitioned operations with local armies. Their stories are compiled here in their own words and with minimal intervention or framing by the authors. Our aim is to narrate what Vietnam veteran and writer Tim O'Brien calls a "true war story," one without obvious purpose or moral imputation and independent of civilian logic, military goals, ideological propaganda, and even peacetime convention.

But what do we mean by "ordinary" as opposed to "sensational"? Most deployments do not meet the expectation of war experience laid down by stories from Appomattox, Ypres, Iwo Jima, or even Khe Sanh. Stuck behind a desk or the wheel of a truck, veterans feel they haven't been to war, though they have listened to mortars in the night or driven around improvised explosive devices in the day. When a drone is needed to verify a target's death, when bullets are sprayed like grass seed, even war offensives lack immediate combat authenticity. As hard as it is to remember the ordinary, it was our project to memorialize it so as to recognize the lives of the men and women who deployed to war.

Every day during a deployment is lived in anticipation of that "golden moment"—to quote one participant—of the return home. As good as home is, it's not exactly the same as the place from which the veteran departed; you do not step into the same river twice. Children have grown, spouses have changed jobs, sweethearts have been unfaithful, parents have aged. The sense of purpose and urgency that deployment impressed is lost to the muddle of civilian life, amorphous new projects, or the return to ordinary jobs and careers.

As much as veterans are changed by war, it is not always in the ways they may have expected. Post-combat stress may inspire nightmares or anxious crowd navigation, but no veteran wants to be treated like a "ticking time bomb," a label by which one former airman was described. An amputation might seem tragic to a witness but a "blessing" to the amputee, as a returning soldier testified.

Veterans can join together in the comfort of familiarity to swap stories and reminisce. But even in those closed circles there is some suspicion; even then the "decoy story"—to borrow veteran and writer Phil Klay's term—can be replayed to distract attention from more pointed attempts to glean information or elicit profound emotions. How are veterans themselves to know what their comrades experienced or how they privately remember a deployment?

This project aims to bridge such gaps by telling war's unvarnished stories. Participating soldiers, sailors, marines, and airmen (released, retired, on leave, or at the beginning of military careers) here describe combat in the way they believe it should be understood. They also recount memories, experiences, and views that they do not otherwise voice. In their interviews, which lasted from forty-five minutes to two hours, they spoke honestly with pride in their own strengths and accomplishments; with gratitude for friendships and adventures; but also with shame, regret, and grief; they faced controversy, misunderstanding, and sanction. In these open conversations, they describe thoughts they didn't realize they were harboring, remember comrades faded from recollection, and recall arduous routines since forgotten.

Participants

Beginning with acquaintances and colleagues, we conducted open-ended interviews, collecting memories and stories of deployment and return home, but we found many veterans were reluctant to reminisce. They felt their experiences were not sufficiently important or representative, that their memories might be too negative or too ordinary; they didn't particularly want to be material for a book, their words collected and printed for a reader's consumption. Those who did commit their time and memories to the project often did so with a sense of a larger purpose: to speak for and to the disabled, to advocate for improved training or leadership, to reach out to other veterans. Although we were warned about exaggerated war stories and hidden agendas, we did not ever get the sense that we were hearing lies. Of course, memory is malleable and details might get muddled, but the larger truths remained intact as the minutiae of life in a war zone rose to the surface of recollection in the course of conversations.

Not long into the process we began to see the uniqueness and import of anonymity. We found in the middle of several early recordings that an individual would come to a detail or even a revelation and decide that the comments to come should probably not be attributed. There are things veterans do not want to talk about with family or friends, decisions that don't translate well from the theater of war to the home front, events haunted by a feeling of failure. Additionally, we wondered if the young men or women sharing their experiences would be haunted by a particular story in their later years. Certainly many of these stories have been told by a veteran before or shared among comrades, but many would not be told without the promise of anonymity. With the guarantee of anonymity, veterans could speak difficult truths that couldn't be communicated to family members or friends. As a result of our investment in anonymity, the design of the project changed. Rather than focusing on individuals, we are creating a collective sense of narration. For that reason, as you read the chapters, you will find breaks between stories; each break introduces the voice of a new veteran. None are labeled by speaker.

We conducted the interviews in person in offices, hotel rooms, and family homes; we traveled to meet several veterans and talked to others via phone, Skype, and FaceTime. We made an effort to preserve the sense of voice from the recordings onto the page, to maintain the oral profile and character of each participant because we were struck by the individuality of these voices—not just in their aural qualities of timbre or resonance, but also in the oral patterns that make an individual's speech unique and in the associations and ideas that emerge from conversing with an interested interlocutor.

We were surprised by how many men and women told us that no one had sat with them for just an hour to talk about their experience of war. As a nation we thank veterans for their service, but as individuals, it seems, we do not know quite how to give a returning soldier our time and interest. What is the etiquette required to listen to stories of deployment? Do we even have the right to ask, "How was your war?"

"Ordinary deployment" may seem a contradiction in terms; deploying to a war zone is by definition extraordinary. Even something so routine and familiar as deplaning can be extraordinary if it is to the sound of mortar fire, a sound that most of us will never hear and that veterans hear only for a brief, formative moment in their lives. But even in this extraordinary context there is routine; each day may have the same patterns of sleeping, waking, eating, physical training (PT), patrols, repair, and preparation. When we asked veterans about their routines, there were a lot of similarities in sleep deprivation, PT, waiting, and camaraderie. For example, one group came across an abandoned clothes iron in their barracks. Such an ordinary item seems completely unexpected in the context of war. Yet almost everyone irons a uniform before going out to meet with community leaders to plan civic projects, gather information, or broker agreements. When a civilian imagines war, does he or she picture a young man with an iron in the heat of a desert morning carefully pressing the creases out of a shirt to show respect for the elderly man he will meet in several hours to talk about water for home use or irrigation? Back at base, we were told, one can become quite "crafty" with needle and thread. Can a hole be mended, a loop fashioned, a pocket added? Sometimes the uniform isn't as durable as its use demands, and seams must be reinforced to avoid the kind of embarrassing moment one lieutenant shared when he met with an elder and tried to cover the rip along the midseam of his trousers. And where did that iron come from? Did you know that Amazon delivers to the Afghan mountains via Army Post Office (APO)?

Most veterans found conversing with us engaging, productive, or illuminating, though for some of them, recollection was mostly frustrating or pointless. Some left with a new understanding of what they had experienced or communicated, though as many concluded with a sense of continued misunderstanding and futility. A few cried for lost selves or lost lives; others continued to experience a muting of emotion or dissociation; almost all laughed at their own antics or errors. Most conversations left us with a rich sense of the complexity and honesty of the men and women we met, even when, and perhaps often because, they guided us through the hardest or most defeating experiences of war.

Some thirty veterans participated in this project, and together they represent many races (Asian, African American, European American, and Latin American, as well as combinations of all the above) and a variety of ages and genders (five women participated). They come from the enlisted ranks and also include officers. Some had poor educations, and others graduated from the finest universities in the country. They live all over the nation, and a few live abroad. They were raised in various regions, with some having the greatest privileges and others in the most straightened circumstances. Some prepared seriously and faced stiff competition to gain entrance to a particular branch or Military Occupation Specialty (MOS). Others came to the service as a last resort or only chance out. Several came from military families, though some have never known anyone in the service and remain the only veterans in their communities. For a few 9/11 or love of country motivated commissioning. Others enlisted to test their mettle or conquer the challenges that, they believed, make a boy into a man. Others cannot really understand their own motivations, their complex, even inchoate, drives.

There are excellent oral history projects that collect information about the wars in Iraq and Afghanistan. Two of the most important are the Veterans History Project at the Library of Congress and the StoryCorps Military Voices Initiative. Those contexts give the recordings their particular strengths; the intimacy of a shared history warms veteran interviews gathered in the StoryCorps project, for example. Our contribution lies primarily in anonymity, in the opportunity we gave veterans to remember both publicly and with the promise of confidentiality. We are continuing this project now in a digital form at After Combat: The Voices Project (http://aftercombat.tamu.edu), where veterans and those still on duty can share their experiences with each other and with interested civilians.

Author Backgrounds

Mike Gibler: I have deployed on multiple occasions to both Iraq and Afghanistan, so several years ago when I was serving at Texas A&M as the professor of military science, I was asked to speak to a group of first-year students about the university's common-reading selection (also known as the Common Ground project), a book about veterans from the war in Iraq. I had read the book very carefully, as the marginal notes in my copy could show you,

and with mounting irritation. It isn't just that the book was riddled with the kind of errors that come up when civilians try to
adopt military argot and when people unfamiliar with military
equipment and procedures describe our work and aims during
a deployment. There was a more significant problem: the author
took a very serious issue that armies have faced since the beginning of war and wrote about it in the most gruesome and sensational terms by describing some very extreme cases in Colorado
Springs, situations that don't represent soldiers well, if at all. A
page turner, the book could be the only one an average civilian
might read about military engagements since 9/11. More important, this story of a few broken and violent men might represent
the scores of us who have managed post-traumatic stress over
numerous deployments; who raise our families and contribute to
our communities; who serve our countries while navigating the
daily challenges of unpredictable crowds, loud noises, and roadside debris. Moreover, I know many young men and women who
have served and seamlessly returned home to continue their educations, rejoin family businesses, or pursue careers in each and
every corner of this nation, their military service known to but a
very few. Was this book going to be the version of them every single first-year student at Texas A&M had in mind when meeting a
student veteran? When I visited with this particular group of sixty
students—Regents Scholars who were the first in their families to
attend college, like many of their fellow first-years who had gone
to war before they came to campus—I wanted to make sure they
didn't look at a veteran as a broken person or a walking threat
like the few men in Colorado Springs whose anger and trauma
cascaded into a violence that blighted their community. I set out
to carefully detail the book's factual errors, as I knew them, and
gave the students a more balanced view of both military combat
and battle fatigue and how one copes with such events and memories. I acknowledged that the military was slow to react to the
physiological needs of the returning forces but that the actions
described in the book were more a reflection of individual char-
acters and morals than those of the vast majority of service men

and women with whom I served. My true objective was to impress upon the students to think critically, intellectually challenge what they read, read differing points of view, and, most important, talk and listen to others. As outlined below, Marian Eide and I entered into this project from differing perspectives but with the same goal: to let the veterans tell their own stories. I must confess that Marian has done the lion's share of work, patiently guiding me and others throughout this process.

Marian Eide: I grew up during the cold war, like Mike Gibler. My parents were in the foreign service, so we lived abroad for many years; my sisters and I went to schools with "army brats," got our groceries from the commissary and our jeans from the Post Exchange (PX). By the time I was ready to graduate from high school, I had a deep knowledge of military red tape and had become a committed pacifist, in part under the influence of the military men and women who led our community and saw war as the very last resort for addressing the kinds of political conflicts that sometimes lead politicians to rattle our considerable cache of sabers. It was one of life's better ironies that I ended up following my career in literary studies on a campus that started out as a military academy. When I volunteered to work with a team of faculty on a critical-thinking seminar for the Regents Scholars, I was delighted with the Common Ground book selection precisely because it focused on post-traumatic stress. We invited Mike to talk to the students about the book from the perspective of a military leader and combat veteran. I'd heard great things about Colonel Gibler from everyone who had had a chance to work with him, and I wasn't disappointed. His lecture was gripping and erudite, delivered without notes and with incredible fluency. He is a born teacher. But he hated this book with which I was so enamored, and my pacifist hackles went up. When he emphasized that the author had told a sensationalized version of the military experience and cast a shadow over the real and varied stories of men and women in the service, I thought, a little defensively, "Well, if you don't like this version, why don't you tell the story?" And then something clicked. Not only did I find I really wanted *Mike* to convey the stories of the ordinary soldier, airman, sailor, and marine, but I also wanted to work with him to collect those narratives. Preposterous. Not only did I have an academic book manuscript faltering along to completion, but I also had no qualifications to bring to the table; I didn't know the difference between a MATV, an MRAP, an HMMWV, and an MRE. (If you're like me, there's a glossary of terms after the last chapter.) But I do know something about narrative, about how to recognize and frame a good story. So I asked Mike to lunch at the university club. I asked him if he wanted to write a book with me. Let's find those ordinary stories, I proposed. Let's collect them from the men and women who deployed to Iraq and Afghanistan. Shockingly, Mike agreed. And this is our book.

How to Read This Book

This book can be read from cover to cover and front to back—the chapters are arranged thematically to follow a kind of narrative arc, from enlistment to homecoming and from past to present— but it is not necessarily designed to be read in an orderly fashion. Readers may choose to dip into one section based on its theme or title but be pulled into another chapter. The real stories happen somewhere between the constant mortar fire on the Fourth of July, the heating of dehydrated rations on the side of a mountain without a stove or fire, ducking into a bunker in flip-flops and boxers in the middle of the night, or traversing a barren landscape that is a combatant's entire world for eight months and to which he or she will never return. We listened to a veteran who thought her recollections would be a burden to her friends and family and another who woke up each morning and tried to tell himself he was not a monster. Their accounts are neither representative nor particularly unusual, but both of them and all those that fall somewhere in between are crucial to a full understanding of U.S. military intervention abroad.

Each chapter is narrated collectively by veterans. The order within each chapter is not particularly chronological but rather associative, as one story recalls another or provides a startling contrast to a third. A set of three dots (• • •) introduces a shift to a different veteran's voice. The mingling of voices also serves to maintain the anonymity of participants so that they could speak freely and honestly about the banal, scandalous, humorous, regrettable, and sometimes brazen. Few told stories of either their own bravery or cowardice.

Either one of us might have wished for a clear moral to this story of war and might even think we have achieved it through these accounts. But our conclusions would probably not be the same. Knowing that simple truth is part of how we trusted each other to tell the story of war. Our differences may be the very source of our sense of balance in bringing the experiences of these veterans to a wider world.

AFTER COMBAT

1

Enlist/Commission

Men and women volunteer for military service for a wide variety of reasons: to pay for an education, to leave a small town, to test their mettle, to rebel against family expectations, to respond to tragedy, or to get out of trouble. The timing of their service is not always in the first bloom of adult life but is sometimes in mid-career. While a select few soldiers speak of patriotic duty, for many the drive to volunteer has complex, personal bases. Some military men and women are escaping financial frictions or personal crises; others articulate a carefully conceived ideal: a principle of American democracy, or capable masculinity; or compassionate care for the wounded.

My mom's side of the family, they're all war refugees from Vietnam. I didn't know until I joined the military that my grandpa was actually a major general for the South Vietnamese, and he didn't make it out. They experienced the war firsthand. So my mom has very different ideas about all that. Which I can understand. And I agree with some of her viewpoints. My entire family, though, were really proud when they announced that I was going into the military. So they do recognize that, coming to America, they were given a second chance because they know individuals who didn't get out. So my family is better off than most; they're not high upper class or anything, but we're getting along. They recognize this country has given them a lot of opportunity. So me going into the military was kind of a bittersweet thing because a lot of them are old enough to remember the war in Vietnam.

• • •

I guess I did not want to wake up twenty years from now and decide, "Oh, man, I really should've done that." It was just some-

PHOTO BY DAVID EISLER.

thing that I really wanted to or had to do. It was just kind of sheer will; I just knew that the Army was what I wanted. I was like, "I wanna be a guy on the ground and doing that stuff." If I had known the career opportunities in some of the other forces. . . . But I basically said, "You know, if I'm going to be in the military, I want to be where the action is, and the Army is the place to be." As opposed to the Marines—and we could debate that.

• • •

I was about seven when I knew I wanted to be a marine. There are two reasons for that. Both my grandfather and my great-grandfather on my father's side were marines. They both passed away before I was really old enough to know them well. I always watched the History Channel growing up. I was always watching World War II videos and such. It seemed really honorable and like a cool thing to do. By the time I went to high school, it was pretty much set in stone, so I didn't really apply to any colleges; I talked to a recruiter. I knew I needed the discipline as well because I wasn't a very good student or . . . person, I guess. I was

　　　　　　　　　　　　　　　ENLIST/COMMISSION

seventeen when I signed the papers and all that. I deployed to Afghanistan from November 2010 to June 2011. Camp Leatherneck was our base station, and we operated out of the Sangin Valley. I was with a marine reconnaissance team.

• • •

When they advertised it, when Congress signed off on the CST program—the Cultural Support Team—they called it "cultural support" for a reason because that goes down easier for someone who doesn't want to see women in combat. But that's exactly what I was in; I was in combat. Really before I even got selected as a CST, I started training. I probably put on somewhere around 20–25 pounds of muscle so that when I would get there, I would look the part, and they would feel confident that I could hold my own. As soon as I arrived in Afghanistan, I had to meet my strike forces, my platoon. It took a lot of time to get them to trust you because their lives were on the line out there if you did something stupid. For most of them this was their sixth, seventh, eighth, twelfth deployment. Special operations, generally speaking, deploy more frequently but for shorter times, so they may deploy for three months. But this is their twelfth time doing it, so they're really a close-knit team, and in order to be prepared for that, they pushed us pretty hard in the training course to make sure we were prepared before we deployed. My personal opinion is that we still weren't prepared; what can you learn in three or four months that these guys have been doing for their entire careers? So you're not ever really prepared; there was a lot of on-the-job training. I was nervous as hell, but they taught us the basics, and we learned the rest when we got down there. There was a lot of physical training too because it was a very physically demanding job, so physical training was one of the biggest priorities. One of the things we were advised to do as soon as we got to Afghanistan was go to the gym and let them see how much you can lift. As I'm a woman, no one expects to hear the stories that I have. I'm not even sure a lot of people believe me. This was before the combat ban was lifted for women in the military, so we weren't supposed to be doing those kinds of jobs. It was not legal, by

Congress's standards, so we weren't supposed to be on the front lines; we weren't supposed to be in combat roles, . . . and I think a lot of people still don't really know what we did and don't really believe us when we talk about it, so most of us don't talk about it.

• • •

To be honest I kind of felt like I was wasting my life; I wasn't dedicated to school; I was just getting by, you know, a C student. And one day I just felt I needed more direction in my life, so I looked for which one could add the most discipline to my life, and for me that route was the Marine Corps. I felt like if anyone could beat it into me, it would be them and kind of get rid of the bad habits that I had. . . . And that's what kind of drew me. Maybe I was kind of motivated by what happened on 9/11, but more so, I guess, I wanted to develop myself personally.

• • •

Rumors to dispel. We're not in the Army because we didn't have any other choice. We're not in the Army because this is the best we could do. I think there's a feeling that it's not for the well-educated; it's not for the people who could make more money. It *is* for them. You have bigger reasons; you prefer to feel fulfilled in what you do; it's not just because you had no other choice or you wanted to pay for college or get out of a jail sentence. It's a real, viable choice, and it's not just something that you're pressured into.

• • •

I was eighteen. I was a mediocre student. I didn't know what I wanted to do, but I knew I didn't want to sit in Alabama. . . . Let me be even more honest. I got into severe trouble in high school. I actually went to jail. After I was released and not charged, I joined the Army.

• • •

I originally wanted to go into the Marines because they have this image that they're the first to fight, but then I discovered that they don't have their own medics. So then that's when I found out what a corpsman was, found that it's the most decorated job in all the militaries. I grew up close to hospitals because I have a

ENLIST/COMMISSION

little brother that I love who had a lot of medical issues growing up. Both of my parents worked, so me and my siblings actually learned to take care of him when he first came home. So I knew I was good with medicine. Honestly, I lied to my parents. Yeah, they had no idea that the Navy corpsmen were with the Marines. I pitched it to them that I was going to be in a hospital or on a boat somewhere, knowing full well that I was not. There was only one spot to go with the Marines, and whenever you're cutting orders, you choose where you go based off your class rank, so I actually graduated valedictorian from my class just so I could pick that one spot. I'm super-competitive in a lot of things, so that helped. . . . I joined for five years in the summer of 2008, right after I graduated high school. I got into all of the colleges I applied for, and I actually got a lot of scholarships to go to school. I was a typical boy at the time; I knew there was a war going on, and I wanted to get to war and see what I could do and be a part of history.

• • •

I joined because I couldn't pay for college, and that was the easiest way to get my schooling paid for. I was twenty. And I had already done two years and racked up quite a large debt slip and needed a way to pay it off. I got a call from a National Guard recruiter, and that was it; I signed the paperwork a month and a half later and shipped off for basic training not too long after that.

• • •

I was actually a youth pastor, and my wife and I had one kid and one on the way. I lost a position at our church, and I didn't have the money or the family resources to pack up and move to another place for another church, so we started looking at a guaranteed paycheck alternative. I was twenty-three years old, and the Army was a viable opportunity, and since it was the summer of 2001, we weren't at war or anything. I actually said that to my wife; I was like, "We'll be okay, honey. It's not like we're at war or anything." So that was how I got started—one of those "I-needed-a-job," honestly. So I signed up for six years because it was a $20,000 enlistment bonus at that point, and then I deployed to Iraq in 2003 and was there for the invasion of Iraq.

. . .

I'm the first in three or four generations within my family that commissioned as an officer. Everyone else has been enlisted.

. . .

I just kind of always thought that's what men do is go to war if there's a war, so that's what I decided to do. When I was a kid, my dad wasn't there. So I was obsessed with what it means to be a man. Some tribes, they cut your back with a razor blade, and it looks like alligator skin, and some tribes have a fire thing. I didn't know what it meant to be a man in America. So in all the books that I read, all the men'd gone to war, so I just thought that that's what you did. That was the generation I guess I looked up to, World War II, my grandfather's generation. My grandpa was Navy, and my dad was a marine. I definitely didn't want to end up like my dad. Drunk. I wish I could say now that it's different, but if there was a war that was major today, I'd probably go. I don't know if I drank the Kool Aid of the World War II generation or what, but . . . I don't think that that's what makes you a man. This sounds horrible, but before, I didn't really respect people that didn't serve their country, and now what I've noticed is that everyone has an ability to give back, to contribute something. For me, I can contribute that way. It's debatable if that's even contributing, I guess.

. . .

The reasons for serving were . . . there's a multitude of reasons. Mainly, the first reason was because I needed leadership experience. I'm the youngest of three, so up until that point I've pretty much been told what to do and just kind of did it. I'm a pretty good rifleman, but I knew that I was behind on managerial experience, leadership experience, decision making, planning, and I've never been put in charge of anybody for the most part. In high school, I played golf, an individual sport, not a team sport. So this was something that I recognized early on, very quickly: there's an experience gap here, and it's got to get fixed. And what better place to do it than the military in a time of war when my country needed me most? So the fact that we were in a conflict and they were needing people and I needed leadership experience, I felt like I would get as much out of it as it would get out of me. And so I made the decision. My mother wasn't really happy about it, my father wasn't surprised, and both of my siblings—my brother and my sister—were pretty apprehensive.

• • •

Why do people serve, why do people elect to serve in the military? I would love to see research on that; I would love to see if there is a difference between the opinions that veterans and soldiers have of themselves for why they joined . . . and why everybody else thinks they join.

• • •

Coming from an Ivy League undergraduate institution, when somebody asked me, "What are you doing next?," the typical answer should have been, "I'm going to graduate school; I've got a job here or there." My answer—and the answer of about seven of my classmates—was joining the military. This is back in 2007, so maybe opinions have changed since then, but only at that time did people say, you know, "Why would you do that?" And I don't know if the incredulity was because they couldn't imagine that somebody *like me* would want to join the military or they couldn't imagine *anybody* joining the military. But the general sense that I get is the inability to talk between the groups. I'm concerned that this generation of veterans will end up behind their peers the same way the Vietnam generation did. They were never able to quite catch up in life expectations, quality of life, earnings, anything like that, whereas you should say that the military should help you succeed as opposed to hinder you from success.

• • •

Right out of high school, I went to a military junior college in New Mexico, and while I was there, everybody was talking about . . . I don't know, nineteen- and eighteen-year-olds playing GI Joe and everything like that. So everybody's talking about all these different things that they want to do in the military. They want to be a Ranger; they want to be Special Forces; they want to be 82nd; Navy SEAL; whatever it is they say they want to be. But 95 percent of the kids commissioning out of New Mexico Military Institute are going into the National Guard. I'm not knocking that in any way, shape, or form, but that's a far cry in my mind. . . . My year and a half career at NMI ended very abruptly when I got in trouble one day, but we're not going to go into that. So I came home, and I started wondering, "What am I gonna do?" And I decided that basically joining the military did two things for me. It allowed me to take control of my life. I didn't want my parents having to pay for everything, dictate where I was going, and things like that. . . . And then it also allowed me to go and do all the things we all said we were gonna go and do. I got an infantry contract that would send me to Ranger Battalion or at least give me an opportunity to go to Ranger Battalion. I thought, "That's what I wanna do, so. . . ." I went through infantry basic training, and early in 2000 I went to 3rd Ranger Battalion. Not the same thing as becoming a Ranger; I don't have a Ranger tab. I spent about six months at 3rd Ranger Battalion before I got sent to 82nd because I had a propensity for drinking under age. Ranger Battalion was 170 percent strength at the time, so basically if you did anything wrong, you go away. I was a little bit of a troublemaker back then. That was a long time ago, but yeah. I arrived in the 82nd in November, right before Thanksgiving. The rest of my active duty enlistment was in the 82nd. I did four years' active duty. Then I came into the Texas Guard with the intention of going to college, and three months later I was in Iraq with the Texas Guard, and from the day that deployment started, with the exception of a two-month break in 2006, I was active duty with the Texas Guard until I separated in April of 2011. The Guard had what they called Title 32: Active Duty for Special Work. So basically they can bring a soldier in and activate your status rather than just doing the one weekend a month.

• • •

I wanted to be in the military ever since I was little. I don't know; maybe it was me watching movies or something like that or because I lived in San Antonio, which is a big military place. Yeah, I don't know for sure, not off the top of my head. I've wanted to be in the military ever since I was little.

• • •

I think I'd just finished seminary when September 11 happened. I was working as a youth minister in a church at the time. I was really called to ministry. I really loved the books, the old languages; I liked the history; I was really into the past. I was really into bringing the past into the present. When September 11 happened, I was looking at full-time jobs and searching, and nothing seemed to fit. Then the invasion of Iraq happened, and they needed chaplains. I'd just gotten licensed to be a minister. I'd just had a baby. We needed health insurance. A lot of things moved me into the Army chaplaincy. That was where I really found the calling to be with people. I didn't realize that ministry was about being with people in their suffering and pain. In the Army chaplaincy, the first day I was on the job, there was a guy who'd just been caught with child pornography, and he was about to go to jail, and he was on his way out, and they were like, "We need you to talk to this guy." First person I ever talked to in the Army. I was shocked by that. And then everybody had a marriage problem, a relationship problem, a breakup, money problems. It was a group of people that were really suffering. The unit I'd joined had just gotten back from a deployment. I was the first chaplain to be there in many, many months. They had so many personnel changes. And there was literally a line of fifteen people outside my office my first day there. . . . They sent all these people to my office, fifteen of them, to just line up. And I was just overwhelmed by that. But it was great; I needed to learn how to do initial pastoral counseling, to triage people. I'd had counseling classes in seminary, but I wasn't as excited about those. I went to the family-life chaplain training center, where they did lots of really good trainings for chaplains, so I went and studied there for a while, while I was doing this ministry in the unit, and that really got me up to speed, just being with people in their suffering, in the pit, when they're in crisis. That was good for me to realize that it's not just about the books; it's really about meeting people in their need right now.

• • •

I grew up below Pittsburg in West Virginia, in the panhandle of West Virginia along the Ohio River, and my dad was a coal miner, so I grew up in the steel industry and aluminum plants, and all of that was slowly dying there. I worked at the aluminum plant swinging a sledgehammer. I tried to go to college for the first year and a half after high school, at eighteen years old, and I was able to do that, and I did my freshman year, but . . . I didn't have any more money because I played football to get a scholarship, but I had my knees injured in spring ball, so I had knee surgery that ended my hopes of getting any money that way. . . . I had Pell grants, full Pell grants to go, because I was one of eight kids, and my dad was a coal miner and he never graduated high school; there was no chance for them to pay for anything. But he claimed me on his tax returns, so I didn't get my Pell grant money. So I ended up at the steel plant right in line with all my uncles and my dad. So here I was swinging a twelve-pound sledgehammer busting carbon off rods, and I got in the United Steel Workers of America union, and I thought here I am; I'm going to be stuck here, and it's the same thing day in and day out, swinging a sledgehammer, your back hurting, coming home all dirty and dusty, like my dad. I just felt like there was just two hills and a valley with a river, and I was stuck between those hills, and I wanted to know what was on the other side of those hills. You know, it was just filled with smog, and with the pollution along the river, you couldn't even eat the fish out of the river any more. I just wanted to see more and do more than just that. I just felt it was going to be a mundane life; it was just going to be in and out, that same groundhog-day life that I kind of grew up seeing, and I just wanted something different. I was making more money than I had ever made in my life, and I didn't know what to do with it. I was making twelve-something an hour, which was a lot then in the steel workers' union. I was going to be there the rest of my life. I said, "I'm joining the military." My family was upset, thinking, . . . "You lucky little SOB; you get this job, and here you are leaving. Are you kidding me?" But there's a lot of veterans from Vietnam working there at that aluminum plant, and they were all very supportive: "Hey, you're going to serve your country; we'll see you in four years." I thought they were going to be mad, like, "You just got hired here." A lot of them, I played ball with their kids; I mean a lot of them were much older than me. They knew who I was, you know, because I was big in that town. So I was going in because they paid 75 percent of my tuition, and I was like, "Wow, are you kidding me?" Today it's 100 percent, and they pay for your books, but I thought that was a great deal. So I'm taking night classes for six years. I was enlisted for six or seven years, made it to the rank of staff sergeant.

• • •

In 1995 I'd started graduate school, and by 2000 I was pretty much swimming in student-loan debt to the point that I was wondering if I'd ever be able to pay it back. I'd heard I could get money from the military. So after worrying about it for several months, I ended up going to a recruiter and finding out that for three or four years of service I could get $60,000 in student-loan repayment, which was about what I needed. The money was really kind of hard to say no to. I chose the Army because student loan repayment for Marines, Navy, and Air Force was $10,000, and in the Army it was $60,000. I don't know why there was such a big difference. So I thought about it, and I thought about it, and I thought about it. It wasn't just that. I was midway through my dissertation, which is a weird time for anybody. It was going, but I felt like I was kind of spinning my wheels, and just personally in my life, I was kind of spinning my wheels too. I wanted a change, and I wanted to get away from a series of failed relationships. The money kind of greased the wheels, and I decided I needed to get out of the academic thing for a while. Once I made the decision, it seemed like a really good thing. At the level I was educationally, I could have gone an officer route. When I went to the recruiters' office, they tried to steer me in that direction. But I decided I didn't want to do that; I just wanted to enlist. For all kinds of reasons, ranging from drama on one side—an almost clichéd desire to say, "To hell with you, world" and do something no one ever dreams I could even think about doing. But also I took class issues very seriously, and I didn't want to rely on my education; I wanted to go somewhere where I was dealing with what I was before my education and see if I could make it, and that was a good decision. Let me be clear: I don't really perceive myself as a big manly man; that wasn't what it was all about. I didn't learn the lessons I expected to learn, but it was a really good decision. It was October 10, I think, of 2000 that I signed the paperwork. But I did delayed entry. I didn't want to start right away because I had a fellowship, and I wanted to at least finish out the academic year. So I didn't go to basic training until May 29 of 2001. How's that for timing? Everyone was worried about China at that time.

• • •

One of the reasons I enlisted in the Marines years ago is because I knew that I wasn't a very courageous person.

• • •

I wanted to have that experience. It's an opportunity where you can't go back thirty years later and be like, "I want to go back and check that box." And people tried to dissuade you, mostly to see if this is something you actually want to do and for what reasons.

• • •

I didn't take the oath to defend this country. I took an oath to fight and defend the Constitution of the United States, which is an idea. When you read the oath, we don't say "our country"; we say "the Constitution of the United States." Big difference. We say "the Constitution of the United States" because we support the idea of freedom; that's what we support.

2

Mission

For an individual within the vast military machinery, it is not always clear why each day is shaped the way it is. Sometimes the particular responsibilities and unit goals are clear, and the long day's tasks feel meaningful and productive. For units facing a clear enemy in firefights that test excellent training, the import and honor of the battle are concretely confirmed. Some units can even point clearly to the innumerable lives their particular mission saved. In other situations, the task is like that of Sisyphus rolling the stone up the hill each day, only to watch it trundle down from its apex each evening. How else to describe the pervasive experience of route clearance: making a highway safe for trucks to move equipment between a forward operating base (FOB) and a combat outpost (COP)? Each day there is a new pile of debris in which an improvised explosive device (IED) may be hidden, an obstacle possibly monitored by an insurgent team waiting to strike. Yesterday's controlled explosion leaves a crater in which today's explosively formed penetrator (EFP) may be planted. Yet even the truck-driving Sisyphus realizes that food, water, and equipment have to make it out to the peripheral units, no matter the small part this repetitive, dangerous work plays in the stated mission of bringing American-style peace, democracy, and opportunity to a troubled region halfway around the world. The terrain and the people bear little resemblance to home and neighbors, but surely those children by the side of the road deserve the same freedoms and share the same basic needs as the kids back home. And so another impossible day's work begins on the heels of an abbreviated night's sleep.

I WAS IN KUWAIT when we were ramping up. They were shooting Scud missiles at us, and we were firing back at them. And then we were pretty much just a couple weeks behind 3rd ID when they went into Baghdad. I was an intelligence analyst. That became interesting because in traditional combat operations a corps-level unit would always be miles behind the enemy lines. Of course, that's all very nice, but when we got to Baghdad, there were no such things as lines any more. When we were outside the wall, we were in the same situation the infantry units were in. They had up-armored vehicles; they had all this protection. We had nothing; we had HMMWVs that were vinyl . . . terrible equipment. We were doing the same kind of job that they were, but we had nothing to stop to the bullets. HMMWVs are designed to go about sixty miles an hour, but we'd drive them upwards of ninety. Going fast, that was our defense. Generally, our operations were very small: getting from point A to point B. Not to engage to anybody. Our job was to disengage, not engage. Even though I was an intelligence officer, we lost all our drivers to other duties, so, ironically, because my commander liked the fact that I had some education and thought that was a good thing, he made me his driver. What that meant was that for five months in Baghdad, I was outside the walls every day. Usually no more than two HMMWVs in a convoy, maybe four or five personnel, and nothing heavier than an M-16, maybe, so that was crazy stuff . . . ; kind of felt like the Old West. We would gather data about what happened when and where and make predictions about what was likely to happen. The way I think about this kind of stuff is based on the way people live their lives. People who do ambushes on convoys are people who also have lives; they tend to have times when they're free to do this sort of stuff. They tend to have areas where they feel secure because of terrain, because it's close to home. So things tend to fall into patterns. What we would do was ever-increasing statistical analysis to try to find hot spots, places to avoid, places we might then go after people. And then we started extending that stuff so that we could start trying to stop indirect fire, by which I mean folks who would drive up with a mortar in the back of a pickup truck and try to lob a mortar over a wall, which was a real problem. It happens so fast. What do you do about it? I'm told that this stuff that we came up with has become standard procedure now. Our main goal was to try to find Scud missiles that might deliver chemical weapons. That was the real threat. All of us believed that at some point we would get hit with chemical weapons. That was a real belief. It wasn't unusual; during major combat operations before and shortly after the Army started moving north, it wasn't unusual for somebody to call out the grid, and the grid was right where you were. And eventually something would hit the very place where you're standing. So you're relying on the patriot missile to take this thing down, and at any point those might have chemicals on them. So procedure was that everyone runs to the bunker. The problem when those things started going off is that it's tough not to come unglued. If there's one thing that scares people, it is chemical weapons. I remember the first time it happened in particular; the alarms didn't go off. They had malfunctioned. So there was somebody running around going, "Get to the bunkers; there's chemical alert, potential chemical alert." We're all just kinda, "What?" And then when it strikes, everyone leaves the bunker and goes back into the tent, and you start putting on your chemical gear, and that's the moment when stuff gets real. You're in these Kuwaiti Bedouin tents that house about sixty people, so they're big. You're watching your entire unit start to put on chemical gear, which takes about eight minutes to put on, if you're good. That's when you start to look around, and you see people you respect as pretty hard-core starting to look worried. There were a number of times when I thought, "How the hell did I get myself into this?" I'm thinking like, "When I trained for this stuff in basic training, I had thought this is the most silly thing in the world; I will never have to wear this chemical weapons gear; this is like World War I stuff happening." This was so far away from anything real. That moment, where it became real, where you really start passing out live ammunition, that's a weird moment.

• • •

In 2001, when 9/11 occurred, I was stationed at the U.S. Army Burn Center in San Antonio. So I was in the intensive care unit beginning to start rounds with our multidisciplinary team of people that take care of severe burn survivors when 9/11 happened.

We were all seeing it on the TVs in the intensive care unit, so we knew there was going to be stuff coming, but we didn't know it was going to be at the scale that it ended up being. So the burn patients started rolling in in 2003; that's when I felt like the war really began for me. It was scary having guys come in with no hands; missing an arm; severe burns; 60, 80 percent of their bodies burned. These people never survived in the history of warfare, and I was to rehabilitate them? What a huge responsibility; I was totally overwhelmed. Iraq was a break for me almost. I mean, yeah, taking care of detainees; the workload wasn't near as intense as it was at the burn center.

• • •

So there were trenched-in artillery pieces, there were tanks and ammunition just lying around or stored up in various places that they shouldn't have been, that they had no business being in, places we wouldn't have bombed as Americans. . . . You're not gonna bomb a school so you can hide all your ammo in that. One guy, a farmer, they took his chicken coop, and they put huge artillery rounds in there—floor to ceiling—and they walled up his chicken coop. And as soon as we got in there, he said, "Can I get my chicken coop back?" Yeah, it's a chicken coop. Really? It was just one of those, "Look, the Iraqi Army wanted to use my chicken coop. I want it back. I'm losing chickens to coyotes." I don't know if it was coyotes; I don't think they have them, but predators. "And I want my coop back." So we were finding all those things so the insurgents couldn't use them against us. . . .

• • •

My job was to scan the road ahead and possibly look for IEDs and things that just didn't look right: tires on the side of the road not facing us; dead animals that were on the side of the road; things that just weren't supposed to be there. Or recent highway work, empty propane cans sitting there on the side of the road. Especially in the city that was a big thing, just so much trash within the city.

• • •

We were a field artillery unit, so we were trained not to be support but actually to be the bullets. We were training to be trig-

ger pullers. And that's how we saw ourselves. Our role . . . what we should have been doing was killing hajjis (for lack of a better term), and instead we ended up picking up ammunition. So after that initial push in, where there was a lot of engagement; there was a lot of, you know, "There's the enemy; fire the cannon at him" or "There's the enemy; pull the trigger." That lasted maybe three weeks to a month. After that you turned into, "Okay, let's go find some ammunition over here. Let's go find some over there." We spent eight of our ten months picking up.

• • •

The first time I was, like, terrified: we're going to go into this building, and everyone's going to be ready for us. But the reality is we went in and smashed the gate with the HMMWV; everyone hopped out because at that point they know you're there. It went smooth, like the training just kicked in; we all stacked up on the door—I was not first man, thank God—and kicked it in and cleared the house in what felt like half a second, but it was probably about two minutes. The first room, there was a male and a female (I'm assuming his wife), and that was it. The second one had two kids, and then it is kind of like this weird balance. Nobody wants to yell and be violent in front of a kid, but at the same time if you're not yelling, then the target isn't scared, and then he might do something. So yelling, yes, it scares the kids, but it also prevents any actual bullets from being fired. Nobody got actually hurt in either of those cases, but you hear stories, with obvious validity to those stories. Maybe you smashed in the gate; they know you're there, and if they're up already, then it's just the time it takes to get their AK and just sit on the door and wait for somebody to kick it in.

• • •

I guess I don't talk about the interrogation process because it was unethical, but I felt justified. I felt justified. Yeah, we know right and wrong, but it gets skewed, and you do what you need or want to do.

• • •

I must have kicked through sixty to eighty doors, you know, raiding houses with tons of ammunition, anything from explosives to bullets and guns. Definitely bad guys. I'm aggressive, and I think I was twenty-four or twenty-five at the time, and, I mean, I loved it. . . . I was more excited about it because you got a result. The proof was there right in front of me, very concrete evidence. I was really excited about it. Definitely those first three deployments; I was stoked. Just waiting to get that. I really had the energy. Just wanted to get back: "Okay, let's do it." So, yeah, I was happy. It was fun.

• • •

The thing about Iraq in 2004: I don't know how many guys were there—maybe a hundred thousand. So whatever you're doing, in the big scheme of things, it's probably utterly irrelevant. If you're, like, a private sitting on the guard tower, okay; that's fine . . . but when you're a lieutenant colonel on the staff of a multinational force in Iraq helping to craft the next version of the campaign plan, you're like, "Well, this is total stupidity. What are we even doing? None of these objectives are even achievable." Within a

week they found Saddam hiding in a spider hole. So the immediate objective—find Saddam—okay. But remember: for seven
months the Coalition Provisional Authority existed as the executive hierarchy for Iraq. Ambassador Bremer was there. The CPA
was an occupying authority; they issued orders; they issued policy
not just for the U.S., but they issued them for the Iraqis: "Anyone
associated with the former regime forces in the rank of lieutenant
colonel or higher will immediately be eliminated from the books
and no longer be allowed. . . ." That kind of thing. I was an individual reservist, augmentee. I wasn't in a unit. So by the time you
got to Kuwait and—"Okay, yep, there's no plane, whatever"—you
kind of wanted to get there, so you just hung around, and finally
you get on a plane; you land; you're kind of looking around: "Okay,
who's supposed to pick me up?" So we got on a plane full of cargo,
and we just flew in. You sleep in the hallway of some office. Then
you sort of start walking around, going, "Yeah, these are probably
the people I'm supposed to work for." So I found these people,
and there were some individual mobilized reservists within the
civil affairs architecture. I'm supposed to work for them somehow. So I walked in: "I'm supposed to be working for you." "Well,
you're going to be replacing that guy, and he's the plans guy." I'm
like, "Great. Can we have a little handoff?" He's like, "Yeah, man;
you've got twenty-four hours because I'm leaving tomorrow." So
he told me, "Look, you've got to go to this meeting, this meeting,
and this meeting. Here's stuff I've been working on." Then he's
like, "I got to go." So I'm, "Are you flying back?" He says, "No. I'm
driving my rental car back." Okay, so these are the kind of people
who took these Nissan Pathfinders that they rented in Kuwait,
drove them into the battle space, never bothered to turn them in,
never bothered to retrograde them, and had them hidden in their
little carports around the Green Zone, so they had personal vehicles. It's just. . . . It was epic. This is why you hate a lot of people in the Army because of a lot of this kind of ridiculous crap. I
mean why on earth would you even think that you should be able
to do that? You're not a cowboy. It's a circus. Those are the kind
of people that get other people killed in both the metaphoric and

the real sense. So I'd go to these planning meetings and I'd say, "Hey I'm from the Civil Affairs Directorate." And they're like, "Oh, well, we've never had anyone here from that office." And I'm like, "But Nissan Pathfinder guy told me that. . . ." He's like, "We don't know who that is. He's never been here." The guy lied. He never did anything. He never went anywhere. I mean this is just typical; with nothing to do, people pretend they're doing something. So he lied about going to meetings; he submitted little activity reports. It was all just a tissue of lies. But why report him? I would have had to report everyone that I came into contact with because they're all idiots. So I was in a bad way in this office because I wanted to do something; they did not want to do anything. So maybe three weeks along in this purgatory, I walked in one morning, and there's a kind of rumpled Marine lieutenant colonel with the old black-rimmed glasses on. He said, "Get your stuff. We're leaving." I thought initially, "Well, anything can be better than this." I didn't even ask. He said, "We're going down to the Green Zone; you're going to work for me." I'm like, "Fine." It turned out someone had called him and said that I had been causing some problems up there. So I went down to Baghdad, worked in the Green Zone at the big palace, the presidential palace. So behind the palace, if you can picture it, is the poorest trailer park that you can imagine—and they're not really trailers; we call them CHUS (containerized housing units), so essentially a forty-foot Conex shipping container with a bedroom on each end and a little bathroom in the middle, and they're all fitted out. So there are just hundreds of those out behind the presidential palace, and that's where everyone lived. There was a gym; there were the trailers; there was the palace. And so that was really your existence. You left your trailer in the morning; you walk into the palace; you did your work. Then you had all these ridiculous embassy people because the embassy was there; the CPA was there. And this was the infamous group of twenty-somethings that had come over to join the CPA and do great and wonderful things. So they're cavorting in the pool after hours, drinking alcohol because CPA and CENTCOM had two vastly different policies. General Order num-

ber one: no alcohol, no fraternization, blah, blah, blah. CPA, it's like a frat party. I got really pissed one night; I don't know why; there's the guys, the soldiers, out guarding the perimeter of this Green Zone so that these retards can pretend they're on some sort of Peace Corps freaking holiday.

• • •

We replaced the 5th Stryker Brigade Combat Team of the 2nd ID. They are now well known for having the kill teams and being a unit that lost quite a few people because of their strategy: the guys who went out and were purposefully killing civilians. That investigation is pretty well documented, but in any case, we had to replace them, so that posed its set of challenges. That Stryker unit was tasked with providing freedom of movement along that road for our forces as well as for the population. So we fell in on the same mission. I was responsible for counter-IED operations and intelligence, so essentially I would take all of the data that was out there for roadside bombs and categorize it, analyze it, and make recommendations on operations that should happen to facilitate either a relief of these attacks or try to figure out what was going on with them. I went on patrol maybe once a week, just to kind of get out; I hated being on the base the whole time, so just to get out and sort of see the terrain that I was analyzing, which is an important part of it. It was a lot less physically stressful, but mentally it was different for me because any time there was an IED that blew up and killed somebody, I felt like I was partly responsible for not having prepared enough information for the people to avoid it.

• • •

There were a hundred of us initially; they selected fifty women for a three-month training course where our job, once we deployed, would be to deal with the women and children on an objective when Special Operations Forces were doing a capture or kill raid. There were twenty-six of us total that were selected of the original hundred, and I deployed with the Ranger Regiment to Afghanistan. I was there for six months and went on somewhere around fifty capture-kill raid missions. Basically, intelligence would lead us to a bad guy—some Taliban, some terrorist type, someone we deemed to be a threat. We would find where they were going to be, probably where they were going to stay for the night, and under the cover of night in helicopters we would land near that place, and we would either capture or kill the individual, depending on what our mission was, depending on if there was a firefight or if they fought back. So we'd get there with a strike force of forty or so Rangers. We'd land. My job would be to handle all the women and children. The ratio of women and children to men in that country is probably about ten to one. Everybody has a lot of kids. So I was getting all of them, searching all of them, and then tactically questioning/interrogating the ones that I thought would be of good intelligence value.

• • •

By that point we had gone into Petraeus's counterinsurgency doctrine. So it was a lot more partnership with both the local military—so the Iraqi military police—as well as essential service assessments of villages. We always called it bridging the sectarian divide because in our area of operations there were Sunni and Shia towns. So there was a lot of bitter fighting: the mayor of this district is a Shia, but there are a lot of Sunni towns in there, so there's a lot of resentment between the two whether or not they were getting electricity or water or things like that. So we did a lot to help them build their government's capacity, as well as making sure that the services they were supposed to be providing as a government were flowing to all of the different areas. As an example, in one of the towns that had been more or less abandoned by the entire Sunni population because of the Shia governance in that area, one of the major objectives during that part of my tour was the resettlement of the town by Sunni families. So any time a few of them came back because they felt it was now safe enough for them to live there, that was a big deal. So we had some big celebration, like a reconciliation is what they called it.

• • •

I knew that as these children grew, life wouldn't be the same for them. They're completely faultless in this; they were just born into it. I knew that even if we could do something makeshift for them; for example, a child with a prosthetic limb would grow out of it, would never run, would never play. I mean, we have people who go to the Olympics with prosthetics. Those children will never see that opportunity. That's why I've taken the course of working with amputees because that's close to the heart for me, because children are the ones that when you ask, "Give me everything you've got," they're gonna give you everything they've got.

• • •

Interrogation produced results: where IEDs were in place, how they had been placed, where the funding was coming from, who was funding in certain locations. You know, really operational and somewhat strategic information. Did they lie? No. I don't think our aggressive procedures caused them to lie, and we didn't act that way either. But, no, we didn't allow them to lie. We acted on their information. We actually took them with us, especially if we were going to uncover an IED. I wasn't prepared to dig it up. One time, we had the guy dig up his IED on the side of the road. He planted it, so. . . . So we had engineers, and our engineers would accompany them to find where the trigger device was going to be. I mean, it was a methodical process. It wasn't like you just go out there with a shovel, and maybe he blows himself up, and he's a martyr. No.

• • •

If they said, "Oh, Joe is a bad guy," we didn't just go to his house and detain him. If we went to Joe's house, peacefully, knocked on the door and said, "Hey, we're here," and we found contraband, then we detained him. It wasn't, "Hey, let's arrest everybody and anybody." We definitely took too many people off the objective sometimes, you know, so I do feel like we detained people who weren't necessarily involved, who were in the wrong place at the wrong time.

• • •

I probably know a lot of inappropriate things, being one of five females to deploy with a bunch of dudes. I have quite a mouth on. I didn't have anyone dropping bombs on my head. I didn't have an aircraft flying over my head. Granted, we had mortars coming at us, but I didn't have someone standing across the line shooting at me. It was different for me; I wasn't security forces; I was an aircraft maintainer. It made me realize how much grit it takes to stand across from someone when they want you dead. Just the fact that they want their families to live through another day.

• • •

In terms of killing Taliban, we killed a lot of Taliban. But the British had pulled out of that area; the Estonians had pulled out of that area; it's winding down, but we helped make that town safer, that little bubble of safety. But outside of that bubble, there's not much you could do. The Afghans don't care; they really don't care unless you're giving them money. You can't make them go protect some town that they're not from. Like I said, we had the Kabul police there when we first got there, and they couldn't care one penny about that town. But once we got the people that were from that town as policemen, you could see a difference. But that's only in that area. You take them somewhere else, and they're not going to do anything. What happens in Kabul will never affect what happens in Musa Qalaand Nowzad. Their biggest priorities are their family, and then their tribe, and then maybe where they're from.

• • •

I was in the surge in 2007. They were pushing marines and soldiers into every square inch of Iraq, as much as possible. That was actually the most violent period in Iraq. The highest level of attacks was going on in 2007. At that time the insurgency was at full force. They were on the verge of a civil war at that time, and I felt that that's what we were there to do. These towns wanted democracy; they genuinely wanted to be able to pick who ran the town, and they didn't want to live in fear. And that's why we were there, to help. We had the "Sons of Iraq," but they were the villagers, and they would get out there and man their own posts. And afterwards that was awesome. Iraq was a very dirty country; there is no sanitation system; there's no trash cans; there's trash everywhere. Well, we got these people to clean up their own town. They would clean the whole town on Thursdays. They'd stop everything after their morning service and go out and pick up trash. You could just see the difference from five months apart, from January of '07 to about May of 2007. You could just tell you were making a huge difference.

• • •

It was right before the surge. It was when the sectarian and civil war. . . . We weren't supposed to say "civil war," but that's what it was. It was an internal conflict that had a huge effect on our mission. That was really discouraging to be involved in that part of it because things got out of hand, out of what we thought the war was going to be at that point. And that was the turning point where things really, historically, got difficult. As one of the people who were living it, I wasn't aware that that was really happening. I thought this would be the beginning of the end of war, that once we realized that things were getting messier, we would all leave. It was the opposite; it meant more troops were coming, more strategies for dealing with a huge city, Baghdad. I was stationed at a base right there at the airport, west of the city. My soldiers operated all around the city, almost in a ring around the city. We had a platoon that would go out and fix IED craters after they were exploded. We had a lot of heavy equipment. My engineers were a heavy construction unit for the most part; they could build buildings; they could build roads. A lot of what they did was clear debris from the side of the road so they wouldn't plant bombs in it; they were just picking up garbage, dirt, logs, knocked-down trees next to the road so you could sweep them for IEDs better. Or they'd repair the craters after an explosion. The medics would pick up body parts. One company was doing that for weeks and weeks, maybe several months even.

• • •

I was in a Marine reconnaissance battalion that augmented SEAL Team 5. Our mission was to promote the foreign, internal defense; to train the local nationals there; to provide foreign support; and we did foreign internal defense, a lot of reconnaissance work. My life was a video game, to be honest. Most of the time they were night missions, so sun goes down, couple hours later, we get all geared up; once we get the green light, the local nationals would lead, and we would be intermingled with them.

• • •

The drones that you hear in the news? I did that before I deployed. So I was already making the impact from home by directly affect-ing those missions. I was already running those missions for two years prior to my deployment. So for me to actually be in theater, it was just the same purpose in a different way.

• • •

I was in Afghanistan, and our unit was in a lot of—I don't know about "a lot"—but we were in conflict. But most of the time I was in the combat operations center, indirectly experiencing it, like calling in Medevacs and stuff like that. So I probably didn't have as bad an experience as some other folks.

• • •

Well, the reputation of the scouts is terrible. Scouts are a fantastic combat force but terrible when they're not in combat. The night before we deployed, we had a party, which I didn't go to. Just to clarify that now. My mom's birthday was the day we deployed, so I spent the day before with her. We had this party, and it was pretty much, "See how much you can drink." And we had a sergeant who was either tough or drunk enough. . . . He got tased eleven times by cops and was still standing. I don't even know how that's possible. I'm sure a normal person would have a heart attack. That guy personifies what scouts are. We're supposed to be . . . rough. But all that being said, we're like that for a reason. In the field, we're one of the most efficient units out there with the exception of Special Forces. I know the Army keeps trying to get rid of scouts. They've gotten rid of 'em like three times, but every single time they got rid of scouts, they brought 'em back. While we're terrible people, we're efficient at what we do.

• • •

My very first patient I ever treated was actually on my first deployment. It was a local national who got run over in front of our convoy. We didn't hit her, just to clarify that. (This lieutenant, it's his first deployment; he's just flipping out because this is the same spot where another convoy of ours just got ambushed about a month before.) But her head was split open, and she was bleeding all over the place. My staff sergeant is setting up security; they park one of the trucks so it will cover me from one side, and I'm doing my work, and as I'm doing it, I just kind of went into autopilot, and I reacted; I processed what was happening, and I reacted. I didn't hesitate to get out of the car, and my team was already out. We call in the Casualty Evacuation for her, and our side approved it, but the local national government did not. So we put her in the back of our truck. I'm holding her airway open at this time because with a head injury you can't do any type of artificial airway because if you dislodge something, you could kill her. So I had to manually pull her airway open—just simple CPR stuff: head tilt, chin lift. I know she's breathing. So we get back to our base, call it in again, it gets denied, and then we actually had to take her to a local hospital because we couldn't do anything, and then I saw her a couple weeks later. She lived. So that was good. But that was my first ever—no one's helping me; it was my show. I thought it was cool because I didn't realize at the time, but after it was all said and done, I got to reflect on that: I got out of the truck when the lieutenant stayed in, and so did the driver, who was also a SEAL.

I think most of the short-term pastoral counseling I did was effective in that it helped people know that they weren't alone, that there were other resources there. They could go to mental health and start an ongoing counseling relationship there. Most of them got medication when they went there, lots of it, and that helped them. As far as the chaplaincy part, I was very present for everything; I was praying with them. When I came back, I decided to stay with my unit longer rather than go to career school so that I could get promoted, and I turned it down so that I could stay with my soldiers and be there with them as they reintegrated.

• • •

Our initial responsibility was just a little base halfway between Nasiriyah and Baghdad called Scania—basically a truck stop—and the sole purpose for its existence is that the HMMWVS can't drive from Nasiriyah into Baghdad without refueling their trucks. So that's why Scania was there. It served no other purpose. So our company was based there, and our job was to run convoys. So we'd either be taking a convoy down to Nasiriyah or bringing one back. Really monotonous. You'll bring a convoy up, and somewhere in that convoy will be a truck full of sodas and stuff for the PX. I don't wanna say it's all that trivial stuff, but it's literally just the stuff that makes people work day in and day out. The really critical stuff, ammunition and stuff like that, that's run on the military convoys. Most of the convoys we'd get are called TCNs, Third Country Nationals. They're Pakistanis, Bangladeshis, maybe somebody from Africa, all over that sort of region of the world. You know, semi-trucks just loaded with the stuff we need day in and day out. Paper, I'm sure. Ink cartridges.

• • •

The first six months I was in Afghanistan, I was the operator of the mine-detecting equipment. I was just a rifleman, and a rifleman is just the most useless thing in an infantry squad. You just have an M-4. You've got guys with 40-millimeter grenade launchers; you've got machine guns. Then you've got a guy with an M-4. Typically, an infantry squad likes to move in a formation, but you can't do that because that's way more paths to walk to step on an IED, and we stepped on a lot. Finally, we just had to walk in a ranger file, basically a straight line. I was at the front with the detecting equipment. That was miserable. A couple of my buddies and I have talked about it since then. We're not sure if they put me on that position because they thought I was expendable because I was a new guy or if at that point they'd recognized that I took my job seriously and they wanted me there. We never really did figure that out.

• • •

I spent a lot of time with the chaplain. His office was close by mine in the hospital. He had a very tough job there because a lot of peers of mine were going through a lot of financial or personal problems at home, especially if they were on more than one or two deployments; you just saw families fall apart around you. He so wanted to feel like he didn't miss something, somebody's body language, so he's constantly just talking to everybody, keeping an eye on everybody, and developing these good relationships where people feel comfortable coming and talking to him. His whole goal: he didn't want anybody in his unit to commit suicide while he was there because it was so common, and nobody in our unit did, and he felt so proud of that when he came home. Yeah, he had one of the toughest . . . he and the psychiatrist, I think, had the toughest jobs there. The psychiatrist not only took care of us—U.S. forces that were there and the coalition forces—but they provided detainee ops too. Some of the detainees had severe psychoses and psychiatric conditions and could hurt themselves or others very badly. And so the psychiatrist and chaplain had a very difficult time.

• • •

South of our position in the Sangin River Valley was the city of Sangin. We had marines there that were getting hit with small-arms fire; they were taking IEDs, so they were losing marines pretty rapidly, so the command decided to put us north of the city and kind of interdict the flow of Taliban fighters from north to south. They basically just put us in the middle of an ant line and sat us there to take fire and kind of alleviate the pressure on the marines to the south. All their training was done in Pakistan or northern Afghanistan, and whenever they're done with training or whatever, they'd follow the river down south where Americans were. So they put us right in the path they would follow in the hopes of tying them up or taking fire and either killing them or at least slowing them down so that the marines south of us were not taking as many casualties. So we were basically kind of a target. They said our mission was to gather intel for the area, but it wasn't really our mission. Maybe it's beyond the scope of my enlisted rank, but we set up in a position, and we left there without gathering any detailed intel, and they were like, "Okay, that's good." And we'd move to another position and take fire. We took up five or six positions; they're all along the main route there on the hillside overlooking the route right next to the city and living areas. We did a decent amount of reconnaissance but not the kind we trained for. The kind we trained for was to watch from a distance and write down what activities are going on, but what we did was knock and talk.

• • •

And then, I think, I always question: "Did I do enough?" I don't know. If I sit there and think about World War I and World War II: wow, like, these guys did a lot. So what are you doing when you're not in combat? When you're not going down the streets with anxiety? Well, in Special Forces, alcohol is plentiful. You can find alcohol, and you can find girls if you want to. So there was a bit of that. That's not to say we weren't mission-focused, but there's a big difference between the first three deployments, when there was really combat; Al Qaeda was strong. Then there's after the surge of troops; then you found yourself sitting around, not doing things, drinking, just trying to pass time. Different. Totally different.

• • •

We were tough on the detainees, and we were tough on the detainees because we caught them in the act of setting in IEDs, or we caught them with thirty-six mattresses in the house and tons of explosives. They were housing Al Qaeda or other terrorist groups coming in through Syria. It would just be a holding house, and then they'd move out. Another guy we caught in Al Qa'im—the assistive team was in Al Qa'im doing operations, and they were hit with an IED. So this one Iraqi was on Al Jazeera news, waving his arm. We took that video, and we found the guy in Al Qa'im. Needless to say, he wasn't treated very friendly.

• • •

The funny thing is that when I first got to Iraq, I got sent to the wrong unit, so that was pretty crazy. They were an airborne unit, and what I did with them is that I was basically a driver. It was pretty interesting. The OP order is known as the Solomon Island. Basically, like a couple months before, there were soldiers who were kidnapped and then were killed and then buried in Iraq. We were supposed to go and find them because they thought that they had found—through sensors or thermal or whatever—mounds that the bodies were under. We didn't actually find them. It was the first time that I've ever been in combat; it was the first time that I'd ever been in a Blackhawk; it was the first time that I'd ever been in a situation where people were shooting at me. But I didn't have to shoot at anybody; I didn't have to kill anybody, which was pretty cool. But I enjoyed it; I really did. That was fun.

• • •

We went on a marijuana-field-denial mission. Basically we hired this random guy, a local national with a bulldozer, to come bull-doze a pot field. None of us could figure out what we were doing this for because we walked past two pot fields to get there. We were just ruining some family's income. So we get out there; we bulldoze this pot field; we walk back to the COP past two other pot fields and never do another marijuana or poppy-field-denial mission again. I don't know why we did that. There was no rhyme or reason to it at all; we took a couple pictures and sent those to Higher. They had their mission accomplished or whatever.

• • •

I think that's where I had my discontent. I mean, we just never changed from being kinetic to stability operations. Our command-

PHOTO BY MICHAEL GIBLER.

ers preached, "Hey let's do humanitarian interventions" and stuff like that, and we did those, but if we weren't doing kinetic operations, "You guys aren't doing a good job; do I need to send somebody down there to replace you?" You know, "hey, we need to pick it up." I'll just share what I felt. They didn't feel successful if their units weren't out there doing kinetic.

• • •

2010 was a really tense time for security contractors in Iraq because you had the jury acquittal after the Blackwater charges. A lot of the security contractors would roll around like they own it; like it's their country, which the Iraqis didn't appreciate. We provided high- and low-profile security for senior DoD civilians and military personnel. The vast majority of our training was focused on conflict de-escalation: "So how do I get out of this situation and make this guy think that he won and make him happy?" The complicated part of this is that we're in civilian vehicles and in civilian clothes, so he thinks that I'm a contractor, or he thinks that I'm Blackwater or I'm CE or whatever they named themselves this month. You're never going to reach a point where you can move around in a hostile area and be completely unnoticed; that's not going to happen. I can't walk through Baghdad, no matter what I'm wearing, or drive through Baghdad without people knowing that I was an American. What I can do is reduce the amount of time that they have to react. Instead of spotting me at two kilometers because I'm in a HMMWV, now I'm in a civilian vehicle, so I blend at two kilometers. Well, the vehicle is still going to look a little bit different, right? So maybe at five hundred meters, they think that's a little odd, but then there's the question: "What is it that's odd about it?" So by the time they know that's not Iraqi, I'm already gone. Instead of a Suburban, it was the type of sedan that you might see on the streets of downtown Baghdad. My two tensest moments of that entire deployment? One was dealing with an Iraqi police officer. He didn't want us to go through his checkpoint. He was threatening to detain us. We were under some really tricky rules of engagement. . . . We didn't want to go kinetic on anything, but if the mission or if circumstances dictated, I had the authority to use lethal force against even coalition force members, which included the Iraqi Army, Iraqi police force, and Americans, for that matter. So he was really stuck on wanting to search the vehicles, and I hadn't been able to talk him out of that point. And then he decided that he wanted to detain us, and he drew his pistol on me. I was the only person outside the car. I'm trying to talk him out of the pistol. He's getting really agitated. Nobody else on his patrol had drawn a gun. He decided to look another way, so I relieved him of his pistol, and immediately all of my guys came out of the cars with HKs and drew down on everybody at the checkpoint. At that point the Iraqi policemen were going, "Whoa! What did we just step on?" And I just . . . told the guy, because I had the linguist there, "Listen, we're on the same side, so I don't really want any problems, so I'm going to give you your pistol back, and we are going on our way, and we don't have this discussion any more."

• • •

I was a forward observer, which is the guy who calls in the helicopters and stuff. Whenever the infantry goes out, they need one of me with them, so that when stuff hits the fan, we can call in air strikes. The intent with Iraq at that point in time was to train and assist the Iraqi Army. The reality was that we were still conducting operations, either presence patrols or actually going in and getting somebody out—like if there was intel that there was a person of interest, a high-value target.

• • •

We were outside a town called Marjeh in the Helmand Province; it was supposed to be Fallujah-style battle. We were an artillery unit, so we had all of our artillery set up prepared to shoot into the town. But it didn't end up being the kind of battle that they really wanted it to be, where you just go in and kind of face the enemy. It was more about what the insurgents had learned to do by that point in the conflict, which was just to lay a ton of IEDs and just wait around, which ends up being more effective than facing the Marine Corps the way we like to fight. But then it was halfway supposed to be that, and then it was halfway supposed to be civil affairs. We were supposed to be helping the local people try farming instead of opium; we were trying to give them corn and stuff like that because the Helmand Province has a lot of opium going between Afghanistan and Pakistan, which was funding the insurgents. And then we were setting up votes, you know, so they could vote . . . have democratic elections.

• • •

At that point the CLC, the Concerned Local Citizens (which is essentially the Sunni Awakening), those guys had come out, and so we would meet with the leaders of those organizations and try and figure out how they would provide their own local security and stuff like that. It was always a discussion for a couple hours about what are the current problems, what are the current projects. So money had been given out; we called them micro-grants; they were $5,000 that we would give just as a grant to somebody for a small business to stimulate economic growth, that kind of stuff. We did a lot of that project assessment as well. Keep in mind, at the time, I was twenty-three years old. I knew nothing about projects; I knew nothing about economic development. But you learn quickly; you figure out kind of the human element of it, figure out, "Okay, is this guy just trying to get money from us?" And then that's why we would try and make sure that we followed up with them, and say, "Okay, we gave you $5,000 to start a small business; show us what you've done with it."

• • •

Great example: we had a detainee. Apparently he was a high-value target. We didn't know; we had no idea who he was because the fingerprints, the retinal scan, all the biometrics data were inconclusive. His identification said something else—obviously forged—but even the real thing looks like a forgery. So you didn't know; the only photograph we had of the high-value target is a thirty-kilobyte jpeg file; literally, we did not know who we had. No idea. Very quickly high-value target goes from being, like, Osama Bin Laden, like Zarqawi—really big; this is actually the guy who's running things—to, "Well, we picked this guy's fingerprints off an IED that blew up, so . . . ipso facto, he's a high-value target." If the top 10 percent are always high value, but you kill all the 10 percent that actually matter, then it slowly just starts to filter down. And so you had that disconnect. We're at the end of the game when we've already signed the withdrawal. We're leaving by this date; we're doing this; it was just running out the clock and making sure that fewer people died on whatever side.

• • •

Like I said, what's hard about that bubble around our town is that about two kilometers north and south of our patrol base it was the safe zone; insurgent tactics and the Taliban ambushes hardly ever happened. You may have the threat of an IED or something. But once you've passed that bubble, it was Taliban territory, and you knew it. It's weird because this is 2008, and I'm thinking the Taliban have to be done; they really don't want to be messing around this much, but once you hit that bubble, you pick up the chatter on their radios. They'd be like, "Oh, the Americans are coming; let's hit them when they're taking a break." Stuff like that. Then you go out to a certain point, sit around and wait, and try to get contact. You just sit there and wait, and if you didn't get combat or contact, you just come back.

• • •

When I was winding down my Marine enlistment time, I was reading a lot of John Howard Yoder and other pacifists. The American military-industrial stuff is making the world such a bad place. I was getting really discouraged about all that. I was never going to tell anyone I'd been in the military; I was going to start this other life. Then I joined the Army, and it's been my whole life. I'm still in the reserves. Now everything I do that's church-related is somehow veterans-related too. That's my identity now. I have to be willing to accept that. A lot of times I want to be distant from that. The military is not a really intellectually sophisticated place, and I like that. I wanted to be with the smart people. And yet there's this other part of me that has an overwhelming sense of compassion and drive, and I need to stay engaged with this community because this is my community now. There's no undoing that.

• • •

The objective of our deployment was to go from base to base closing down American bases, escorting those troops out, escorting their equipment. But if Libya did anything, we were supposed to go in and be the first ones in to be a beachhead, sort of, for the rest of U.S. forces. That was the hush-hush. That was if-needed, as an emergency, because we were one of the only combat units there. There were units in Afghanistan, but those units were supposed to stay in Afghanistan. We were the threat of what could happen.

3

Every Other Day

Life during a deployment can be "infinitely boring," to quote one veteran. Over time even the squeal of mortar fire and the boom of the C-RAMs (counter rocket, artillery, and mortar) becomes familiar. The days and nights are unvarying: shifts of work, physical training, too little sleep, the same food in the same place with the same people, video games, and Tom Clancy novels. Emails from home and Skype calls with a loved one, when possible, offer some punctuation in the routine. The unit may patrol the same stretch of road or deliver goods to the same COP; the view from a guard tower offers an unchanging panorama, so a foot patrol could be a welcome variation. Yet it is in the details of this everyday boredom that a deployment carries its unique character or forms the memories of a particular veteran's war, the material for camaraderie in the years to come, the nostalgia for a precise time of life.

I REMEMBER WHEN I first landed in Afghanistan. It was surreal. You saw everyone running around on the flight line. And they hustled us into a little room, and we didn't see the mountains or anything because the dust had kicked up. So I get in there, and basically the briefing we got was, "If you're not in shape, you're going to die." That was one of my first briefings. Right after that followed the intelligence reports and how much of a threat you were actually at while you were on base. So that was my initial welcome to Afghanistan. I worked the one p.m. to the one a.m. My first night there was my first attack. You heard the bombs in the background while you were on the truck where we were waiting for aircraft to take off, and of course they ground us when that happens. We were sitting there, and we could hear everything going on. We looked at each other like, "Is that bombs going off?" As they get closer, you realize what's happening. Everything was very overwhelming when you first come in. But then the sun comes up, and you get to see everything. We're driving on the perimeter road, which is called Disney, and it circles around the base. So it's my entire group; we're on the bus; we're driving back so that the other group can trade off with us and go to work. As we're going by, they've started putting up concrete barriers outside of the metal fence that goes around; it just has the concertina wire on top. As you're passing by that, they're putting up these giant concrete barriers. I noticed there was a little spot; I saw the little crack, and I could see children off in the distance between the barriers. So I realized if I timed it just right as I passed the concrete barrier, I could snap a photo of these children. Just as we passed it, I took the photo, and a rock hit my window; it would've hit right in my face if the window hadn't been there. I looked back, and these little kids are just chunking rocks over the perimeter fence at everything that's passing by. I learned later that it was an issue for people who were exercising, running the perimeter. There was one lady in particular who got a concussion because they'd hit her in the head. But something baffles me when I look back at that photo: the rocks that are surrounding these children, each one that's painted white denotes a land mine; it sits on top of that land mine, so you know not to step on it. Seeing the age of the children, especially the smallest one, who had to be about three; I think the oldest one was maybe around seven or eight. . . . It blew me away about their ages because there's no city near the base, and everything that surrounds it was completely destroyed by the Soviets. You can tell where the cities used to stand and the rocks are crumbling, rock walls with giant holes in the sides of them. We can't see any type of city off in the distance, so there's no telling how long it took these children to walk there. It was a big realization: just how different it was. There wasn't a gas station that you could go to; there wasn't a Walmart you could run to. There was just . . . there was nothing. I can only imagine what these children think when they look at us every day. I remember we used to run; for our PT we'd run the perimeter of the hospital.

If you ran it so many times, that was a mile. For the most part I really liked running around there. I liked watching people come and go and watching the helicopters take off, the emergency stuff coming and going. When you see soldiers, when you see adults, it doesn't hit you as hard as when you see children. So there was one day when we were running around, and there were children who had stepped on the land mines. They brought them outside to get air, to get sun. And so I just remember seeing those kids standing outside and we're running laps around them the entire time. That was probably the crappiest feeling I've ever had. Guys would make jokes, and I know for the most part we joked to deal with an awkward situation, but I mean very inappropriate jokes. When those kids were throwing rocks at us, the guys made a comment about shooting the children. And me. . . . I don't know if it's just because I am a female or what it was, but I made the comment that given another scenario, I don't know what I would do, but in that situation it was unwarranted; it was the wrong thing. It wasn't going to kill you. So then the guys made the jokes about, well, I would just shoot the land mines. And that's something that's always stuck with me. That comment has always bothered me ever since then. That was day one. Every other day was not like that.

• • •

We were picking up all this supply food for a ship. And the ship food is way better than the Afghanistan food at our outpost was. But the steaks had "Class D. Not fit for domestic sales" or something like that. I told my mom that, and she was so mad. She was like, "I can't believe they give you Class D meat!" Like there was an atrocity there.

• • •

FOB Kalsu was a pretty nice FOB. There were four corners; there was a nice security wall that had turrets on the top, and people pulled security. Within the actual FOB, within the walls were (we called them) tin cans where we lived, and then you have contractors living in the same place with us. You'd have base of operations in the middle of the base, and then you'd have chow hall. There were other things like the communications building and stuff like that. But the FOB that I was at, it was nice. I think the first time I ate in the chow hall there was steak and shrimp and stuff like that. So it was nice. It was always hot there, like a hundred-degree-plus weather. Then when the sun would go down, it would be like eighty or ninety degrees; it wouldn't be hot, but there'd be that lasting temperature from the day. There were a couple times where our base got mortared; we weren't always protected because of the wall security. We would have mortars and rockets being shot into our base all the time. We did have to carry our weapon everywhere. Within the tin cans there were sandbags and stuff to protect us, so we weren't like exposed-exposed. But with the mortars in Iraq, you don't really know where they're going to land. The other cool thing was in the actual base they had these cement blocks; whenever we heard the alarm for the attack, we'd get underneath the cement blocks. We got up early, did physical training, and then if we were going out of the wire, if we were leaving the FOB, the base, we would get orders, and we would basically make sure that we had everything in order, and then we would go out of the wire. What that would entail would be me sitting in the HMMWV waiting until we got to the location we were supposed to be at, getting out of the HMMWV, and basically pulling security so that nothing happened to the sergeant major or the colonel. Any time we were leaving the wire, leaving the FOB, we had to go green, which meant that we had live ammunition and everything. Once we left the FOB as a guard, our eyes were constantly open, while we were driving, for any sort of hint of movement or IEDs or anything like that. And then when we stopped, we would get out and we pull a complete 360 security of the HMMWV because there were four HMMWVs. So we were constantly on guard, constantly looking for any sort of threats, and then when we actually arrived at our objective, we would all get out, and then we would all pull that 360 security looking for any potential threats while the colonel or command sergeant major would conduct their purpose for being there.

• • •

I was taking some classes for my masters online at the time.

• • •

It's called multi-cam. It's supposed to camouflage for any environment. If someone laid down in multi-cam, they could disappear, which we tested. It blended in with these little shrubs. So you have a front plate and a back plate, and you have two side plates under each arm that're supposed to protect your ribs. The standard load-up—most people use this load-up—you can have seven mags across the front, and it's easy to grab whenever you're firing. I didn't because I was a machine gunner, and my kit was altered. On my back I have extra mags for the loader. So he could grab it. If I ran out of ammunition, then I still could fire. Besides the Kevlar . . . I'm trying to think. That's pretty much it with uniform. A standard combat load weighed something like seventy pounds. Mine weighed closer to two hundred with the amount of rounds I carried. And I carried batteries for the radios and all that stuff. The heavy stuff.

• • •

It always smelled so bad anywhere you went on base. There weren't any sophisticated plumbing systems. There was just this hole that all the poop and all the water would go into, and they would empty that out in the mornings. And you always would smell that everywhere.

• • •

Afghanistan is like a combat vacation . . . well, compared to Iraq. The constant patrolling, the monotony, Iraq just wore you down because it was the same thing day in and day out until you got attacked. Afghanistan was, "Hey, we're going on a patrol," and you'd go on about two or three patrols a day and maybe one at night. You couldn't enter the houses of the locals without a police escort, and you never wanted to take the police because they were crooked, and you didn't trust the Kabul police; they didn't know what they were doing. We had vehicles, but you could only patrol up and down the wadi, which was a north-south riverbed in that area, and then you may have convoy duty once a month to resupply the other FOB that was a couple clicks away, so you'd get in a convoy and go over there. But most of the time you were either on guard or you were on patrols, and there were two platoons that were on patrols. One of them was a day-patrol platoon, and the other was a night-patrol platoon. And that night patrol would go out around ten thirty, and they would come back around three. And their whole job is to go out for a couple of hours and sit up and watch and just try to catch people doing stuff. Day patrol was to go around and get a census and see what's going on in the morning, and in the evening you'd try to do a combat mission.

• • •

The food that we were eating was indigenous. One of my guys didn't take to the food very well, and I actually thought I was going to fly him out because I wasn't able to break his fever for a while, and I had him constantly on IV fluids. Fortunately, it broke, but I really thought I was going to have to fly him out because he was in bad shape. All my guys, it was not uncommon for them, during that first period, to be vomiting and have explosive diarrhea. To be completely honest, the remaining two-thirds of that deployment we actually lived off of macaroni and cheese, tuna cans, peanut butter and jelly sandwiches. Every now and again we'd get a pig or an animal that we would cook ourselves or have a fish fry with the more trusted units. But we lived off of care packages for the remainder of the deployment. And protein shakes out the butt. Life would have sucked a lot more if we didn't get those care packages.

• • •

In Iraq a lot of it is constant patrolling, and complacency is what kills you. The person stands up in the turret for too long, or the one time that you miss seeing that tire on the side of the road, that kills you. And that's what pretty much messed me up for a long time because attention to detail is life or death over there. The little things kill you. The one time that you don't set the concertina wire right, that vehicle can go right through it. So it's always good to feel like you're getting back at those people who are doing that to you. When you know 100 percent in your mind that they are the bad guys. In Iraq it was snipers, and then there was the IEDs, the main ambushes. You're dealing with the smart guys that are ex-military, that constantly work around this; they've been studying you, they've been watching you, and they decide when to attack you. So it's out of your hands when they do stuff to you.

• • •

The first three months in Mosul during the invasion—three months of MRES. Nothing; that's all you ate. That little pre-packed meal ready to eat, that's what it is, and they could pretty much survive a nuclear blast. Those things, they're like space food. Y'know, everything is dehydrated, and you're gonna have to heat it. Three thousand calories per meal in those things, but there's only twenty-four options of what your meal is, and after four months you're like, "I'm getting chicken and mushrooms again. Whatever." That's one of the things that they changed then too; when we started having to eat more of them, soldiers started to say, "Can we get something besides this? Nobody liked this in the first place." When you did have an MRE during the second tour, there was a lot more variety to it. I want to say it was near the end of our first tour (it's hard to remember that one sometimes, some of the pieces of it); KBR started to take over a lot of our food and equipment and where our water came from and all these kinds of things, so you got better supplies. You got higher-quality foods. The second tour, one of the guys I was standing in line with—we're going through this chow line, y'know, getting food, and you look at it—somebody said, "What? Lobster again?!" And you stop and think, "What is wrong with me?" Really. He just said "lobster" like it was a horrible thing. But every week they would have lobster tails and steak once a week, like they were trying. . . . "See? Life is good. Life is good." Never mind the fact that we didn't care about the lobster. We wanted the mortars to stop. That's what you really wanted. And that was the other change. That first tour, I think we got . . . my camp got attacked once, and that was near the end, when we were getting ready to leave. We had one . . . no, there were two . . . there were two rocket attacks . . . that happened separately over the walls that somebody shot a rocket in. But then that second tour. . . . It was like three times a week they were shooting mortars at us, and you had a whole plan for getting in bunkers and . . . it was, like, we're just surviving through that. So while you had these higher quality things, y'know, better stuff, it was a more persistent antagonism, basically, than what was there initially.

· · ·

In Baghdad, it was seven days a week; you kinda just get into the routine, y'know; you get back from your mission at night, you bed down, get some sleep—probably about four or five hours of sleep—get up, go hit the gym for an hour, get some good work-out time in, then you come back, you start checking your equipment, you check your vehicle, make sure everything's in working order, spend a couple hours on that, go to do mission briefs, discuss where we're gonna go tonight, what the dangers are, who's seeing what IEDs have been where—y'know—what are the dangers along this route. This is the route we're taking; why is it dangerous? Where do we need to be careful? What do we need to watch out for? . . . Make sure our equipment's in good working order, get with the armor and take care of any problems. . . . It was a constant focus of, "Make sure this is all in order. Now we're gonna get ready, get back on the road, take off, come back." Do the whole thing over; get four or five hours of sleep. I don't remember what the rotation was, but occasionally we'd get a day or two off where it's just, "Okay, stop and rest." But . . . then it's, "Okay you've got twenty-four hours. You're going to spend the first six of those working on your vehicle and taking it down to the maintenance bay and talking to mechanics and getting that done, and then you're going to have to make sure that you get some face time with your wife on the Internet or somewhere. . . . At some point I got moved to an administrative position where I was more on-post and got to do more communication with the wife, but during mission time, when you're out on the road, you don't get that. I would talk to my wife then about two to three times a week, and it would be, y'know, maybe during my chow time. I'm like, "Go on, I'm gonna skip lunch and go talk to her."

· · ·

We had heard about it in training, but I never really thought it happened like that. But we were told if no one is out in town like

PHOTO BY MICHAEL GIBLER.

normal, then that means there's an IED. And that's real. The town would all of a sudden be a ghost town, and yesterday there were kids playing in the streets. (A) It's super obvious that something's about to happen, and (B) it's kind of, like, eerie because you don't know where everyone went; you don't see anyone in the windows.

• • •

Intelligence is more reactive than proactive; we were trying to change that while we were there; we would take all of yesterday's information from the guys out in the field. Y'know, this is what they saw. This is what happened. This is what we discovered. Yadda, yadda. All these details, put it all together, and go, "Okay, based on this information, at this time and this setting, we can forecast that if this is another typical day, this is what's gonna happen tomorrow. This is what's gonna happen the next day." So we'd sit there and put all that information together for eighteen hours. At any time, we'd present probably seven or eight different briefings throughout the day, whether it was to commanders of units who were going out into the field or the air crews that we supported. And then . . . somewhere in there we ate lunch and dinner. It was more of a blur. And then I'd go back. Work out again. And then . . . go to sleep. And it got to the point . . . it got so routine, that I could tell you the number of steps I would take between each spot, how many steps I would walk in a day. It got that detailed. Because this was my first deployment, no one really gave me the heads-up that "Hey, you should probably, like, bring a Gameboy or something." And I left most of that at home because I was like, "I don't wanna bring all that over there and destroy it." So I got there with almost no entertainment. I had three books, and I finished those in the first day. So I worked out from the necessity of needing something to do. I ended up reading close to eighty-six books while I was there.

• • •

You have a lot of solid waste that needs to be dealt with. When we got to Camp Victory, each unit had certain buildings that they could occupy. The one we had had no working plumbing, but we had toilets. Somebody came around and counted toilets and said, "You're good to go." The problem is that none of them worked. This is fine for a couple of days; you can dig holes. But you've got upwards of sixty people in a small area digging holes; that's not going to work for too long. So the way we deal with that is you have these big oil drums cut in half, and you use one till it fills up, and then you go to the duty roster, and you get up in the morning when it's marginally bearable—between four and five in the morning—and you mix four parts diesel with one part regular gasoline, and you stir that stuff until it burns it up. It's good too. You learn a lot from that kind of stuff.

• • •

Most of the time we were sleeping out in the desert, you know, just random spots in our vehicle. I was on a light armored vehicle. We were a four-vehicle platoon, so we would travel eight hours away from our camp at a time, and we would sweep the highways, whether it's getting out and walking the highways and kicking tires or reacting to a bomb strike that a convoy experienced or sniper fire. Four- to five-hour patrols; then come back, sleep, get up again, whether it was the middle of the night or during the day. Most of the time, we didn't come back, so we were very . . . I don't know . . . we were very transient. We kept all of our equipment in our vehicles, so we were just ready to go any time, and they always told us, "We might not come back, so make sure you bring everything with you," so it was just patrol after patrol after patrol.

• • •

The Golden BB Theory? If some guy gets shot with a BB gun, but it hits his artery, he dies. Golden BB Theory. I'm on a twenty-acre base; where's the mortar round gonna land? I'm standing at the right place at the wrong time, and that mortar round decided, y'know, BOOM! right here. And that was kinda how we were. And we made a game out of it, to try and cope with it. We mapped out the base, and we sectored it off. Y'know, A, B, C, D, E, F, G, 1, 2, 3, 4, 5, 6, 7, 8, 9, 10. We narrowed it down to a certain size, and we bet money on where the mortar round was gonna land. If the mortar round landed close to your sector, you won the pot. If you were in the sector when the mortar round landed, you got double the payoff. I lost most of the time. I mean, we'd only make dollar bets; it was like one dollar per zone. Every morning we'd come in and go, "Okay, next mortar, here's my bet." I won maybe a handful of days. We had an E-9 over there who was just absolutely outstanding for some reason, so we started watching where he was guessing and started avoiding that area of the base until the next one came through.

• • •

That was the number one stress in Iraq: a troubled relationship back home. Number two was the people I work with, I can't stand. Three—it was way down—was, "Oh, I worry about dying." "Somebody's trying to kill me." "I got hurt." The whole time I was there, I noticed that most of the soldiers dealt with death pretty quickly. It was really obvious how you would die. You'd get blown up and WHOOSH! it'd be over; you'd be dead. You probably wouldn't even know it had happened. Most people just had that awareness. I could see that within a week they stopped being nervous and just got real used to it. I noticed that about myself too; I wasn't worried about dying any more.

• • •

I ordered a bicycle online. It was delivered in a box through our postage system. You could order anything there; it was amazing. So I got a bicycle and put it together. I just wanted a regular sand bicycle; you know, no gears because the sand there is like talcum powder; it's not like the sand you think of here, where it's grainy. It's been beaten for thousands of years, so it's just very fine.

• • •

We called it a hooch, and it was sort of a trailer-looking thing. It was, you know, kind of a bad seventies-style-esque look, and I shared it with one other individual, which I was really glad for, particularly at the beginning because it was very nerve wracking—the sounds, you know, the mortars and what have you. I remember the first time a mortar went off, and the C-RAM and sirens, and they gave us these little cards that said, "If a siren does this, you do this," and I remember being on the ground looking at my card trying to figure out what I should do. So it was bare bones, but it was comfortable; it wasn't a tent. We were all just sort of sardined in this little trailer community. Essentially it was very quiet; you know, if they were in their trailers, they were sleeping.

• • •

One guy had a ten-thousand-dollar cell phone bill because he kept arguing with his wife. It had been more, but the phone company cut it down to ten thousand.

• • •

If a diesel truck goes by, the sound of that engine, the smell of the diesel. . . . I have all these . . . they're not horrible flashbacks; I'm just transported back. It was so hot over there, even at night, crunching through the gravel, going truck to truck to talk to everybody, pray with them before the convoy. I would just do that every single night. We'd all gather for prayer; everyone was smoking; it was like this incense. The headlights, the smoke, prayer. They'd stand around in a circle; some would kneel, though. Soldiers are extremely superstitious or faithful, however you look at it. I remember one of them said, "I don't want to be turning around and walking the other way when the prayer happens, knowing what we're facing, the uncertainty of it." I'd pray for a successful mission; I'd use some language from the prayer book. In the beginning I would thank God that we had the opportunity to do this so that our kids wouldn't have to. I had some of those thoughts in my head. Mostly it was for safety. I'd always pray for the people back home, the families. Then they would joke, "I'm glad you're going on the convoy tonight." And I would say, "You know, the founder of my religion died five hundred miles from here. He was killed by soldiers. He was crucified. Right over there; it's not far; just go across that desert and you're there." I'd always say, "I don't think I'm the lucky charm; I just think I'll be here with you when things happen. I'm going to be here with you." That seemed to make sense to everybody, which is what I think we really want in life. We don't want an easy life; we want somebody there for us.

• • •

It's a lot like Vegas; there's no time there; everything's open 24/7; the lights are on; there's no clock. You're just in this gamble. It's an unlucky lottery; if you win it, you die or get injured, but ultimately you're just gambling on the odds. The more times you roll the dice, the more or less chance you have.

• • •

You get up at four o'clock in the morning, and you do the exact same prep stuff and then go through the exact same briefing, and then get basically the exact same trucks and drive down the exact same road, through the southern desert of Iraq, where there's literally nothing. I mean, it's just nothing. And you try and stay alert. As a leader trying to keep my soldiers alert and focused and not wanting to just go to sleep, I can't think how many times I elbowed the guy in the gunner seat because I knew he wasn't paying attention, you know. And how many times somebody probably kicked me in the back of the head because they knew I wasn't paying attention. I mean . . . I don't care how disciplined you are when you reach a point where it's just impossible to just. . . . Same stretch of road, two, three miles and nothing happens. You know?

The vast majority of these guys driving it every day literally have never been in an engagement. A lot of these guys have never seen something fired in anger, and now they're three months into this tour and have done the exact same thing every single day, seven days a week, without stop, without rest. . . . And they're spaced out.

• • •

That's kind of what I enjoyed about the reconnaissance thing. They call us cowboys. We kind of got to do our own thing, and we did it well, so no one really told us not to. Most of the time we didn't bathe. If we did, it was poor. It was bad or just nasty. Especially going that long without doing it; I mean just baby wipes and water bottle baths. It was a really long time. We didn't shave; our military grooming standards went out the door when we were out there, which we were happy about too because we got to grow our beards out. It was just more fun. You didn't have to blouse your boots, and, you know, we didn't really wear our protection until we were shot at. We just walked around. There was one time a general flew out, and we all had to shave, and we were all pretty pissed off about it.

• • •

At night it was a little bit better because Iraqis go to sleep, and they sleep hard. And we weren't kicking in doors; you could easily unlock the doors and just walk into somebody's house, and you surprised them. You'd wake them up and say, "Hey, we're going to be here for a little bit. Go back to sleep. We're going to have guys up on the roof." And just sit there and watch and try to catch somebody planting an IED. And it's pretty much every day for seven months. You switched; you'd go from vehicle to dismount to post to vehicle to dismount to post. When you were on a vehicle patrol, after your eight hours of patrolling you were on eight hours of QRF, which stands for Quick Reaction Force, just in case that vehicle mounted patrol or dismounted patrol gets injured or they get ambushed, something happens and they need help, you have to be outside ready to go in ten minutes with all your gear on. Well, we'd been there for four years, so these people are pretty much used to it. They're frightened, but, like I said, we weren't kicking in doors. The first thing is in the daytime you just knock on the door and wait for them to come, and you say, "Hey, can we come in the house and talk to you?" We always ask them and accept it kindly. We'd sit around; they'd bring us chai, which is tea. They were very cordial toward us. Their little kids would come sit by us, and we'd mess with kids, and I really felt like I was doing something. The kids are the biggest part of the war effort to me. To me, it was interacting with those kids and making them enjoy seeing us and being out there and giving them candy and stuff. As a parent, I can't be upset at someone who's giving my kids candy. I can't be upset if they're coming out with soccer balls and that's all they're doing. But the minute they start blowing things up. . . . So during that whole time frame it was about reaching out to the community and showing them. One of our mantras was, "No better friend, no worse enemy," and you want to show them that you're there to help.

• • •

There was one town we called Hatersville that we literally just drove through because we knew something was gonna start and figured that was the easiest way; if we killed enough of them, maybe they'd stop. That was three clicks away from the FOB. I never did figure out why those people were so pissed at us. We weren't hurting them at all. The piece of land that we were on didn't have a real problem with AQI or some of these groups coming in from other parts of the country or other parts of the world influencing it. So whatever issues they had were primarily theirs. Now there was some Mukhtar Militia influence, and they were getting weapons and materials out of Iran pretty clearly. The first attack in July was when my truck got hit by an EFP that was Iranian-made. We'd never seen anything like it. It was one of the first ones in theater, so that one kind of threw us off. And basically we just kinda got lucky; they set it off a couple seconds early, and it hit the engine compartment rather than the crew compartment.

• • •

You go to the gym when it's not stifling hot, and it's in this huge tent, is all it is. It's like an eighty-man tent or something, which we lived in the first three months we were there. We had eighty guys in one tent with bunk beds. It was very difficult—not for me as much because I was a day-shift worker; I felt it was much harder on the nurses that worked swing shifts and night shifts because you can't sleep during the day when it's ninety-something degrees and it's in a tent. So there were people that had chronic sleep deprivation because they'd just worked a night shift and then they couldn't sleep during the day because of the heat and people coming in and out of the tents.

• • •

It was gray in the very beginning because we went during the rainy season, so in addition to the fact that we had bombed the heck out of the base in order to take it over, so there was really no life; they would also always shoot all the birds because they don't want them getting in the planes. So there was just death everywhere; it was real, and you just couldn't get away from it.

• • •

They would helicopter in these big palettes of boxes of MRES. They had cold weather ones, which you put boiling water in and let them cook for a few minutes. But we didn't really have boiling water, so we'd take a plastic water bottle and throw it in the exhaust pipe of a MATV and let it heat up. I don't know if it's healthy or not; I'm sure some of the plastics. . . . But it'd get pretty hot, and then we'd pour it in and let it cook. So we did that. We just didn't have the materials to make fires. We burned all of our trash and poop and piss and stuff in a big pile, but other than that we didn't have spare wood to make a fire. Beef Stroganoff was my favorite cold-weather MRE, and spaghetti and meatballs was my favorite regular MRE, but by the end of my deployment I wasn't able to eat anything. They come with these really high-calorie milk shakes or protein shakes, and I would just eat those a few times a day, so I ended up losing over twenty-six pounds by the end of the deployment. Month after month of these MRES, processed, I would feel sick to my stomach; it was too much.

• • •

I managed to procure a very rusty bike, and I would put on all my gear, and I would ride that. I became very strong. I would put on all my gear and walk or bike, and my trip was always punctuated by seeing the sharpshooter's tower; the hospital is right next to the wire, and, you know, I'd always go and hear the sound of machine gun fire typically, and it was, other than that, pretty lifeless. I'd go into the hospital. I'd ride my bike to the back of one of the ICUs, park it, walk in, take off all of my gear, and immediately just go and start seeing patients. That was when I wasn't on call. So I'd start to see patients and see how they did overnight and if there were any new admissions and how they'd be divvied up from the evening. And then we'd have rounds with the whole team, all the ICU staff; physicians, nurses, respiratory therapists, and the higher chain of command would come through, and then we'd have our tasks for the day. Then we'd stay until the work was done, and then if I weren't on call, I'd leave the hospital—I'm not sure when; I'd never really look at the time—go back and change, and then I'd immediately go to the gym. I went to the gym every day. I was in fantastic shape. So I'd go to the gym and then come home and have dinner and then just read or write. I wrote a lot in my journal. And then the same thing would happen, unless I was on call, which was every fourth night, and that's where you're the one ICU attending that stays behind and handles all the admissions and covers all the patients overnight. And that was busy always. We always had our patients come in at night, and it would just be one after the other, after the other, after the other. It was a very busy time when I was there.

• • •

The route that runs along the Sangin River is called Route 6, and at the time it was the most heavily IEDed road in the world. We would have to drive down that every once in a while to go south to pick up MRES, or mail or something, or do a mission. So we would, you know, be prepping for a mission, and they'd be, "Hey, so there's twelve possible IEDs on the road." Being the lead vehicle driver, you're like, "Holy shit. That's a lot. I don't know if I want to do this mission." But you have to, so that was very nerve-racking. So you'd drive, and you'd use the thermal, and you'd see these little dug-up holes in the road. And you'd be, "Is that one? Is that one? I don't know." Avoid them if you could, but sometimes the road was so narrow that you couldn't.

• • •

That was one thing that I was proud of. Our first sergeant was insane; he was nuts, just off his rocker crazy, but he had us work so hard to fortify that COP. Sometimes you can read about American positions getting overrun. I just don't think that would have been possible; it would have taken a battalion of Taliban to overrun our COP. The flip side of that was that we were always miserable; we were always filling sandbags, always digging. We were just miserable, but no different misery than in the books you read.

• • •

So IED denial or cache denial. That was a typical mission; it'd be, like, me and a guy or me and two other guys. Because that's how they do it; they just bury weapons or whatever and come back to them later. We found a lot of stuff. We found hundreds and hundreds of pounds of ordnance. We found a lot of things. We found a couple IEDs that had been set up but not ready to be detonated yet. One time we were walking through the village. The southern part of the village comes right up against the green zone. There was a culvert, drainage thing, which the path went over. Pretty much every COP has an eye in the sky. It's a big tower; it's just a very, very expensive camera that they control from the COP, and they look around, and it's got thermal, night vision; it's got everything you could want. It's a very high-definition camera. And they were like, "We see two guys doing something suspicious." We were just around the bend of the road. We were walking south, and the road cut east. They were like, "We see some guys doing some suspicious activity; you might want to check that out." So we kind of spread out, and we tried to go around and come up behind them. But you can't in a village; you can't really sneak up on anybody. At least in the situation we were in, it wasn't going to happen. They escaped into the green zone. We walked up onto the area they were in, and they had completely dug out in the mud. I remember it so vividly: the mud was so perfectly scooped out. They'd dug a line for a wire detonator. Underneath the culvert were three big jugs. . . . I don't know how many gallons they were . . . but big, emptied jugs of vegetable oil is what they used to put homemade explosives in, and there were three of them. It was 150 pounds of homemade explosives is what it was. We blew it up. And that was that. It was really satisfying finding that because that would have been horrible; that would have cleared out maybe a whole squad. When we were on roads, we had two guys with detectors in front of each line. It could have taken out like four or five people. We called EOD. We removed it just about twenty meters down in the green zone. We just put it down in a grape row, blew up some guy's grapes. But . . . I just wish we could have shot those guys. But I don't know. If somebody comes into my country with a gun on their back or on their shoulder, I'm going to do whatever it takes to get them out. . . . At the time, we all just really wished we could have caught those guys. It wouldn't have been pretty. But I mean, really, I don't blame any of them.

• • •

The scramble. . . . It was like the TV news. You're writing the script all day to give the news the next day. So people are working the phones: "Hey, did you certify any teachers in your AO? Did you give away some books? Do some inoculations?" So that was all within our staff responsibility. So you're looking at all these nuggets, and I was sort of like the editor. All these colonels were all bringing me things to put into the script, and I was the scriptwriter. I'd say, "Yeah, no, that's no good. That's no good. Yep. Nope." And if I took something, I didn't have time to verify it. So it's like, "Colonel, if you're giving me this nugget and I get asked a question, you're going to be there." So this is the deal that I made with all these colonels that couldn't stand up in front of this general. I said, "I'm not going to take the hit for you. I'll brief it, but you've got to give me as much information as you can, and you've got to be willing to stand behind it." Just like a good reporter. And they'd be like, "Yep. Okay. That'll be fine." So I'd write the script; it'd be brief—maybe about two minutes of talking about civil-military activities—and then on my own I decided, let's give him a little more, sort of like a Sunday special. So I would write something a little more extensive, like five minutes with some slides, about a particular topic: education reform and how, across the theater, various bits are contributing to training teachers or rehabbing schools or whatever. So that went over okay. I kind of did that on my own, and people sanctioned me to do that.

• • •

I was the watch officer . . . where all the communications would come in and out. There was me and one other guy, and we would just shift. I would do all day, and he would do all night, and then after a month we'd shift, and he'd do all day, and I'd do all night. It was pretty boring. We'd just sit around in this little room. It was like a plywood building with sandbags. Everything else on our base was tents, but this was like a little bunker structure because it was where all our comm equipment was. They had to have an air conditioned part so that the computers wouldn't burn up. So I was in there. We'd keep track of all the units coming in and out, do a bunch of reports. That boredom would be punctuated by a few really stressful moments. We had units all over the province, some pretty far away. If someone was hit—by an IED, for example—they would call us, and we would call one of the bigger FOBs because we didn't have any aircraft or anything like that. We'd have to call a bigger FOB and ask them to send a helicopter to go get them. That was always really stressful because you're trying to talk to someone, and they're actually taking fire at that time or someone is bleeding out at that time. You're trying to get everything exactly right, and you're worried: are they giving me the correct coordinates, or are they giving me the wrong coordinates? There's a ten-digit number for where they are, and if they send it wrong, the helicopter is not going to get there; the person is going to die. So it was really boring and then really stressful.

• • •

I was a 240 gunner, which is a machine gun. We have the 249 SAW, or squad automatic weapon, which is a smaller gun, and then the 240, which is a bigger bullet. I would carry that and set it up and shoot it when need be. Everyone had to do security. In the middle of the night, you'd have to stand up on the top of your truck or on the wall, just to make sure no one is sneaking up on you. On a couple occasions we had someone come up to us in the middle of the night, and that made us kind of nervous, but he had just wanted to talk to us without anyone knowing he was talking to us. So he gave us information and stuff, but it's kind of scary seeing a guy through night vision walking up the hill toward you. There were a lot of foxes and wild dogs and stuff that you'd see at night. They'd let us do target practice at them. They'd sneak into our area and steal our food, so it was good to keep them away, but a lot of times in the middle of the night you'd just hear POP! POP! and someone was shooting at the dogs because they're pretty vicious over there. They're just running around; these dogs are huge.

4

In Country

When we think of military occupation, we don't generally imagine it as a cultural immersion experience for young Americans. For many who deploy, the time in country is spent on a base among other Americans, where all the food and equipment is imported from the United States. But for others, the objectives are to win hearts and minds, to explore not just the geographic, but also the human, terrain. They might live among the people of Baghdad, blending in as a Special Forces unit. Or they might be working with communities to restore or improve civic infrastructure. They may for several days occupy a family home and maintain vigil alongside mothers and fathers, children, and grandchildren. Or they may just visit the local bazaar to collect souvenirs for the folks back home. These men and women have the unusual experience of living in a war zone but also of sharing in another culture's customs in a way that no tourist could. Soldiers have been invited to ceremonial feasts and family dinners in Kabul. Marines have acquired a taste for the particular brew of Baghdad chai, a beverage that no American coffee shop replicates. Marines have lived in the warrens, passages, and stately chambers of one of Saddam Hussein's palaces. One soldier swam in the Euphrates, a river once irrigating the cradle of civilization, now a rather polluted waterway. Some memories of Iraq and Afghanistan are violent, gruesome, or just plain grinding. Other memories are exquisite: sunrise above the Afghan mountains or the oceanic green of a child's eyes. When soldiers come home changed after combat, it is not only from the burden of war but also from the enchantment of seeing the world at another angle.

THERE'S THIS ONE TIME we went down south of the Arghandab River, and we were in Kandahar, Zhari District. We were stationed in a village called Kandalay. We had this area south of us called the green zone; it's where all the irrigation from the river was. We had a good mix of everything: very lush pomegranate orchards, grape fields, cucumbers, melons; there was a lot of pot; it was a farming area. There was an orchard. They're really beautiful compounds in a way. I mean, they're made of mud. It's kind of like a look back into history. In this part of Afghanistan, which is pretty impoverished, they'll have a compound with an orchard in the back and a really beautiful garden. It's really cool. The Afghans grow grapes much differently than we do; they do not use fences; they use a series of trenches that are just miserable to cross. There'd be an irrigation channel and then a big mud wall that can be anywhere from two to three or four feet thick; then there'll be a two-foot ledge where they'll grow melons or cucumbers. Then they'd have another irrigation channel. The grapes just kind of grow over the wall. I'm sure they've been doing it the same way for generations, but it's just horrible terrain to cross. You can't go through. There're paths around them, but that's where the IEDs are. Then there was the village and then a highway that ran east-west, and then north of that highway was just a desert, barren. Really weird.

• • •

We had one particular week we spent clearing out a school in a small village—I couldn't point it out to you on a map. It was Mosul somewhere. We were clearing ammunition out of the school that they had—a pretty sizable school for such a small village: four good-sized classrooms, chalkboard at one end and everything. Desks that were all pushed to the side, but these boxes are lined up here. You'd be having boxes of ammunition. It'd be thirty-caliber rounds and 7.62s, which are what shoot out of the AK-47, and rockets—huge rockets, eight feet long, in boxes. And all these things just piled up in a place where there were supposed to be kindergarteners learning how to write Arabic and memorizing the Qu'ran. They were supposed to be doing these things, and there's rockets everywhere. We loaded all these things up into our trucks, and we got everything out, and it took us about a week. But after we cleared out this one guy's village, you know, you talk with the people occasionally. They speak a smattering of English. You might have an interpreter—a "terp"—there, and if you do, you get a little more conversation. So then the sheik—the sheik is just a village leader—was so grateful for it that those of us that were there that last day, he took us in and he fed us a feast. And we sat around with this old man and we got to eat—and that was awesome. This guy, he was so thankful that we cleaned out his village that he—I mean, they slaughtered a goat for us; they had Iraqi domas; they would have this big thing of rice that was wrapped in foil like they cooked the whole thing at once. And in there was, y'know, vegetables that were stuffed with lamb and stuff and you knew that this guy—that this village—didn't. . . . I mean they were a third-world country, stereotypical; it was very typical of what you'd expect of a third-world country, just very basic subsistence. They went out of their way, and about thirty of us got to sit in this man's courtyard and eat food with him. It was so not what we were experiencing everywhere else.

• • •

I'll wake up, and I'll be in either Iraq or Afghanistan. . . . I'll be there again, and I'll just remember all of a sudden and get a sense of what it's like. I used to joke about the heat in Iraq; it's like taking a blow dryer in the summer and just putting it on your face. And so any time there's a blow dryer going on and I feel it on my face, I kind of remember that. I kind of remember that's how it felt.

• • •

We went and raided around the area and stole a bunch of unripe melons. They were the most refreshing, delicious thing, so juicy. The melons were so cold; I don't know how because they were in the hot sun, but it was amazing. Totally unripe; they were green on the inside, but it was so good. We each got about half a melon. It was awesome. We would regularly raid the farmers' fields and eat their grapes. . . . I didn't really feel too bad about it. I mean, I knew that this was their income. I didn't feel like we should be there, but at the same time I felt that we were there, and if we needed water, I wasn't going to *not* eat those melons. I don't know.

• • •

In some of the palaces in Iraq, there were working spaces, and then there were still people sleeping inside simultaneously. So in the vast middle ballroom there were a bunch of double bunks that they'd put in, and there was the mess side on the other. So in the morning, you'd walk in from the back, where these trailers were, and there'd be dudes walking down the hallway in their underwear because they left their bunk, but they're going to the latrine. So the video that was circulating for a long time when I first got there was called "underwear man," and it was some dude who'd gotten out of his bunk and was just walking down the hall like you would walk down the hall to go to meetings an hour later, and he's like wandering through the mess hall getting coffee. . . . So this was the whole strangeness of it. The Marine guard company was living in the basement, sleeping in these crawl spaces. You'd go down there; they were like moles. I'd go down there to try to—I don't know why. Oh, I'd heard there were some good latrines down there. So that's the other thing. Private latrines. Trust me. Very important. What we did discover was that they had the pool, showers, and then a hole in the floor. They were trying to convert it into an effective office space and get the people who were living there out. So by February, March of 2004, there were no longer people living in the palace. They'd pushed everybody out to these trailers.

• • •

It was so gray and barren. I love birds, and the fact that we had to kill off all the birds was crushing to me, you know? I was like, "We can't even have birds around." I mean, I understand that you don't want them flying into the engines of a plane. I understand that, but, boy, what a drag. Everything had to die over there.

• • •

Well, the kids are the greatest thing in the world. In Afghanistan, they're beautiful. They're just blue piercing eyes, covered in flies though; they're filthy as heck, but there's something; they're just beautiful to look at. It really stands out because the whole country is a shithole, but you have these children that are just really good-looking kids. The kids would never attack you because they know you've got candy and stuff. If the kids are around, it's a good thing because the insurgents and the Al Qaeda, they're never going to attack you if children are around. It's just a bunch of innocents walking around in a war zone.

• • •

I'd go back to Afghanistan in a heartbeat. Definitely. I was intrigued by the country because it hasn't changed. If you take out cars and the occasional power grid, nothing has changed there since Alexander the Great. They still live in the same type of structures; they still have the same irrigation systems. I was always fascinated that I would pass by these structures and wonder how old could this be because it looked like something out of a medieval movie. How much has this seen? I've always been intrigued with the idea of time in the first place. Just to think, for example, someone else has been sitting here telling you a story that they experienced. It's only separated by time. That was pretty cool. Take away all the terrorists, and that was pretty cool.

• • •

There were a bunch of stray dogs. They weren't really dogs; they call them something else, but I forget. We got an suv, not a hummer, not one of the big up-armored vehicles, but an actual suv, and we just drove around—and this sounds horrible—but we could shoot them because they were tearing everything up. And that was kind of fun, I'm ashamed to say in front of normal people.

• • •

Geez, talk about the dust storms. I mean, those things are incredible in and of themselves because they have distinctive smells, which is odd. You can always tell the dust storm, where it came from, based on its color and its smell. Whether it's from Syria-Turkey, Saudi Arabia, or from the south. The south always smelled like oil because it was always from Kuwait. The northwest smelled absolutely terrible, and then it was always like a dark brown. And then the west was always a light color and no smell. You could still see. I mean, when the ones from the northwest came in, not only did it smell bad, not only was it miserably hot, but you couldn't see ten feet in front of you. I've got pictures where you can just barely see headlights, and I'm probably three or four feet from the car. Nobody took showers during dust storms. Everything was nasty. You had this fine layer of sand over everything after it was all said and done. Car wouldn't start because it would be sand logged. HMMWV would be stranded. Aircraft wouldn't start. It was miserable. It was like, "Oh great, now we have to go, y'know, clean out the generators and clean out the trucks and clean out the aircraft."

• • •

A lot of those people that we interact with, when they were younger, they were fighting Russians. And they were fighting each other in mujahideen battles. So they're used to constant warfare, but they also know that the Taliban have time, and that's another thing that we can never control. The day we pull out of the cities, all the Taliban have to do is show up. And they could just be some teenage boy in a black mask and an AK, and he's automatically in power because he waited until the Americans were gone.

• • •

They invited some local village elders from around the area onto the base, and they were all in the market. We called it the "Hajji Mart"; people think that's insulting, but they considered it almost . . . some of them considered it a compliment. They're like, "Yeah, I've made the hajj." It's like, "I'll take that nickname." There was an officer. He was a major. I wanna say he was a major (I can't remember), and he was talking with one of these elder gentlemen, who was the elder of some small little village just north of Balad. I guess this particular gentleman had kind of stayed out of the conflict as a whole. The major was trying to explain what they were trying to do in terms of bringing electricity and water and freedom to this gentleman. And this gentleman was using his son as a translator. At one point they were explaining indoor plumbing, running water, and the old man started crying. Just this seventy-year-old man, in tears. I was like, "This is odd. I don't understand. It's not my culture, but I don't understand." And I was sitting there witnessing this event in this little local marketplace that they had set up on base, and the old man said something, and the son said, "Well, sir, I don't really know how to translate this without insulting you." And the guy was like, "Come on, just, y'know, just let me have it." And the son said that the old man had said, "God must love you more than he loves us if you have the miracle of water at your fingertips every day." And everybody who had just witnessed that conversation went dead quiet. Because here's a man who for seventy years, as his son had explained, walked a five-mile round trip every day to the well with his donkey and his camels to fill up the water buckets for that day's water. For seventy years. And we had just explained to him that we get it every day, any time we want it, at our fingertips. Because we have the miracle of life at our fingertips whenever we want. And that's such a significant part of your life too. I mean, if you look at their culture, that's huge. That's how they view their relationship with God and how He views His relationship with them.

• • •

The night was something; especially when there's a firefight at night, that was something. You hear the helicopters; you see the rockets or the missiles flying; you see the tracers going everywhere. There was a firefight right at the gate, so there were tracers going about ten feet above our heads. There was a helo dropping, sending missiles across the base and just rocking the whole base. That was really cool. It wasn't our unit, so we didn't know exactly what was going on other than that there was a firefight right outside the gate.

• • •

I think that, unfortunately, the majority of my comrades . . . their attitude toward the Arabs was much more simplistic and almost racist. I say "almost," but in some cases it was very racist. Arabs, Iraqis, were referred to more in disparaging nicknames than they were anything else. . . . From a lot of the guys that I was deployed with, I know there's this absolute disregard for them as human beings: "Oh, they want the Arab Spring? They get democracy? Good. See how well you screw that up." It's more of a, "Look at the 'towelheads' over there, thinking they're going to be like

Americans, blah, blah, blah." . . . They don't tend to look at the culture as a viable culture, more as just an antagonistic culture. Them versus us.

• • •

We filmed a video on New Year's Day 2011. We were on our base, and it was very dark 'cause they always have light discipline so that it's not easy to target lights and things like that, and we were expecting they were going to do "fireworks," which was just an illumination round from a mortar. So we're all sitting there getting ready for it, and I have the video. It's like, "All right, here it comes!" Someone had counted, and it's like, "It's supposed to be right now!" We're like, "I just see it's dark," and we see up, and there's this solitary light just sitting there in the sky, and it's not lighting up anything, and we're like, "Yes! It's New Year's!" like that was the best we had. And we had our nonalcoholic beers, and that was it; that's all we could do. And it's funny; you drink a nonalcoholic beer when you haven't had actual beer in eight months or something like that, and it feels like beer; you get this weird buzz.

• • •

I was the only health-care provider in the region, so I actually saw a lot of local nationals and treated individuals for all sorts of things. There was a time when local nationals could come see me, and I would see if I could figure out what was going on with them. Most of the time it was really simple stuff, just aches and pains, and then chronic diseases that we couldn't really do much for with what we had, just manage symptoms. I developed my little training program to teach the local nationals; we were paired with trauma care and stuff like that. I taught probably anywhere between two and three hundred local nationals.

• • •

Oh, God, I ate the worst thing in my life. I had only been there for a couple weeks and was trying to make my way into things and didn't really know too much about customs or anything; I learned as much as I could before I got there but not too much. There was another guy who was a captain—I was a lieutenant, so he outranked me—and we were at this large meeting with—I

68

don't even remember the occasion anymore—just tons of people, and whenever they have a meeting like that, they always have a large spread of food afterwards. And it's just one long table with mountains of rice and other stuff on top of it that is just a free-for-all, just grab, do what you gotta do; nobody questions the sanitary nature of just grabbing things like that, but you do. When it's chicken, you can tell it's chicken, and it's okay. In fact, one of the best meals I've ever had in my life was a mountain of rice with chicken and stuff. But this one was not chicken; it was clearly not chicken; it was some kind of weird meat and some other thing that looked like not meat, but it was something. And this Iraqi dude offers it to me, puts it in front of me; and they don't just offer; they just literally put it in front of you, and that is your cue to do whatever. So I was told by—well, let's use active voice—so a friend of mine tells me, "You have to eat that now because it is offensive if you don't." And I'm like, "What is it?" And he's like, "Don't worry about it; just eat it." So I did, and it took every bit of willpower I had not to just throw it up everywhere 'cause it turns out that a delicacy in Iraq. . . . There's a flap on the back of a goat that covers the ass that is all fat, and that's what it was. It was goat ass. I did. I ate that. Swallowed it too.

• • •

They actually offered the GRE in Kandahar. So I actually had signed up for it, and I was going to take a helicopter from my outpost down to Kandahar airfield to take the GRE. And my flight was canceled because there was a dust storm. So there I am standing on the airfield—the helicopter landing pad, which is just a pile of rocks—standing in these rocks, kicking a bunch of them, saying, "Crap, what am I gonna do now?"

• • •

I'm guessing y'all hear all the time that the Iraqis hate us. That's what I've always been told. I don't really watch the news, so. . . . Well, there's always gonna be people who don't like us. But when we showed up at base, they knew that base was closing down, and it was always stunning to me. We would have to get out of our vehicles and lead our vehicles forward because the Iraqis would try to block us in. And we had some of them saying, "Take our children with you" and stuff like that. We do bad things sometimes. People see it in the news: "Soldier Kills Eight Civilians." And so people think that's what we all do. Our gunner would sit there with lollipops and throw them out to the kids as he saw them because, I mean, they have it bad. If there was gunfire in the streets here, no one would know what to do. At least they know to run and hide. And so they try to. . . . They were trying to get us to either stay or take them with us. They know we make it better for them. Running theory among my unit was that as soon as we left, Iran was going to invade Iraq. We were wrong about that.

• • •

People always ask me, "What was it like in Iraq?" I'd just make it a joke; I'd say, "Well, we had a lot of guns, and people seem to be really nice around people who have a lot of guns."

• • •

The only way to get things done in Iraq that I observed was to have a close, personal, intimate relationship with someone that you could go to in the middle of the night and say, "I need these four trucks ready by four a.m. I really need these trucks. I've got this mission." And it was real personable. "Can you help me out?" "Yeah, I can help you out." Another way was just the sheer threat of force and anger. Those were the two ways you'd get things done. You go to that person at four in the morning and you say, "I need these trucks. I've got these orders." They'll say, "That's not my problem; you should have come yesterday." And then you just get angry. You just threaten them, not physically, but I saw people throw water bottles at each other on those kind of issues—just logistical, scheduling issues. Everyone is trying to build a little safety shell around themselves in this chaotic environment. And you build it by keeping your regular meal times; you build these routines like prisoners do. And somebody throws something in from the outside, and people just lose it. I had a water bottle thrown at me by a colleague because I'd asked for something at the wrong time. It was constant emotions going off the charts. Because going from zero to ten was what you had to do all the time. You had to accelerate your aggression just to survive. Or you had to be ready to do that.

• • •

The detainee camp was huge. It's typical: the watchtowers, the concertina wires around. There are about thirty different compounds. There was a schoolhouse there in the prison for them to be educated and, of course, the dining. For that theater of war, we were the TIF, the Theater Internment Facility. We had physicians' assistants (PAs) that would go to the wire. We called it "the wire" because they would go to each one of the wired compounds, and they would triage anybody that needed care. Then people would come to the hospital on a regular basis. So I had certain rehab people that either had an injury or something we were rehabbing. Upper or lower extremities were very common. . . . The PA would make sure that they were coming to the hospital to see me or my team all the time. The dentist if somebody had teeth problems. . . . Or hernias are real common there. A lot of them are just chronic stuff that just needed care. You know, our general surgeon was able to help a lot of detainees just with some really simple surgeries. And the dentist too; just pulling teeth was his main thing; I mean, he made those guys feel great. So we took care of them just like anybody else. The International Red Cross would come through and inspect us. I really enjoyed their visit because they really helped with advocating and showing that we need to do as much as we can and be as humane as possible. Were there people in the hospital that had a really hard time taking care of detainees? Yes. There were just a few. There were just one or two. They were usually tasked to do other things in the hospital because some people just had trouble working one-on-one with the detainees. They would just do another support role—maybe supply or logistics or something. The people that were face to face, providing care. . . . I don't know of anybody that didn't just. . . . I don't know what else to do when I see a burn injury; I take care of it as I would anybody else.

From what the interpreters explained to me, Takfiri were the ones doing a lot of the damage, the violence, to those that didn't believe in their extreme ideologies. It really calmed down once they were segregated. We knew to bring them into the hospital separately. We knew they would cause problems; they could potentially cause a fight or something in the holding cells because there was a holding cell within the hospital that the security guys brought them in and out of. Only so many could come to your clinic at a time, you know, four or five that the security officer felt he could keep control of. So he stood guard there with all the proper gear to respond to anything that might happen. They would get their treatments, and then they would be escorted back out by the guards.

The violence within the compound was no less than probably in our own prisons. Prison violence was very bad there, just like our prisons here. There were certain factions within their community, so they injured each other. They fought a lot. A lot of the injuries we were taking care of were severe fractures of the elbows. They would put their arm in a backward position, and two guys would hold them down, and they'd break their elbows. So the orthopedic surgeon and I. . . . He did some of the most severe elbow fractures that I've ever seen in my life. So they'd have very stiff joints and elbows. And they did that so they couldn't pray.

Walking into the compound every day was very intimidating because you just see how organized they are. I mean they face Mecca at certain hours of the day. What I mean by "scary" is that they have a certain ideology that they believe in, and I know I'm the infidel, and I know they want to kill me, a lot of them. The ones that don't are very cordial; they're moderates, but they would support it if one of the Takfiri guys could possibly grab a pen off my desk and stick it in my throat, and you know that, and if you start getting that feeling, you can ask them to leave your clinic, but that happened very rarely there.

Most of them loved coming to the hospital because it's air conditioned; it's a different spot, and they enjoyed coming there just to see what we were like. So the relationship with them was very cordial, very nice. I was never armed; as medical providers, we always left our weapons at the checkpoint when we're going into the hospital; we wanted to feel as nonthreatening as possible. So we even took our jackets off and wore a camouflage smock, you know; we even wore our medical smock with a pocket. During Ramadan, our chaplain was very good about educating us about our religion and their religion and making sure we didn't offend them and respected their rights. We wouldn't have food in our clinic during that time that they were fasting and things like that. You know, they tried to respect us; they were always thankful, you knew, through the interpreter. . . . So I think that was the biggest frustrating thing for me as a health-care provider: I don't speak Arabic, nor can I read it, nor can most of them speak English. There were a few high-profile-type detainees that were very well educated; some of the imams were very educated or just more educated than the other population. Most of them are illiterate, just like our prison population; most people are illiterate.

Now there were different jumpsuits; there were people in yellow jumpsuits, orange jumpsuits, and red jumpsuits. The red ones were very rare because they were on death row. So there were certain people that were already convicted; they were waiting their time out, and they were going to be sent back. That was through the Iraqi court systems up in Baghdad. So they were sent down to just stay with us mainly for their protection from other factions within the prison system up there, from what I understood. Then there were people in orange, and they were prisoners per se, but we still call everybody "detainees." If you call somebody a "prisoner," they're already guilty. I mean, it's just the language. I'm sure it had something to do with the translation to Arabic.

Speaking of the language, they all got a Qu'ran when they first got to the prison. We had first grade, second grade, third grade, all the way up to fourth grade to try to have them become more literate, so they can see what the Qu'ran really says, so that maybe they can become educated and read it for themselves, so they don't follow certain ideologies from the imams that are very radical. They loved going to the schools because the schools are air conditioned; they got to learn. They loved learning how to read. They never had anybody give them that kind of attention before. The food, a lot of them thought the food was better than what they had regularly. That was all produced from people that were brought in to work as contractors from other countries, not our military—for instance, to make sure that was appropriate for them.

I think the biggest thing was the communication barrier with the interpreters. We had twelve interpreters in the hospital. It was hard to keep interpreters because they would either be scared and quit, or they just had other things going on or death in their family because violence was so bad there. So you had turnover all the time, chronic turnover. Out of the twelve or eighteen interpreters we were supposed to have for the hospital, there were only about four or five that were consistently there the whole time I was there. The other ten or so interpreters were constantly turning over. You had to develop a new rapport with a new interpreter. We all shared interpreters, like the dentist and I would. . . . A guy would be running back and forth across the hall; he'd go over and translate for the dentist and then come over to the rehab clinic. And you always felt like your message was being filtered or translated differently than what maybe you wanted it to be. Because education is one of our best modalities in rehab. You've got to be able to educate them about what to do when they're not in the clinic, so I was always concerned whether that was being done clearly, and you had to just keep bringing them back every few days to make sure that they understood what was going on with their condition.

The first six months were the most violent. They were burning down their compounds; very crazy, the first six or eight months I was there. Then we were able to separate out, to filter out, who the moderates were and who the radical jihadists were that were causing a lot of the issues. Once that happened, it all calmed down. Once the extremists were put in their own area and spot so they can be together, and they won't hurt each other. . . . They were causing so much violence. That's where all these severe elbow fractures came in. This one gentleman, he wouldn't tell who did it to him for the longest time because he was scared for his life. He so wanted to be able to put food in his own mouth. His elbow was so stiff that he couldn't even touch his mouth with his hand because it was just stuck. It was his dominant hand, and, well, both elbows were totally broken. One of them was just worse than the other. So he just wanted to be able to get his hands to his face. But both of his elbows were severely fractured. So his biggest goal was to just be able to touch his face, you know, touch his mouth. One of them was just slightly better than the other; one he never got to his face. But one of them we eventually got to his face. I see him vividly in my mind because he came to my clinic frequently. He was in the hospital; we wouldn't even let him go back to the compound for fear of his life. So he stayed in the hospital, and I would go see him in the evening too to make sure he was wearing his splint because we'd make gains during the day, but if he didn't wear his splint at night, he would lose the gains we made because tissue has to be kept at its longest length to get it to elongate; it's basic biomechanical science. So to get that joint to move, it had to be kept elongated. I was glad that he was kept in the hospital because he was so severely injured; he couldn't take care of himself. He had a very great sense of humor. He was constantly making people laugh through the interpreters, so I remember him very vividly. Eventually, once the people got moved out of his compound, he was able to tell who injured him, so the authorities could prosecute those people for what they did to him.

I just remember this real big guy, like six-foot-five, six-foot-six huge guy. I remember him really well because he so didn't want to come see us; he so didn't like us. But when he came in, I was able to help him with his finger, and the surgeon did a minor surgery; he had a bad fracture that needed to be fixed, and it made him better, and he just so . . . loved to come see me. I mean, the relationship just totally changed from the first time I saw him. And that happened. I can think of about five or six other ones that happened with. So I think it was just those really rewarding relationships I had with some of the detainees.

Then there's another one that lost his leg and his arm; he got hit by a rocket that was fired by one of our helicopters when we were in a battle with them, and he lost his arm. I remember—I don't know why I remember this—but I remember asking the interpreter, "Can he tell me what happened, and how did he lose his limbs so I can kind of understand what type of injury it was?" Because it was real fresh; I mean they were still shaping his stump; it was just a very fresh amputation, just cleaned up by the surgeons and closed down. I was trying to make sure it healed without too much swelling and healed without infection because the flies were just everywhere; we were just constantly shooing them off, and they didn't care. That was interesting: flies land on them; they didn't feel it. You and I would be just like, "Oh, my God!" But they were so used to it their whole life that they would let the flies just kind of land on their wounds if they weren't covered. . . . (The flies were terrible there. Eventually preventative medicine was able to get them under control. I mean even in the cafeteria, when you're eating, the flies land on your food. You're constantly shooing at your food and just trying to keep the flies away.) So even with the wound, you're just constantly shooing them away. Anyway, I just remember him looking at me: "Your helicopter blew up my limbs." And I'm just like, "Aw, I'm sorry you had to experience that, but I'm gonna do everything I can now that you're here to help you, you know." And just building that trust with him, that I wasn't going to hurt him and that I was there to help him and that some of the things we did for them were painful, but I was so passionate about explaining to them why we need to do this to your limb, that I'm not doing this to hurt you. I'm not torturing you. "Do you need pain medicine?" We were constantly worried about whether that was a problem or not. They had numbers. The detainees had like a serial number, so I never really knew their names. Their medical charts . . . a lot of private information was HIPAA controlled.

• • •

There was no time to reflect over there. There was just no time. We had a guy who died while he was home on leave. So he just disappeared. He went home on leave and slipped up driving his car, drunk probably, on the ice in Dallas during an ice storm. And he died. So we had a memorial for him. We had a memorial for a suicide. My sister battalion, which was the one next door to me, had a lot of casualties. So we were always at their memorial services helping out. But the idea was you get them over with, and then you get back to life.

• • •

The culture shock in and of itself was huge. I went from an over-abundance of things: a home, a place to sleep that's guaranteed. Yeah, there are threats here, but not like over there. Seeing how the Iraqi people live, how they have so little, but yet they thrive and they survive. Being in a temperature that I thought my face was melting off, you know. . . . Being in an environment where I had to be sensitive and open and willing to accept the fact that at any time my friend or I, you know, we could die.

• • •

We had interpreters that generally interacted with the Iraqis. But we would go on a mission, and there would be children who would run up and talk to us and stuff like that, but honestly, we couldn't really talk to them because we don't know Arabic. We knew certain key words. One of them was "car bomb"; I think it actually translates to "car explosive" or something like that. If we heard that, we'd immediately call the interpreter over and be like, "What is he saying to us?" Despite what a lot of people think, most of them liked us because we made their lives better; I mean, there was the occasional person that did not. . . . For the most part, we were over there trying to help people. I think they understood that, and they would try to help us. I think there were two occasions that we probably would have suffered casualties if someone didn't come up and say, "There's a person in there that has a gun." Or we had one person come up and say, "Car bomb." And there was a car bomb like fifty feet ahead of us.

• • •

I was at Camp Victory when I was in Iraq; it had a bunch of water diverted from the Tigris, and it had been stocked with fish for people in the palace, so we'd spend a little bit of time fishing. . . . I really don't like fishing. I border on the bleeding heart, and I see it as mean to fish. But after a while you realize that's kind of stupid, or even if it's not stupid, you're going to do it anyway. There are a lot of guys who know a lot about that stuff. So they started making fishing gear out of anything they could get; I mean, fashioning hooks out of paper clips. The fish were so hungry you could put anything on it and get them out of there. The goal was to eat the fish. The orders came down that the fish might be poisoned, so we couldn't eat the fish until about two months into this. Our first sergeant was like, "What the hell? Screw it. We're going to cook these fish." So we ate the fish. The great thing about Camp Victory at first was. . . . Later that became, like, this fortress, but when I got there, it wasn't a tight perimeter. The walls had been knocked down in all different kinds of places, so that 3rd ID could get in there. There were no guard towers. So it was really just sort of like this very porous border. What would happen is that the Iraqis were really hungry, and at first it was like kids, and then more. They would come in, and they would fish because they wanted food. That wasn't really that big a deal; they would come in, and they would come out. But then the question became: What do we do about this? They could be a security threat. So what we would do was have some men who would stand there and kind of watch them while they'd fish, which was kind of cool when you could talk to them a little bit. If you can imagine. Six month after this happened, it would be undreamable. But we'd just gotten to Baghdad, and I was exhausted. My body felt like crap, so I passed off my rifle to someone and said, "Look, I need to go on a run." I needed to get away from people, so I put on my PT uniform and just went on a run. And without realizing it, I ran outside the wall and ran out into Iraq and into Baghdad. I'm running, and at the point at which I realized this, there's this Iraqi guy trying to salvage corrugated metal from a bunker that had been destroyed, and I see him, and I look around, and I realize what had happened, and he sees me, and we both do a double take and just run in opposite directions. But that changed over the course of time I was there. First there wasn't really that tension. When I got there, it was still people jumping up and down and waving American flags, and it wasn't really the hostility that kinda slowly evolved. Oh, it was heartwarming to be pulling into Baghdad and seeing women (I focus on the women because the burka with a full face covering seemed so culturally distinct) jumping up and down and waving American flags; I mean, wow! Maybe there's something good that came out of this craziness after all. At least you feel like. . . . There's all kinds of emotions that come with being an invader. And that made it feel a little less horrific, what you were doing. For a long time, I would try to apologize to Iraqis that I would meet under these circumstances. I think they were just kind of shocked. They're not really used to soldiers addressing them in that way. I feel like, "I'm really sorry we had to meet under these circumstances; I have no desire to be walking into your country with a loaded weapon."

• • •

We had two Afghan National Army guys with us. Sometimes we'd buy chickens or lambs from the local populace. They'd slaughter them and cook them for us. So I got to taste the food, and we'd eat the flat bread that they'd make by stepping on it. Whenever they make it, they'll, like, stomp in a circle. It was really good with the rice and stuff. We got to see their crops and their growing seasons; we saw it from winter to summer. One time we took over a compound, but the people wouldn't leave until the morning, and they had three kids, so it was two parents and three kids. When we took over their compound, we got there at two in the morning. So I ended up having to babysit the three kids for four hours in the middle of a war zone. We'd try to teach each other the language and stuff. And they'd start grabbing stuff on my gear, and I had to push them away. But they were very interested in us. They were very excited because we were all there; they stayed up all night. They weren't scared; they started to get a little too brave and wanted to run around, and they were like, "Dave, keep them over there! Keep them over in the corner!" I had to corral them. It was a unique experience.

• • •

Poppies? They're tall. Blooming, they are a bunch of different colors. I thought it was gorgeous. When they're not blooming, they just have the bulbs. And how they'll make the heroine out of it, they'll slice the bulb and let it leak out; then they'll go through and collect the sap. They'll be in their fields all day, slicing them and collecting. The Taliban gets all their money from the opium harvest. And right when we were leaving, the opium fields were done, and they were starting to grow marijuana. Some of my other team leaders had been to Afghanistan previously and said they got six feet tall, these fields of marijuana. We had heard that sometimes people would go through and destroy the fields, but that's the villagers' livelihood; if we destroyed that. . . . People want them to grow rice and corn, but they can't make the money off of that, so if you want a bunch of pissed-off villagers that are going to shoot at you, sure, go ahead and take away their poppies.

• • •

Especially by Sangin River, we'd call it the green zone. We were right on the edge of the green zone, so kind of in the brown zone, a lot of sand and dirt. It was beautiful to look into, especially in driving; we drove a decent amount across the country, and see-ing the mountains and stuff was very pretty. I thought it was a pretty place, a very beautiful country. I absolutely thought it was gorgeous.

• • •

You read about Islam and Baghdad being the center of the world in the Middle Ages. You kind of see that.

• • •

One of the coolest things I saw was this massive sandstorm blow in across the Afghan desert. It was, I think, the most amazing thing I've ever seen. It was this towering wall of just dirt. You had to go into your tent because if it came through, you could get lost even if you were six feet from where you needed to go. People would get lost. There were a couple people we found after the storm was over, and they were like ten feet from their tent, and they couldn't find their way, and they were, like, completely covered in sand; their pockets were filled up with sand; their goggles and every-thing. It's just kind of a different world environmentally. I'm sure they were scared; I would have been terrified. Mostly people just made fun of them. There's not a lot of compassion.

I equate Baghdad to New Delhi or Mexico City but not quite as big. And relatively cleaner than the other two cities I just cited. It's crowded, there's traffic, and part of the reason why it's crowded and there's traffic is there's security checkpoints everywhere. What it potentially could be is an amazing urban sprawl with infrastructure and incredible mosques, buildings that I didn't even know existed, that are just gorgeous. And really cool war memorials from the 1980s Iran/Iraq War, the crossed sabers, and the Green Zone that you've seen so many pictures of soldiers being underneath. And then Sadr City. And you see some of the poorest people I've ever seen on the planet; they just have nothing. Well, Sadr City isn't as poor as just north of Baghdad. Sadr City is exactly what you read on Wikipedia or anywhere else on the Internet. You've got a lot of people living in a small space, and they don't have very much. But that's not as bad as maybe twenty minutes north of the city, in between Camp Taji and Baghdad. There are people literally living in trash. And it's sad. And it definitely makes you thankful for what you have here in this country. But Baghdad is an impressive city. You see historic sites; you see where the towers of Babylon once stood, according to the Bible. And you see some of the most fertile soil in the world, and that's incredible. It's like gray silt. It's like nothing you've ever seen before. And there are eggplants just growing out of it that are, like, this big. I loved the chicken and the lamb and the rice and the eggplant-tomato soup. And on Christmas, this is a cool story: on Christmas Day, we went to a sheik's house, and he had three wives, and he had one house for his wives and one house for himself. That was a cultural experience. One of the wives cooked for us, and they were like, "We want to feed your soldiers." And we were like, "Well, they're kind of pulling security right now." And they were like, "I'll give you plates, and you just take it out to them, and they'll do it in shifts, or whatever." And I'm getting all of this through my translator. I was like, "Okay." And my platoon sergeant told me, "Sir, you need to go in there, and you need to eat with these people." And I was like,

"I don't want to eat before the soldiers." And he was like, "This isn't training. This isn't like that. You go in there, and you go eat with them. You're going to insult them if you don't." And the food was just . . . that was one of the best meals. It's just incredible when you're sitting there eating something that rivals one of the best steakhouses. And you're in Iraq, eating in Baghdad, eating homemade chicken and lamb and rice and eggplant-tomato soup and falafel bread, and it's just incredible. And you just walk out of there stuffed, and your soldiers are happy they got what they got. Every time I ate Iraqi food, I loved it.

5

The Best Job I Ever Had

A deployment is not necessarily uniformly dreary or dangerous. For some the conditions on base are surprisingly luxurious, the food plentiful and delicious, the work imbued with a sense of purpose and meaning. The responsibilities assigned to even very young men and women allow these soldiers to rise to the demands of the occasion, to become the best version of themselves. The bonds among soldiers in a unit or on a particular assignment can be one source of fulfillment, but the mission purpose itself may be the strongest source of satisfaction. In a deployment an individual finds him- or herself in the position to save hundreds of lives; to improve living conditions for families in an occupied territory; to rebuild a country, region, or economy; or to keep a city or town safe from tyranny. Living in a war zone is also living abroad; for some, deployment is a first exposure to a country radically different from their own; to customs and circumstances that are startlingly foreign or startlingly familiar; to values and beliefs that are memorable and inspiring; and to histories and landscapes that bear the ancient signs of advanced cultures and the modern edifices of industrial, artistic, social, and cultural accomplishment.

I JUST REMEMBER A lot of negative stories about the war in Afghanistan and the war in Iraq: how it was a terrible thing and that we shouldn't be there. I'm not saying that we should have been or anything like that; I'm just saying they always highlight the bad stuff that is happening in the war; they never highlight the good stuff. But it is what it is. This kind of stuff you'll never read in the newspaper. We visited all the local hospitals and clinics, and we wrote to these care package charities requesting just simple stuff like bandages, diapers, simple antibiotics, and everything like that. We collected all of it for a couple months, and then come Christmas, we went around and distributed all these health-care supplies that we got from these care-package communities and charities and gave it to all these local clinics and hospitals. But that was a great thing that we did, I feel.

• • •

Great people I was working with. The people that I protected were very loyal, and I didn't really feel like I was protecting some celebrity that I didn't care about. And the mission they were doing felt good. "Feel good" is kind of not the right way to put it, but it's really the only way to put it. We felt like we were making a difference. And I got to see a different part of Baghdad every day, even though that's dangerous in a combat zone. The farming communities that I saw were really cool; the health-care facilities just blew me away. Dental equipment, dental chairs that are here in the United States, that probably rival the level of health-care that we get here in the United States. You know, the zoo was incredible; it was pretty cool to see that. And then the Green Zone. We went to the Green Zone maybe two or three times on average in a week, and that embassy is just incredible.

• • •

We had the opportunity to be a part of a really big mission: Operation Matador, which was in, I believe, Al-Qa'im, Iraq, which is on the border of Syria. At the time we didn't know what kind of mission it was; we were just told to show up. Al-Qa'im is a fairly large base, and we showed up, and it just seems like everyone was invited to the party. There were tank platoons, special forces, Navy SEALS; pretty much everyone showed up, and it was just a big push through the city of Al-Qa'im. We were told at that time that this was the biggest movement since Fallujah. So we thought that was neat. The experiences there were pretty amazing as far as what we saw and what we experienced because it seemed as though I had a front-row seat.

• • •

First of all, I wanted to get the hell out of Baghdad. I was with a tactical Marine unit in Ramadi and Fallujah. I had a good opportunity to work with some really smart guys, Marine reservists.

One was an investment banker, and one was a fund manager, so we started talking about economics and economic redevelopment. We wrote a plan—an economic engagement plan for Anbar Province; we got a general to give us some buy-in, and we actually pushed it up. We were doing some crazy stuff on our own: making contacts with people out of the country, with Iraqi ex-pats that were contemplating bringing foreign direct investment back into Anbar Province. We talked about exclusive economic zones inside of Anbar Province, rehabilitating the entire agricultural sector. Iraq had been independent in terms of its agricultural requirements up until the time of the Gulf War. We tried to get in front of a three-star general to talk about how important the agricultural sector was, so we made a chart that had Iraq's agricultural production 1900–1991, and then we overlaid that with the agricultural production of Iraq from 1991 to 2004. Right? Very simple graphic. Dave was the fund manager; he had an undergraduate degree in economics and an MBA, and he goes up to brief the three-star Marine general. He says, "Sir, we're here today to talk about economics and agricultural redevelopment," and he had this chart with these two axes; within twenty seconds, this general goes, "What the fuck are you talking about? Who are you?" Explanation. He goes, "Get out. Go away." And then you have his chief of staff, who gets up and says, "Thanks. Thanks for your. . . ." And that was it. All of these things are nested into winning a counterinsurgency battle. It's economic development; it's public health; it's all of those things. Well, we all understood that. But to try to impress the traditional military—especially in 2004, when they just wanted the traditional kinetic fight— was pointless. So we were on our own and doing good stuff and working some good deals, and we got some buy-in but not a lot. So we go back to Baghdad and meet with our State Department colleagues. But at the time no one gave a damn about Anbar, frankly, until the two dudes were hung off the bridge in Fallujah, and then it was all Fallujah all the time. Right? So I went back and forth. I think I did some good work with some good colleagues that may have been useful if we'd been able to get it into the right hands. And then the local stuff: you help a guy; you fix something that's obviously broken.

• • •

The strangest thing is that my mom will tell you that when I was in basic training and when I was deployed were the happiest times she's ever heard me in my life. Because life is simple. It's a routine. You know what time you're getting up. You know what time you're eating. You know what time you're going to work. You didn't necessarily know that you were going to make it through that day, but you knew when you did get back, you had a bed that was yours.

6

Explosion

There is an incredible din in war, as one veteran phrased it. First, there is the high-pitched whistle just before a mortar round lands and sounds off its low, reverberating boom. The roadside IED, probably the signature weapon of these wars, has its own complex range of sounds, and the objects these improvised devises explode make noise as well. EFPs are designed to pierce metal, to explode large vehicles by penetrating their armor. The roadside bomb can be hidden in almost any way. It can be in the debris along a highway. It can be hidden in a crater made by an explosion yesterday. Some bombers cloak their explosive devices with the corpses of the deceased. It is possible to become habituated to explosions or to the sound of a rocket-propelled grenade (RPG) overhead, but you still have to react, to check the perimeter, to take shelter in a bunker, to call in Explosive Ordnance Disposal (EOD) or Medevac, and to look out for the bomber who might be standing by to set another explosion or pick off survivors with an automatic rifle.

WE LANDED AT BALAD Air Force Base; they dropped the ramp of the plane; I took two steps off, and the mortar rounds started walking down the runway, literally 80–100 meters away from where we were standing. They were essentially following the path of the runway. Basically it's like artillery. They lob it into the air, and it lands and explodes, sends shrapnel everywhere. Everyone else in the unit that I was going with had already been overseas at least once, and as I stepped off the plane and it happened, I stopped because I was in shock. And I was like, "Oh my goodness, it's already happening." I thought, y'know, "Give me a couple days here." So I stopped, but I had the full bird, who was a colonel, who was also on the plane. And he walked up behind me, patted me on the back like nothing was wrong, and goes, "Welcome to Iraq," and then just kept walking. They weren't even worried.

• • •

In my company, which was eighteen vehicles, only one vehicle came out of there without being struck by an IED. And I would say, easily, my vehicle got struck five times. We would walk these highways, with burning tires, moving dead animals.

• • •

This is a stupid, stupid thing that we had to do. This detail was to go around the outpost and pick up wag bags. Wag bags were shit bags, like the one you took a shit in. So we were literally just picking up wag bags. We were outside the wire, in a known heavy IED place, just to pick up shit bags. So that was refreshing. It was me and four or five other guys that I was put with. We were actually going to support them because this was supposed to be a joint thing, so I wasn't even with my unit. This was really frustrating because I don't know any of the guys and how they operate. I'm the third man in our little column thing: the point man looking for mines, the dude right here, and I'm the third guy up. And we were like, "One of us is more or less getting his legs blown off" because Upper Sangin Valley was a mine-field. It was stupid just to pick up shit bags. So we're walking, and BOOOOM!—just a huge, huge explosion, close enough that the concussion actually rocked me; I was jarred, my ears were ringing, my insides were just. . . . The trucks dropped us off on the road, and I thought the trucks got hit, and the trucks thought we got hit. But it was actually a controlled detonation on the other side of the 611. No one told us, but they have a five-hundred-pound bomb and a controlled detonation. EOD was detonating; no one told us this. I had one guy with me, but the rest of my guys were in the truck, so I started bolting back, and by the time I got to the end of the line, they were finally able to tell me it was a controlled det. The other unit, the staff sergeant or gunny who was in charge of this little detail that we were doing, he was on the radio: "What the fuck was that?" And they found out it was a controlled detonation right there on the other side of the trees.

He was in a convoy, and they hit an IED, and they stopped. Someone got out and stepped on another IED, and it blew his legs off.
Then this guy, he got out to help him, and trying to help him, he
hit a third IED, and it killed him. And another guy tried to help
him, and he was killed.

• • •

I was based in a place called Zabul. Highway 1, the main highway, runs bottom to top throughout our entire area, and for a
while it was the most heavily bombed road. Eleven people were
killed in the span of ten days. There was a morning where these
guys—they were route clearance, they were engineers; their job
was to go out on the patrol; they would basically just drive slowly
through areas where they thought there were potential bomb
emplacements, and they would go, try and find them, and clear
them. These guys were driving on the road, and I think a five-
hundred-pound bomb blew up and killed four people in the same
truck. . . . We had an airfield, so the helicopters would fly in,
and they would load them on the helicopters, and then fly them
back to Kandahar, and that was their way of getting out. I don't
know; the first time that happened, it was the worst because . . .
I hadn't seen it like that before, where you're standing on the airfield, and then they're carrying out the stretchers with the bodies, putting them on the helicopters and then taking them. . . .
It's just one of those things I'll never forget. I mean, the guy's
foot was hanging out. . . . I can't forget that.

• • •

There was one particular day, we probably got mortared probably about every forty-five minutes. We had a round come in, and
everybody shut everything down, so it was like it caused an interruption of the work day. And . . . it became frustrating at that
point because it was like, "Well, crap. Here we go again. Here
we go again. Here we go again, geez." It got to the point that particular day that we stopped even acknowledging it. They would
launch—y'know, one or two rounds would come in—and at that
point, because the base was so big, we didn't even acknowledge

the alarm and kept working. Keep working. Hear the alarm. Tune it out. No consideration for whether or not it was going to land close to us. They liked American holidays. New Year's Day was rough. Valentine's Day, for some reason, was rough. Just out of, I guess, general psychological warfare. Like, "Oh, it's New Year's Day back home, and we're gonna make you feel bad that you're not there." Other days, it was just random. Maybe that particular day, they woke up and maybe there was an operation in that particular city, and that made them all angry, so they said, "Okay, we're all angry today. We're gonna go over here and do something." I was over there when they got Bin Laden. When that news came out, that particular week was, as one guy put it, "living hell." It was . . . it was rough. We were getting constant—constant—indirect fire. When we get attacked, we send out a reaction force to try to figure out if we can catch the guys who are doing it; they kept the reaction force outside the base perimeter that day because it was so constant, so heavy. I remember seeing mortar explosions closer than I'd ever seen them before. That particular day I feared for my life. The particular instance that I'm recalling, my mind went blank for about a good ten minutes. I had no thoughts. Nothing. I just kind of zoned out and sat there and, like, didn't care where I was, didn't care what I was thinking, didn't care about anything else. I was like, "Okay." And my first thought after that was, "Call home." That was the first thing I did when I finally came to my senses. I called home. Talked to my dad. I was like, "Hi, Dad. How are you? Good?" It's just very basic conversation.

• • •

A busful of guys were going on recreation R&R, so they had left their helmets and body armor and weapons behind at camp and were on the bus headed up to the Kurdish mountains. An IED struck, and it was near our base camp, so we were the responding team, and there was so much blood and bone and so much. . . . I mean, you don't encounter things like that, so you don't . . . there's nothing that comes up. It's just, you actively think about it. God, the amount of destruction from that, the amount of lives ruined and changed, and people. . . . I didn't know any of them personally, but I didn't need to. When you see that, . . . there's nothing that really compares to it. Nothing is gruesome any more. You're numb to the rest of everything. The rest of life is just, "That's not bad. You want bad, let me tell you about this bus that got hit."

* * *

Holy crap. That was an eighty-millimeter explosive right off; we had ten of them coming in at a time sometimes. BOOM! BOOM! BOOM! And there, in the midst of it, you don't think, "Oh, crap, this is something that's gonna kill me." You think, "I don't wanna get out of bed; I've only had three hours of sleep." You put your equipment on; you grab your weapon; you get to where you've gotta be. Everybody gets accounted for, and you're so focused on the process of accountability and making sure everybody's there that unless somebody gets hurt by it—unless somebody is missing—the idea of the fatality of it never strikes you until later, and you're like, "Oh! Hey! That was dangerous." You learn to hear it; you know: *phweeeeee.* You're lying in bed, and before the first mortar strikes, you're grabbing for your Kevlar, and you're grabbing for your weapon, and you're headed for the bunker because you know. You would have a unit there doing the job already, and you had us coming in and learning the job, and you shadow the person who's doing your job for a little while, and they told us the first two days, "Okay, here's what we do in a mortar attack." And the next day there was an attack, and they're like, "Goodie! You get to learn; no better way to learn than practice!" And that was a little freakish. . . . As artillery men, we're used to the BOOM!— we're used to explosions. We're used to hearing that SLAM as it comes out of the tube, and you hear those BOOMs, but it never has a negative connotation to it; it's like the pain of hitting somebody when you strike, and I'm sorry if that seems really crass and isn't a very good analogy. It hurts to hit with a fist but not nearly as much as it hurts to get hit, so it's not the same thing. So having it come at you—having it come in—you're like, "No no no no no. This isn't supposed to happen this way." And in your head you've got that going on the first couple times. And I remember that first attack was, "Wait! What? Huh? You can't—they're attacking *us?* No no no no no. It doesn't work this way. We're the good guys. We're supposed to do all the winning."

• • •

I definitely have a very different conception of the body and what it means to be mortal after a night of suicide bombers' remains and in the Baghdad morgue. This is one of those dark stories that I really only pull out if it's getting late at night and, "Well, she's really attracted, but I wanna just set that last little hook in." Suicide bombers—Al Qaeda in Iraq and the Sunni terror (it's death-wish guys), probably Chechnyans actually (those guys just *love* to fight), walk in with suicide vests on, explosive vests. Al-Najaf Church. October 31—it's Halloween night—October 31, 2010. So it's in downtown Baghdad. They walk in and take the whole church hostage. One of our interpreters, his brother was there, so he's on the phone, ducked down, and it was a ransom situation. U.S. intentionally stayed back; Iraqis kinda went in. But, I mean, they were just looking to wait for the media to show up before they killed everyone with the Army outside. So while he's on the phone, and we're listening in, all of a sudden it's gunshots, gunshots, gunshots. BOOM! BOOM! Signal gone. And it was sixty-eight men, women, and children killed. So it was very, very brutal. I mean, it was the church service that was basically taken out. So then afterwards we were trying to figure out, well, who are the guys behind it? But it was a great experience where all of the infantry guys were, "Are you gonna be okay when you get around those bodies?" I'm, "Yeah. I'll be good. I'll be good." And it was those guys who were puking in the corner, as I'm sitting there bending over the body, or I'm, "This smells awful right now." And that was an experience where it was, "Wow, that's what guts look like. . . ." And I'm, "This is all the different colors, like you got the fatty tissue that's just kinda yellow; and there's the intestine; you've got the green stuff going on here." I definitely had moments—and this is where the awkward sex and war converge, when you start to look at the similarities in bodies, and it's, "Well, this is a pretty girl. And this is . . ."—you can't help but make those comparisons—and it's, "Well, I really

appreciate flesh that's not torn." What's that phrase? "Eviscer-
ated," I think. And so . . . that awkward spectrum where . . . I
don't want to encourage those connections. I don't want to force
out that the bodies are bodies and breathing is breathing and
very quickly have similarities that are coming up. I want to try
to understand it because I think that's the biggest way you can
get in trouble, when you try to force things out; I mean, you just
kind of force it out of the front of your mind, but it's still sitting
around somewhere in the back, getting stale and musty, and it's
gonna come up at a certain point. You can only push things down
so long. That was—that kind of memory was—like when you
smell. . . . This was five days after—and if you know the power
grid in Baghdad, it is not very reliable; these guys were held in
coolers that were getting electricity for three hours a day. So it
was preserved enough that it wasn't like they obviously looked
like they were decaying, but it was such a pungent smell that
when I walked into the room I was sharing with a captain, he was,
"You're stripping in the hallway, and you're taking a shower right
now. You just smell like death." And coming back from that. . . .
Some Special Forces guy we're working with, he went to some
religious place. I'm, "I have no sympathy for those guys whatsoever." I'm not a good-or-evil type of person, but if I were, that is
the worst thing someone could do. I don't have any sympathy. I
don't really have any feelings one way or the other because it's
bodies; these are inanimate objects. There's nothing—there's
not a person left.

• • •

We had a convoy. We went out on a Thursday, five HMMWVs going
to a local area. Same patrol the next day. We were just tagging
along on another group, but an EFP goes through, kills both the
guys in back. That's the small, cheap IED that's very well made,
most likely smuggled over the border from Iran, very standard-
ized. I mean it's just a little thing; it's like a cone, but as it explodes,
it kind of inverts in on itself and just forms a penetrating round
that's very effective; I mean, it punches through all the armor that
we have. Costs like $250 to make. Sitting in the motor pool and

looking at all these multi-million-dollar armored vehicles, it's, "Ah . . . I'm sitting on the wrong end of this cost-benefit analysis."

• • •

They eventually gave us this cool . . . it was like a truck, like a remote-control car. And I always got to play with it; they had a camera on it, and it was like my favorite thing to do. So if we thought it was a bomb, I would be like, "Oh, let's get my truck out!" So I was playing with my own remote-control car, and, you know, it was usually an IED, and we would just have to wait there for hours for EOD to show up. At the time, I think there were maybe not as many EOD techs as there are now, so it took a few hours for them to come out. So we would just sit there around this bomb and wait for someone, stop any convoy or people that were coming by. But they were sneaky. We found one, or one exploded on this convoy, and we got called to it, like normal, and we pull up next to the convoy, and we're sitting next to a truck, and I kind of pop up, just because it was so hot; you just want any type of breeze. So I remember popping up, and, you know, we're chatting, and I kind of look down next to me, and I just see wires and this radio base, and I kind of tap my vehicle commander, and I'm like, "Look down." And we had to yell at everyone to move, but it ended up being, well, they call them daisy chains, multiple IEDs that were in a line, and I guess the circuit on the first explosion never got passed, so it was just, I think, two other IEDs in a row that didn't go off. And the convoy had just been sitting there next to them for hours.

• • •

We patrolled a particular road called MSR Tampa, which was a supply route. It's like one of the few paved roads in Iraq because we paved it. Along this road there's markets and all this stuff, and it's always packed. No matter what time of the day it is, it's always packed. And then you drive down one day, and there's nothing. Not a soul in sight. That was the most unnerving ride of my life because you know something's wrong. The Iraqi people themselves always know something's going to happen. Their rumor tree is amazing. Their word of mouth is faster than our Twitter. So

every time something is going to happen, they all know, so they all get out of the way. They don't want to be caught in the crossfire. Well, we had to patrol the route. There was an IED, a daisy chain, on the road. A daisy chain is a multiple-explosive IED. It starts on one end, and it'll blow up. It's supposed to catch the underside of vehicles as it goes down the line. It's not all that effective compared to some of the other ones. But, I mean, it does its job if you're a dismounted soldier. We found it, cordoned off the area—that is, go one hundred meters out, behind it and in front of it, and make sure nobody drives down that road—which is essentially what we did. We have all-terrain vehicles. We just went off the road. We called EOD, and they blew it up. They do c-4 packs on each one, each of the explosion points, and then they blew it all up at once.

• • •

Where's the bad guy at? Where's the guy I've been trained to fight? How can I learn to expect this? What are the things I can learn to identify? How do you learn to deal with . . . ? It's infinitely more traumatic when the world just explodes, and that's what I would say my impression of that day is. I'm not kidding when I say that image is fixed: just this black with this yellow spark in the middle. But there isn't anything scarier on the battlefield, because I can't kill the person who is doing it. But this was going to work, this going to the office and doing what I've trained to do my entire military career. And this is reacting to someone else who has control.

• • •

I felt just as scared driving over here today, trusting somebody coming at you in two-way traffic or falling asleep or texting and hitting you, as I would there. However, my person in my pod with me—we had two guys living in one little trailer—he was scared every time he heard a mortar. I mean he was petrified. So everybody has different perceptions. He couldn't sleep the rest of the night if he heard an attack, whereas I'd go right back to sleep after coming in from the bunker. I would just go right back to sleep. Yeah, you never forget the whistling of that mortar; it's a very distinct sound. The alarms never go off until well after. You think that you're gonna have an alarm, and then you run to your bunker, and the mortars start coming in. It's totally not that way. It's *phweeeeee*, and you hear that whistling, and you just know after it happens one time. That siren—the giant voice they call it—the giant voice doesn't need to tell you to get into your concrete bunker outside and get behind the big barricades because that whistling is very distinct. It wakes you right out of your sleep; at least it did me. I just grabbed my helmet and flak vest and went and jumped in the concrete bunker. Outside of all of our pods, there were concrete little bunkers because our biggest concern was not being hit on the head by a big mortar but just the shrapnel and fragment blasts from the device and the peppering (we called it) that occurs from all the flying debris when it hits. So you go into these concrete little concaves, you know, like square little boxes, and everybody crawls in there, and you just cram in there with as many people as are around that area, and there's plenty available. They're strategically stationed throughout the whole compound, so you know which one is yours. We practiced it all the time too, so you know which bunker is yours, and everybody ends up in the exact same spot after a few times. We all respect each other's area because you know you might be there a while; you don't know how long the attack. . . . And then after every attack, everybody has to go to their unit; there's a big accountability thing. So, yeah, you might get attacked at one o'clock in the morning, but you're up for the next three hours because the commander of your unit has to see you, has to know; you have to be accounted for. Somebody was always snagged on the way by the command because they wanted to see if that young captain or lieutenant would check and report that that guy was missing. So you were constantly tested. Because if he got blown up and then they call the command center and say, "Hey, I have 220 of 222 people; I have two guys missing," they'd say, "What's their name?" And it's "Frank and Joe from. . . ." "Oh, yeah, we've got them right here; we just wanted to make sure that you were doing your accountability correctly and you weren't just saying they were here or somebody got mixed up in the conversation." So, yeah, we were constantly just trying to keep everybody extremely agile in their thinking and sharp and not be complacent; complacency's our biggest enemy there in the field. It happens. Everybody gets into a routine, and you forget to be agile when things don't always go the way they're supposed to go.

• • •

It was one of those things where there was this constant fear: "Gee, is something going to drop out of the sky? Am I gonna die?" We had an explosion once in the ICU, so you just never know when you're going to potentially die. And I just remember being paralyzed with fear the very first week I was there. You know, it's not like I could take a cab and go somewhere; I'm stuck here. So I just put my head down and do it, and every time I hear a siren I'd be as fast as I can to hit the dirt, and that's all I can do. That's the only thing I had control over. I had sort of a self-talk, like, "What do I have control over and what do I not have control over?" And so I tried to break it down like that, and that's how I survived. You know, I worked out every day, which I think was a great outlet for me. . . . If I hear a siren, I'm down, and that's all I can do, and I just hope that if I'm gonna be mortared, it's right on top of me so I'm dead, or it's far enough away so that I'm fine. So you have these little negotiations with yourself. That's how it was then; I acknowledged it when it happened, and I just kept working.

• • •

I didn't personally experience it, but we had been told that if they have a dead body, sometimes they'd plant IEDs around the dead body because they know that we'll go check, and it's easy for someone to step on an IED. A lot of guys stepped on toe-poppers, we called them, which is like two pounds of explosives that kind of take off someone's leg rather than kill everybody completely. So that was always a possibility, and that always caused the most anxiety because you didn't know if it was ever going to happen. There's no one shooting at you. You didn't know. You couldn't do anything. They are very well hidden under ground; it's just a chance you have to take.

• • •

I was in Iraq from June 2007 to August 13, 2007, which was when I was actually injured and blessed to be blown up by a bomb. It was my twentieth birthday. It was a pretty fun day. From the moment that I woke up, I knew that something was wrong. The night before I had called my parents (because they have little communications stations). I talked to them, and I was going to call them again the next day, and they were going to sing "Happy Birthday" to me. After the conversation I said jokingly, "Well, not if I get blown up." So that was the night before. In the morning when I woke up, I just felt there was something off. We weren't even supposed to go on a mission that day. We were told that we would have the day off, that we'd be able to rest. But then we came to find out that we were going to go out. So after we got our orders and stuff, we geared up and prepared to go out of the wire. The interesting thing is that I would always ride in the last HMMWV. Always. But my buddy that I was rooming with, his dad had passed away, so he had to leave and go back to the States. So I took his place in the front HMMWV, which was weird in and of itself. So we were getting ready to leave, and we find out that there was an IED placed on Route Christie. So we were informed that there was a possible IED threat and that EOD was going to take care of it. That was kind of. . . . I didn't really think about it, like, "Okay, it's going to get taken care of." We end up leaving. We go to the mission objective. I remember pulling security, and then I remember being able to hang out with my staff sergeant, and we got to try chai tea from the locals, which is really good. So it was a pretty pleasant experience, the mission. And then we ended up packing up and heading back to the FOB, and I remember sitting in my HMMWV behind the driver, talking to these guys; we were joking about what they were going to do to me when I got back home because it was my birthday. So they were going to beat me up or whatever. We were probably about two or three miles from the FOB, and the IED went off. I remember feeling the intense heat and just a complete sense of . . . not realizing that this was a bomb until after the dust settled and I could breath. I was in pain, and I couldn't talk because it had blown open my neck. I looked over and saw my hand, and it looked like a mangled piece of muscle and fat and no blood, and you could see the bone. And then when my neck was blown open, I could put my hand, my fingers, in my neck, and there was just this blood coming and coming and coming. It's pretty intense. I have this huge scar right here. But I didn't pass out; I was awake the entire time. During this whole experience I felt, like, at peace about it. And that's the story within the story: joining the military was to run away from my purpose, and my purpose was to share the gospel. I came from a Christian home. During that time, I felt this peace; I didn't feel as much pain as I should have felt. I remember the moment that we were attacked; my buddies came over, and they took the door off, and they pulled me out, and they started doing emergency care on me. So I remember lying on the blacktop, looking around, feeling this peace, and thinking, "Am I really going to die?" And then looking up, and God's like, "You're not going to die. This isn't your time. You're not done yet." At that point I relaxed, and I was like, "Okay, that's cool." And then I tried my best to be relaxed because I knew in situations like that everybody else is on high alert. I remember the emergency medic Blackhawk came, and they put me in the Blackhawk, and I was in there for maybe two or three minutes, and then I passed out. Woke up in Kuwait, in the hospital in Kuwait, with my hand gone and thinking, "This is not fair; I didn't have a chance to say if I get to keep my hand or not." But I was blessed to be blown up. You know how you have the bones that are right here (at the wrist); it's like someone sliced through the bones. My recovery was really quick; physically it was really quick. My neck: the doctors would say that they wouldn't think that I would ever talk again because of the damage, but after a month and a half of recovery and prayer and all that stuff, my neck closed. I had a trach and a feeding tube, and that was out within two months; and then I began to talk. And then my hand: there wasn't really any significant damage other than just the loss of the digits. I didn't have any residual bacteria buildup; I didn't have complications in surgeries. It went really well, well enough to where the doctors were like, "We've never seen this before." It feels amazing. Yeah. I don't have any phantom pain or anything, which is crazy. I still use it; I do things better with one hand than I did with two: I golf; I snowboard; I play paint ball. Yeah, I'm disabled, but I'm not really. Yeah, I'm a veteran, and, yeah, I was injured. But I say I'm a little different than other veterans who have been injured because I don't use this injury and the loss of my hand as an opportunity to have a self-pitying, woe-is-me attitude because I realize now that God's using it. I'm missing a hand, and people asked me what happened, and I get to tell them that I was blessed to be blown up. And when I tell them that, it throws them off because it's like, "Well, you should be angry; you should be bitter; you should not be where you are." I get to tell them, "Well, yeah. I absolutely agree with you, but this is an opportunity for me to take what has been given to me and use it as an opportunity to share a story that involves rebellion and anger and hate, and the Lord uses it to teach joy and love and restoration and restitution in a family; a young man who went from being a young boy to being a young man who . . . I'm firm in my faith. I know why I'm here. So that's why I say I'm blessed.

7

Low Points

While there are many tragedies in a war zone, the low points often come from disillusion, from tension among people stuck with each other on a COP, or from finding that what you had been trained to do was irrelevant to the actual deployment or that the ideals that motivate you on the most basic level are completely irrelevant to either your peers or your leaders. Sometimes the basic tenet of brotherhood fails, or you feel the most threat to your own safety from the failings of your peers. Soldiers returning home can find that things are not what they seemed on email or Skype.

I CAN'T EAT ANYMORE Skittles. Skittles. They're in MRES. It's just skittles, skittles, skittles, and I can't eat them to this day.

• • •

I got an email. My fiancée emailed me. April 10, 2011, I got that email. That particular day was also the same day that I had a mortar round land maybe about thirty or forty feet in front of me. That particular day I had woken up, and I had already kinda been in a daze because I was getting tired, was getting stressed, had been there so long, been pulling so many hours. My sleep schedule was naturally starting to shift to a twenty-five- or twenty-six-hour cycle rather than a standard twenty-four-hour cycle. I remember going into the USO tent, sitting down to get on email, and I'm reading through emails, reading through emails, and I was looking for hers, but I didn't have any. I hadn't checked the computer in probably close to two weeks, and I was like, "Man, she didn't email me, didn't email me," and then there's one from her. "Ah, there it is." Click. She did email me, and it was, "Dear Dave, I'm sorry to have to write you this, but I've been sleeping with someone else since you left, and I don't think we can do this. I mailed your stuff back to your parents' house, and I hope you come home safe one day." I walked outside the tent. I had to breathe—and this was nighttime—and I'm sitting there outside, and the tears are coming down. And as I'm standing there, I hear the alarm go off. And of course I'm like, "I don't even care at this point." I've got a different problem. I remember hearing this very high-pitched squeal. And the next thing I remember is I was sitting on the ground looking at the sky. I don't know if I sat myself down or if the mortar round knocked me down. I remember the brief instant beforehand when my ears popped; I felt my chest compress; it's like hot air filled my lungs . . . and then it was like a moment of nothing. And then I was sitting there looking at the sky, and some guy ran up to me like, "Are you okay? "Yeah." "Okay." And then he ran off to do something else, and I just got back up and walked into the tent. That was it. Nobody else asked me anything.

• • •

The locals, you saw them as somebody different. You alienated them, so to speak. When we got out of the vehicles and were pulling security, we didn't go up to them and ask them how their day was. If they got within about ten meters of us, we would just scream at them. We basically treated these people as if they were animals. So when I got home, that hit me pretty hard. I felt kind of guilty for doing that. I mean, these people were just trying to live their lives. And here we are disturbing their way of life. I was young and naive back then when I was deployed. I started doing more reading about the war, and this might be a controversial opinion, but I felt that we should not have been over there at all. All the lives that were lost were lost for nothing. I don't want to say my time was wasted over there. I want to say that we did something good, that we did help protect other soldiers from getting harmed or injured. But we could have avoided that whole mess. That was part of the growing-up process, that self-reflection.

• • •

As a company we didn't use enough fire discipline. It's the reason all of our backs are so fucked up. We have to carry so much ammunition because we use so much. You can never have enough, you know. What if a firefight lasts a day? What if it lasts two days? There were situations where we were in two or three days of sustained contact, and there were ammunition issues. Not only that, but the risk of collateral damage goes through the roof when you're just firing rounds blindly.

• • •

We were there with intel on known terrorist groups that we're combatting; we worked with a couple different foreign national units, but their higher-ups would be their cousins or brothers, and they would know that they're the people doing the bad stuff, and we're supposed to be teaching them how to combat that, but they wouldn't do it. Like, for example, the SEALS; they actually cut this unit a pretty large sum of money to buy communications systems they can install in their vehicles so they can talk to each other while in convoys. They went half price, and they bought some piece of junk. The unit commanders pretty much pocketed the rest of it.

• • •

I had a guy under me coming home from his deployment, and he attempted suicide, and he spent a week in the hospital. It was because he came home and his fiancée, she'd spent all his money and left him for another guy. It was all going on the whole time he was gone, and he didn't know, so he attempted suicide. He tried to inject himself with some pretty powerful drugs in the emergency room. He went there saying, "I'm gonna commit suicide," and they left him behind a curtain by himself, and he broke into the crash cart and started injecting himself. They should've never left him alone, so there was a big to-do about that. They had to investigate it and stuff. Anyway, he got his heart rate up there; well, he ended up in the intensive care unit for a couple days, and then he ended up in a psych unit for a while. But he's doing great now, and he was able to reintegrate, but he came darn close to killing himself. He was determined to do it. The thing that he told me was pivotal for him and why he won't do it again—and that convinced me when I was seeing him at the psychiatric hospital. He looked at me and he said, "You know what they told me here?" And I said, "What?" (We're still really good friends today; he's a wonderful guy.) He said, "They told me that if I commit suicide, my daughters, that the likelihood of them committing suicide is greatly enhanced, and I can't ever do it again." I knew from that moment forward that he would never do it again because you could just see the epiphany for him. Knowing that your kid would do that, I guess, really made it click for him that he won't do it again. And so I wasn't worried about him any more, and he's doing great. He's remarried, has a beautiful wife, and she had two kids, so he has, like, five kids. And he's doing wonderfully, and you would never know. That part of his life was very sheltered by his supervisor and me and others because we knew he could make it. We didn't want that to hurt him long term because we knew that he just had a bad time when he came home from Iraq, and he needed time to adjust. But I think a lot more of it is happening as they come home, and what they thought was happening back here was totally different when it comes to their loved ones and their immediate family. There was a lot of infidelity going on. I would say that that's probably one of the biggest drivers, the relationships that they're not able to keep, especially after they've done several deployments, you know.

• • •

It rained one day my first week there, and then about three or four months later I remember I looked around, and it hadn't rained since. I'd seen children swimming around in a big puddle out there outside the base perimeter, and I made the comment, "Where is this water coming from? It hasn't rained." One of the guys was like, "The sewage." And he pointed over by the latrines that were right beside us. Oh, my God. The kids were swimming in sewage. Yep. Because that's the water that would drain off into that lake that they had there.

• • •

Being the only woman, I had to deal with some of the advances that some of the guys would make toward me, and some of it was rather unprofessional, the way some male operators looked at what my job was, what I was there for. . . . Some of them are pretty used to the old boys' club, and having a girl on their deployment disrupted their habits and their team, as they saw it, until I proved myself. My deployment was longer than a Ranger platoon's deployment, so I got multiple platoons. So every time I got a new one in, I had to re-prove myself and re-deal with the gender relations. Some of the stuff I dealt with being a woman in an all-man's world . . . I'll just name a couple of things. What they would say to you or what you'd hear them saying about you, that wasn't really anything. But there were a couple times that I . . . didn't really feel unsafe, but you have to remember we worked at night, so walking from the gym back to my tent or walking from the shower to my tent, it was all pitch black other than your headlamp. So it added a bit of anonymity to any menacing, maybe a little, not stalker-ish, but you'd find a guy who was hanging out right where he knew you would be and just staring at you in a way that would make you uncomfortable. . . . There was one time I was in the laundry shack, where all the washers and dryers were, and I was doing my laundry, and there was a guy who was just in there to stare and be creepy and try to get me, I don't know, to take him to my tent or something. I have no idea. Some of the other things: I'd be sleeping at night, and they'd tap on my wall right where my cot is, right up against the tent wall, and they'd tap to try to get me to wake up. I don't know what they'd expect or what they wanted necessarily. I mean, I think I know what they wanted; they were making attempts to get me to sleep with them. There's reasons why men have these expectations that women on deployment will sleep with them because it's a thing that happens in deployed environments; people sleep with each other. It's well known, and it's obviously no one particular gender's fault, but it is against general order number one, so it is technically against orders in a legal and a military sense. Lastly, there'd just be the belittling, the teasing. It would take a while for them to get the picture that you weren't there for their pleasure. You were there because you had a job to do. Actually, when I first got there, I pretended to be a lesbian, which sounds really stupid, but I was young, and I knew I was going to be in a situation where I was surrounded by alpha males. It wasn't going to go well for me unless I found some out. So that was my attempt, and it was stupid, and it didn't work. You're living with these people, and you're working with these people, and you're not going to be able to hide the fact that you are a straight girl. They're going to figure it out. Every single one of them found out who I was before I even got there. They were all trying to Facebook-friend me and all that kind of stuff, trying to creep in on me and see what kind of person I was because it's exciting to them, this girl who's going to be new and interesting to their world over there, where it oftentimes does get to be boring. Really, the training we got was, "Don't sleep with them." Constant reminders during our training, "Don't sleep with them; don't sleep with them." For some reason the instructors during our training picked me out as the one that was going to mess it up. I was going to be the one to be immature and make a bad decision. I was constantly reminded that that was not what I was there for, which I obviously knew already. I was terrified of doing anything that would be remotely like I had done anything wrong, which, honestly, made for a lonely life. You can't do anything with just one person; if I went to breakfast with one guy, I was sleeping with him as far as everyone else was concerned. Unless I could go somewhere in a group, I was going by myself, so it was lonely. There was no training about how to deal with the constant advances, and it was constant because as soon as you finally got comfortable with a group, as soon as I finally got used to a platoon and they started looking at me as a sister and not as a piece of ass, then they'd leave, and I'd get a new group. I had to do that three times during my seven and a half months there. It was a pain.

• • •

Abu Ghraib is probably why I'm telling you . . . because I'm so passionately wanting to convince you. I'm one of those veterans that volunteered to go. I'll be darned if I'm gonna spend twenty-something years in the military and there'd be a war going on for ten years and I didn't deploy. I mean, what would that say about me? So there were a lot of us who have a lot of pride in what we do, and to see that happen was very embarrassing. It just shows you how things at the tactical level can just infect things at the strategic level tremendously. It needs to be institutionalized at the grassroots level because war is so complicated now. Things could happen at that level that could affect us strategically at multiple levels, and Abu Ghraib was a perfect example of how people at very low levels cause huge strategic problems throughout our whole country and our whole cause.

• • •

My unit was a really dirty unit. There was a lot of racist stuff that went on in my unit. There was really bad tension between whites and blacks, really horrible stuff. I mean people would go after each other, their careers. The army itself tries to control all that stuff, and in training they do a really good job. Outside of training every unit is different, as I learned. The artillery tends to be historically black in the noncommissioned officer (NCO) channels. There's a problem with a group called the Black Masons in the military, and the unit I was in, it was black, and it was organized by Black Masons. I thought this was conspiracy theory when I got there. I thought, "This is conspiratorial garbage." But then you see it's organized, and it's like a shadow group of the Masons. It's not so much about pushing racism for itself but about blacks helping blacks at the expense of everybody else. And it's outlawed; it's not legal for them to do this, but they do it. What that means is that people get promoted really quickly; they get all kinds of special stuff sent their way, and other people don't. I'm not trying to say it was all black and it wasn't white. There was plenty of white crap that went on. There's a lot of tension. Now, in my experience, it was primarily at the higher ranks of NCOs where that stuff mattered.

• • •

Oh, my God: c-a-c-h-e is "cash"; nobody in the Army knows it. Oh, it drove me crazy. I remember the first time we got a new lieutenant. Our old LT had lost his leg, and we got a new lieutenant, and he was like, "We're doing cache (pronounced 'cash') denial," and I remember looking up and seeing my buddy look across the room at me, and we're just like, "Yes!"

• • •

I didn't expect drug use to be as rampant as it was, both among the soldiers and among the Afghan Army and among the local nationals. There was a lot of hashish use. We caught civilians several times smuggling or whatever. I don't know what actual heroine looks like, but we caught them transporting the raw poppy sap. They cut them to harvest it. I don't know what that's called, raw opium or whatever it is. But we caught a lot of them carrying a lot of that. The Afghan Army would bring that onto the COP and sell it to soldiers. I mean, these people got caught. A lot of people got caught. Then marijuana, of course, was brought on by the Afghan Army; they just brought whatever they wanted. There wasn't really any drinking. I don't think anybody really wanted to drink. Actually, we all wanted to drink. We all would have drunk, if we could have, but nobody had anybody send them any booze. Thinking about it, that would be a lot harder to hide than anything else. So that was weird.

• • •

You get shot at. People start dropping. Everybody tries to find cover. Nobody wants any of their friends to show cowardice. Nobody wants to see that, not only because it could put your life in jeopardy, but nobody wants to find out that their friend is a coward. Sometimes that happens, and that's never an easy thing to deal with. I can't imagine being the person who is showing the cowardice. It is horrible to watch it happen. You can just see fear. Inaction is really the main staple of it. It's that they're not doing their job, and they're not responding to the commands that are being given to them. We had a guy who had actually worked for DARPA—that's Defense Advanced Research Projects Agency; he wasn't even in the military. At one point he was, but he worked for DARPA. He wasn't even supposed to be going out on missions with us, I don't think. But he was like, "I'm going to go; I need to find out how this equipment works, see it in the field." He got the chain of command to give him a weapon and plates—you know, body armor. He went to the field with us. He was a total bad ass, but he kind of stepped up and covered that guy's sector, and it all worked out.

• • •

A lot of betrayals. I think it's pretty common for soldiers to feel, "I did all this for you, and look what you've done to me." My ex-wife and her boyfriend, who was married too. . . . I just started drinking a lot and running a lot; it's just what I did, miles and miles. I got good at it and got hurt doing it, but I had to cope somehow, and that's when I started the veterans' writing project. I was writing and reading stuff. Now I look back at those writings, and I can see how disturbed I was at the time. I was just really crazy. I went through a string of relationships for years after the divorce, one every three months. I'd be real committed, and then I'd just disappear; I couldn't be anywhere and feel anything.

• • •

We've got a line of people who want to know where their brothers, cousins, and uncles are in Abu Ghraib prison, and I don't have a list. I'm supposed to have a list, but I don't have a list.

• • •

Tons of problems with drugs. Much of my unit was drunk most of the time because you can buy alcohol from the Iraqis, and they had a whole system set up. I remember a guy on guard duty was so drunk the night before. He had guard duty the next morning; he gets up, and of course it's 120 degrees outside, and he's dehydrated. His job is to follow around Iraqis on post who have been hired to work there and make sure nothing happens, and, you know, he passes out in the sunlight. Now, imagine that you're one of these Iraqis: there's a passed-out American soldier with a rifle. I mean, what kind of situation is that? But that's the kind of stuff. There's all kinds of illicit sex going on. I mean, there's really nothing pretty about it. Truth is, if you ask if there was anything that really inspired hate in me? People in my own unit. Mainly the leadership of my unit, which was just profoundly ignorant in a very dangerous way on the officer level, in a very personal way on the NCO level. I think there are all these crazy myths out there about people bonding in a combat zone, but generally you learn to hate people you live with in a combat zone. That's just the way it is.

• • •

We were mortared twice, both times early in the morning. Other than that there wasn't any . . . there were no issues as far as enemy contact was concerned. Our biggest threat in that tour was roadside accidents. Accidents on the freeway. I had two soldiers that were Medevac'd out of sector, and they were lucky to be alive. They had been hit by a truck that was going approximately 75–80 miles an hour. They were stationary, pulling security. The driver of the truck was an Iraqi who fell asleep, and he was hauling tomatoes. It flipped the MRAP; it turned it 180 degrees and flipped it three times. They were all wearing their seatbelts and their harnesses, thank God. One suffered a collarbone fracture and the other one a severe concussion that subsequently has caused him to be medically discharged on full disabilities from the military. But it's just interesting; you wouldn't think that erratic driving, or drunk driving, or falling asleep driving would be the greatest threat you're facing in sector, but that was it.

• • •

It didn't go well. We found out that most people sold their voting. They had, like, a card that represented their voting, and they would just sell them for what came out to be like a dollar a piece, so whoever was already kind of powerful and influential could very easily maintain that by manipulating the votes, buying them, or just intimidating people. It may be better now; you know, this was in 2011, but I don't know how well it really worked while we were there.

• • •

Coming back, there was a rash of suicides and motorcycle deaths and domestic violence in our unit, and that was really weird. We had a marine shoot himself on post not long before we came home. He was just on post and shot himself and killed himself. And I was thinking, you know, we were like three weeks from going home, and I always wonder what happened to him that made him want to do that because, obviously, I don't think suicide is really rational, but to do it right before you're about to leave was so strange, I thought.

• • •

For the lowest-level enlisted guys, a lot of times the barracks aren't that nice, and they want to get out of the barracks, so they get married and then get a housing allowance, and they can get off base. Then they get married to these people who are just kind of using them. Then they go and deploy, and they give that wife, maybe, a power of attorney over their stuff while they're gone, and then you just hear horror stories about, you know, their wife spending all their money and cheating on them, and then it's bad enough. . . . That never happened to me. I was married. My wife was faithful, and I knew she would be. But when you're there for seven months and you can't even call them, it's really hard; it's really stressful. It kind of messes with your mind, I'll be honest. One of my friends, who was also an officer, he was in another unit, and we kind of missed each other; he deployed and got back right when I left. He emailed me one time, and he was like, "Hey, I hope you're doing okay. I'm going to go and have lunch with your wife and say 'Hey.'" And I was like, "No. Fuck no. You're not going to have lunch with my wife." And he was a good friend. I would trust him now. But over there it was just, like, I really got pissed off. And I was mad at her, and she hadn't even done anything, and she was like, "No, I told him no anyway." But it's hard not to get irrationally jealous, and then if you're one of those guys where your wife is screwing around, or your girlfriend, or whatever, that can be pretty devastating, I think. Because you're so miserable over there; you just want to come home, or at least you're thinking about that most of the time, and then if there's nothing to come home to, or if what you're coming home to is bad, that could be a reason some wouldn't want to stay alive any more.

• • •

I went to basic training where we had men and women training together. I'm as liberal as it gets, but that's a really bad idea for all different kinds of reasons. It really is. Please don't think I'm a nut, but it creates all kinds of problems. For example, in a dumpster out behind a dining facility there were two soldiers, a male and a female, having sex in a dumpster. It's beyond imagination. That's the kind of stuff that goes on. No alcohol, no sex in a combat zone? That stuff went on all over the place. For money and just everything, the real, real dark of human nature. You see people at their best, but more often than not, you see them at their worst.

• • •

We had a marine who tried to get another marine to shoot him in the foot so he could go home; I knew him very well. I had had him on my last deployment too, and he was really good actually. So I had a lot of hope for him when he was with us in Afghanistan. And then I went out to their little outpost one time, and they were just basically living in the dirt. They had some Hesco barriers and some MRES and a couple of bomb dogs and some water, and they lived out there for weeks. And then the marine that he tried to convince to shoot him, I knew him as well. We had this weird thing; it was like a draft. We got all these reinforcements from another battery before we deployed. And they let the officers pick who we wanted. Like, "Okay, you need three comm guys, and we have nine, so you get to kind of argue over which guys you want. I picked this guy because I thought he was really good, and I knew him fairly well. So when he told about this thing where this other marine had tried to get him to shoot him, some people didn't believe him, but I did believe him. Everyone was just kind of like, "Why would you do that?" It was a corporal trying to get a lance corporal to do it, so he kind of like pulled rank on him to try to get him to do something really bad. I don't know. . . . I think we admin separated him (the one who wanted to be shot) and sent him home. It still took about two months. He was sitting around the base, you know. Probably no one spoke to him.

• • •

I gave a targeting packet on a Sunni group. That thing is executed yesterday. I mean, phone call; immediately, guys go out. Awesome. "Yay! We got the terrorists!" This was the fifteen-year-old kid with the fingerprints as opposed to that high-level Shia operative. There was an Iraqi colonel that arrested a Shia Jaish al-Mahdi guy (or it might have been Asa'ib Ahl al-Haq) with ties back to Iran; he had Maliki's blessing to execute the search warrant. Had the approval. Turns out, the insurgent has a cousin in the Iraqi parliament; next thing you know, that Iraqi colonel's in jail. It just was that politically sensitive. Even though the Shia insurgent groups were probably accounting for two-thirds to three-fourths of our casualties, as opposed to the Sunni groups, which would do the spectacular bombings (al-Qaeda in Iraq or whatever), but at that point they were a negligible threat to the U.S., by and large, because the biggest threat was insider attacks and direct fire and explosively formed penetrators; it wasn't the truck bombs that were rolling in. It was the small, targeted devices that weren't going to piss off the population but were gonna do us a lot of damage.

• • •

I'll say this: the hardest part for me during a deployment is not the firefights or the explosions. It was whenever you weren't there. The helpless part. Because you're just listening to your guys on the radio calling for help. Being on base while my friends, my brothers, are calling for help and you know you could help them; you know you're an asset, but I was taken out of the teams to be part of the CO's attachment. The feeling of no control, the helplessness for you as the individual having to listen; it's very surreal in a way because you are, in comparison, safe, while any minute you can hear what's happening; you can see it in the distance because we were on a plateau; you can see where it's happening; they're right there, and you can't do anything because you're here. It's kind of like in the movies when someone is about to kill someone's family, and they have to watch. That helplessness, that anger. Having no control sucks.

• • •

Seeing dead bodies didn't really affect me or anybody else that I know of. During training you're taught that these people are not human, I guess. You're kind of brainwashed to think that. And it definitely kicks in. And in the end you're kind of pissed off. . . . The first mission out, one of our other teams lost a guy; he got shot and ended up dying. This kind of set a precedent for the whole deployment that we were kind of upset and pissed off, and, like, this is really serious stuff.

8

Close Call

Surviving a close call is the stuff of Hollywood. Yet over time in a war zone it can become mundane, part of the everyday routine, an inconvenience or an interruption. But there are other times when the consequences are just too close, and a veteran is left with an enduring sense of responsibility: for someone who died in his or her place, for lacking the foresight to prevent an incident, for the eerie memories of coming close to one's own death, for the training and esprit de corps that saved one from annihilation, or for pure dumb luck.

I FEEL BADLY ABOUT the way I left the Army. When I left, I was supposed to go to Afghanistan, but I was going through a custody battle. So I asked my battalion at the time, "Hey, I just can't make this trip." The warrant officer who took my spot lost both of his legs and one of his arms in Afghanistan. And he, you know, took my spot. So that's the only thing that really sticks with me.

• • •

I was the lead vehicle driver for the MATVs. I once rolled the truck over down a hill. That was funny. We were driving at about three in the morning with the drive lights out, and no one knew where we were. They give you this tiny thermal screen to drive through, and then my driver has night vision, so he's like, "Go left, go right," or whatever. Then I came up to a ledge; it was a very steep ledge. I asked my gunner, "Am I okay to go over this?" And he said, "Yeah, you're good." So I started inching slowly, and it turned out to be a sideways slant, so the truck started turning and just rolled over a few times. Everybody was okay; no one was hurt, but it was exciting. The vehicle ended up on its side. We had to call in a truck to winch it back up; after that it had a cracked windshield, but we kept driving it for, like, another month before we replaced it.

• • •

The first time you're somewhere and you hear this shot ring out, what's always funny is you're like, "Huh. That sounded really close. I wonder what they're shooting at." And it takes you a little while. I've never heard anyone else say this, but I observed it all the time. Whenever you'd get a new person along and something would happen, it just makes no sense that someone wants to hurt you, and at first, before you get used to that dynamic, it's just hearing a bang. It just doesn't make you think that you could be the target. Why would anyone want to hurt anyone?

• • •

As a leader in the military, this is the thing that I regret the most and beat myself up over the most. In some ways I think it's responsible for who I became later in my career, but I was still a really young guy, you know, twenty-four. We had these twelve-hour shifts, and it's really hard over long shifts to keep people focused. We'd been outside the wire for eleven and a half hours. There's this canal that runs east-west through our AO, and we stopped at this little village on the canal, got out, set a perimeter with the trucks; I went and talked to the sheik in the town and kinda chatted with him: what was going on, what they needed. You know, they always want money for something, or food for something, or whatever it is, but that's important to find out what's going on, what the feel is. We got back to the canal road. . . . It's a water canal; they're very wide, artificial, probably fifty feet across. They're a forty-five-degrees sloped bank, and on the other side of it will be a dirt road just wide enough for a HMMWV maybe. And then there would be a berm, like an eight-foot berm sloped about the same way on the other side. So we got back down the canal road, and I noticed this blue bongo truck. A bongo truck is this little flatbed, like a utility truck. Like a little Toyota. A cab with a flat bed in the back, very small.

We're on the north side of that canal. And this is the first thing that should have gotten my attention: this guy's on the south side of the canal, and he's driving like a fool. And I don't mean like third-world driving, where everybody just drives. He's racing down this canal road, which might be the stupidest thing you could ever do. And he runs up on the bumper of this other car, and he's honking the horn, and, I mean, just inches off this guy's bumper, jerking all over the place, and then a couple of my men said, "What the hell's his problem?" He got by the guy, and we didn't pay attention. We stopped at another village on the way for about ten minutes. I really think that's when they set it up. We're pretty sure what happened is that truck went down to the end of the road, came back around, and set the IED in front of us. I think that's why he was in a hurry to get up there and set it, and we gave him the time because we stopped at that little village there.

So we're driving back in, and I was short-changing the patrol. We were supposed to stay out till noon; we'd been out since midnight. Well, what I figured is that I could come in the gate about 11:45, and by the time we cleared the fuel depot, I could call RFP—that's Return from Patrol—about twelve, and that's what was on my mind. I was done. We're, you know, exhausted. And then the world blew up. We were driving down, and I could see tower 12, just the northwest tower of the FOB. There's this image that I'll always be able to imagine. The whole world is black; there's like a yellow spark in the middle of it maybe. I felt the truck start to slow down, and I yelled at my driver to go.

That was the biggest problem we had. You always want to get clear of the kill zone. I had a young, very, very inexperienced driver, who was a mid-tour replacement. He had been mine for maybe a couple weeks, and he told me the truck wouldn't go. So that was when I knew that the truck was disabled. I called for a status report out of the truck. I've gotta back up and say I wasn't wearing hearing protection. They tell you to wear hearing protection. All the colonels will be like, "Wear your hearing protection; wear your hearing protection." I understand why they're doing it, but it's never going to happen at a ground level with the troops. And I'm sure they know that. They have to say, "Wear it," and I understand that. You've got to be able to hear. I'd lost hearing temporarily; I mean, it was ringing. The only injury we sustained out of the group, by the way, was the driver. His left eardrum was popped. So I called for a status report out of the truck, you know: one—up, two—up, three—up; the interpreter told me he was up (we had a local national linguist in the back seat). Picked up the radio: we're struck by an IED four hundred meters west of tower 12 on the north side of yellow brick road. That was just all slang for where we were. They asked me for a grid. I told them to fucking plot it; I'm busy. We basically had an Icom, they called it; it's basically a walkie-talkie. I'm not even sure those things are secure to communicate with the other truck. I could hear Sergeant Smith, who was the second commander for the other truck, call me, but I couldn't hear what he was saying.

We had to bail out of the truck because the EFP set everything on fire. I told the crew to evac the truck. I remember thinking to myself, "Wow, this fire is spreading really fast." Because, you know, there's things you'd like to do when you're getting out of the truck, and then there's things you have time to do when you're getting out of the truck. I've never been the type of guy to carry an assault pack or anything like that; I just loaded my vest down. So I just open the door, grabbed my M-4 and this little stuffed Beanie Baby that we had on top of our radios for good luck, and jumped out of the truck. Ziggy. I still got Ziggy. I threw Ziggy in my cargo pocket—I don't know why it was important to me at the time, but it was, so I threw Ziggy in my cargo pocket, jumped out of the truck onto a forty-five-degree bank and almost fell into the canal, which sucks because if you do, you're probably not getting out wearing all that gear. The linguist came out with me, and he's not wearing all that gear, and I still had to grab him to keep him from going into the canal.

I remember looking up and seeing Sanchez go over the back and over the turtle shell of the trunk, and I started moving back toward the other truck because at that point my concern was, "When are we gonna start receiving the small arms fire?" or whatever it is. Got back to Jones's truck and just started putting out security. Started putting out a perimeter. Jones should've been on that, but he wasn't. Like I said, first engagement that year. And even me, who had seen that stuff before. . . . Six months without something happening, you know. The talk, the log and the talk showed twenty-two seconds between when the IED went off and when my radio transmission went out. In my mind, there's no time period in there. Maybe two seconds for the crew up-drill. I don't know where that twenty seconds went. I always thought that was interesting. Put security out, and then this is where we caught some breaks. The bad guys didn't . . . just bad luck for them, frankly.

The Short Range Patrol—either Short Range Patrol or QRF—was commanded by a really good friend of mine, a staff sergeant. They had gotten tasked with just running the . . . trucks that go around all the port-a-johns and suck everything out of them and then take 'em down to the trash heap south of town and empty 'em out. Well, they were just coming back. They were coming back, and they were literally approaching the south checkpoint when the IED went off. All they did was just bypass the checkpoint and go for the access road, and they were already hauling to me. At the same time, the s-5, which is a civil affairs unit from over battalion headquarters, was leaving the north side of the base with our s-3, lieutenant colonel, in gun trucks, and a detachment of Iraqi Police. They were patrolling the north checkpoint at almost the exact same time. Second Platoon was getting ready to come on shift because, you know, we had the midnight to noon. Well, they had the noon to midnight. So they were in the motor pool, checking everything out with their trucks and everything like that and literally just had to throw some body armor on and roll out. So within five minutes of this thing rolling, we had an enhanced company, plus four or five detachments out into the battle space around the area. We were really able to lock it down, got a little bit of a feedback from some locals.

This is where it was kind of interesting: one of the patrols there, we locked them down on that truck. Well, they had three gun trucks, and I took over one of their other gun trucks so that my patrol was back intact. We were able to respond and capture the triggerman. Caught the triggerman. . . . I have to back up because I have to tell you that up until right about the point when that truck got there, I was fine. I was just doing my job; I was fine. When everybody came rolling in—the staff sergeant, the s-3, the colonel, and all these guys came rolling in—I almost lost it emotionally. I still get really emotional thinking about it because there's just the brotherhood complex. And when everybody comes running to you because you got smacked, . . . that was a really, really powerful thing for me. Literally, there on the battlefield, I've got all this stuff to do, and even though there's people coming out there now that have outranked me, I haven't given control of the battle space over. I started this brief emotional rollercoaster, like, one second I wanted to cry, and the next I wanted to laugh. What brought me out of that was when this local came up and told us, "Hey, there's this guy we don't know here, and he's running south."

We locked it in. We sent more patrols down and just clamped the area down, rounded this guy up in a field. The s-3 wouldn't let me get near him, thought I was gonna kill him, which I was. Interrogated him, got a location on the bomb maker's house, went and did a cordon and search on that house—the most botched entry on a house I have ever done in my life. We looked at the house and set up our perimeter, picked a door, and I hit the door with an s-5. The captain was standing right behind me. Well, a lot of Iraqis in that part of the country had this huge hutch in their house (I guess that's what you would call it). There's two entrances to the house. We didn't wanna take one because we looked at it and said, "That's a kill zone, all day." So we picked this other entrance. Well, they didn't use that entrance. So they had this wall-sized hutch; I mean, these things are like fifteen feet long, floor-to-ceiling, a couple feet thick, and it's got almost everything the family owned in it. You know exactly what I'm talking about; this thing was massive. Your grandmother's wall hutch has nothing on this. It was across this door. The captain and I got it open but stuck in the doorway for a couple minutes. It really sucked, so. . . . Went in and cleared the house. The bomb maker's wife was there. She wasn't happy with us at all. Couple younger family members. Found a whole lot of Mukhtar Militia, pro-Sadr mate-rials. Some things that could be used for bomb making, nothing, really like, "Oh, this is this type of explosive" or whatever.

I think the guy gave us his contact, the guy who had helped him out, because everybody came out—the intel guys, EOD, you know, everybody came out and did their assessment. They said that EFP was probably made in Iran. I don't know how they reached that conclusion off some dust particles, but they did. An EFP essen-tially becomes a plasma dart, so it melts through armor that it wouldn't ever be able to penetrate. It entered at the wheel hub assembly at the front left and exited the top part of the engine block. The HMMWV was a bolt-on package, and it had no armor over the engine compartment or the trunk at all. We actually had some spall in the passenger compartment. Spall is pieces of metal that get blown in by . . . shrapnel created by your own armor or whatever. None of it hit anybody. . . . If you looked back in the truck, there's holes all in the floorboards. Pieces of metal went underneath my legs, over my legs, and things like that, but the vast majority of the EFP was focused on the engine compartment. He just set it off half a second too early.

I utterly failed that day. I didn't pick up on all the clues on all the signals that you've been trained to recognize for . . . years. I had completely checked out. Once I saw that tower, the guard tower (I can see the guard tower on the base), I'm home. I'm done. I wasn't looking at the side of the road; I wasn't looking for people; I wasn't looking for the signal indicators. I can go back through, and I can crawl all over that site. I can show you some of the pictures on my computer; I can show you the markers in the background. There's pictures of the crater; when you look in the background, you can see the flag tied on the tree to basi-cally tell them where to detonate it. The bongo truck and the way it was acting. Even going back to tensions in the last town we stopped at, where everything seemed normal, but it wasn't. I'm certain with the way it went off, and when they placed it, there had to be freshly disturbed dirt. All of the indicators were there; everything was there, painted up like a big fucking pretty sign, and I blew it. It's also something that I'm past. Probably got past it because nobody died. But I would honestly say at that point in time I was a mediocre, decent, okay infantry NCO. I was an E-5— this is going to sound arrogant, but—smarter than your average bear but nothing outstanding, nothing particularly amazing. After that, no way. I was never gonna let that happen again. And I became an outstanding NCO. I mean, I'm not afraid to claim that. I've got the awards to prove it. . . . I never lost a soldier. You know, I led I don't know how many missions since then in a lot hairier places and with a lot more tension. Did some people probably not like me after that? Probably, because I was the type of person who was gonna make sure everything was right. My thing was that this was never gonna happen again. Not to any of my guys, no. Not on my watch. So that's what changed for me. I wasn't gonna let that happen again.

• • •

Being a nineteen- or twenty-year-old individual having to write your death letter in the event that you die, when I did that the first time, I went back and told a lot of people things that I kept to myself before.

• • •

She was one of my best friends, and she was in the same part of the country as me, in the south, where there were a lot of IEDs. After her death for the next couple of months until I came back, I was scared because you can't be protected from stepping on a bomb that's going to end your life. Anywhere you step can be booby trapped or what we call daisy chained, where they'll actually rig a series of IEDs to blow so that you step on one and it blows up a chain of them, so you kill a whole group of your buddies by what you step on. Everything we did was at night; all of our missions were under night vision goggles. If they'd try to hide an IED, you couldn't see it, but even one that was not very well hidden would be hard to see. For a while, I just felt like every step I took could be my last, for a couple of missions after her death. That was really the only time I felt fear on any of my missions. No one from any mission I was ever on was wounded. That's actually pretty incredible. They'd get hurt, honestly, like, by falling through the roof of an Afghan house or stepping into a hole, but it was never a gunshot. So I was pretty lucky when it comes to seeing trauma to my friends. But I saw plenty of Afghan or insurgent dead bodies or people who were hurt, but never one of my guys.

• • •

One time on Route Irish we were three guys in a civilian car, and we were stopped at a coalition checkpoint waiting to get IDed. The guy manning the gate was an Aussie working for Blackwater or one of those security contracting companies. After waiting ten or so minutes, we finally passed through the gate. I shook his hand, said have a nice day, and went on my way. My car didn't get two hundred meters down the road when I heard this enormous boom. The guy that I just shook hands with was no more. The car directly behind mine was the vehicle-born explosive. Why he waited until my car made it through the gate, I'll never know. However, I often think about it, and I'm truly grateful I made it back when others did not.

• • •

We were attacked with rockets a number of times, like I think most people are, but the first couple patrols that I went on, it's weird. It's not like when you imagine a sort of force-on-force conventional combat; there's a line here, and there's a line here, and you're shooting; you're exchanging rifle fire and whatever. You sort of expect that, but when it's an unknown factor, when it's the ground underneath you that could potentially explode at any moment, that's not combat; that's just hope; that's just hoping that something doesn't happen. And the same thing goes with rockets; you hear a rocket coming, and you just have to hope that it's not going to land near you because there's nothing you can do. At least in Iraq there was nothing you could do about it. In Afghanistan it was a little bit different. On the larger bases there was some radar and things like that. In Iraq toward the end of my tour there was a rocket attack right when the new unit was coming in; the unit that was coming in to replace mine was coming in, and the Iraqis always knew, and this was the same in Afghanistan; they always knew because we wear patches, which is dumb. I don't know why we still wear patches. I mean it's cool when you're back in garrison, but I know what unit I'm in. I know what unit all my friends are in when we're out there. All we're doing by showing patches that are different is broadcasting the fact that it's new units, new people. So they knew that every time there was—they call it a RIP, a Relief in Place, and a transfer of authority, they always knew when that was going on because there were two sets of patches out on the road. So when they knew that, well, if they aim a rocket at the base, they have a higher chance of hitting somebody. It's not quite twice as many, but there's an inflow of people before there's an outflow. So there's a couple weeks where there are now more people on the same base, and then if you wait three weeks, that number will be the same as it was before. So in that case they knew, and they shot a couple rockets the last week or so that I was there, and I remember I was in our temporary tent, which had no bunkers outside it, had no protection overhead, and we had nothing to do; our jobs were over. We had maybe four days left before we were going to ship to a different base and then go out to Kuwait, and I was, like, sitting on my bunk watching a movie on my computer or something like that, and all of a sudden there were a couple rockets coming in, and they landed not too far from our tent, which is a scary thought. They ended up killing a couple of the new guys, who had only been there for about a week. So it made me think like, "What's worse? What would've been worse? Killing the guys who had been there for a week or killing people who had been there for fifteen months a week before they have to leave?" That's a question I still don't know how to answer.

• • •

There was not a single round fired. I was doing one of these two-HMMWV convoys on a seven-mile run. It's about seven miles but seven really hot miles. It's not unusual for the vehicle before us or after us to get hit. We'd decided that these vinyl coverings we had on these HMMWVs did more harm than good because we couldn't see to return fire. So we just took them off. It felt like riding dune buggies through Baghdad. So we're on this main drag through Baghdad, and it's a divided highway, four lanes either way, standard middle of the day, hot as hell, and all of a sudden we start seeing civilian vehicles coming right at us from the opposite direction, which is really a bad sign. It means that the locals are seeing that something is up, and they're trying to get the hell out of Dodge. The question is: What happens next?

My glasses had gotten broken, and I need glasses. Normally I'd be driving the lead HMMWV, but I was following at the time. The private in front of me slammed on the brakes out of nowhere, so I slammed on my brakes and just barely missed rear-ending him. I jump out of the vehicle, and I'm pissed off—"What the hell are you doing?," that kind of thing. As I'm in the process of losing my temper, I see a wire stretched across the tree in the median down to something in the road. And there's no way we can get around it now because, with the traffic going in two different directions, there was just a jam. Nobody was going anywhere. At that point I'm looking around, and I'm realizing this is the most beautiful place for an ambush I ever saw. There's one of those civilian walkways that's like a little footbridge that goes across a major road directly above us; buildings all over the place with chain-link fences around them. And we're sitting out there in the open.

First of all, what hit me was: I'm going to die. And you force yourself to spread out. Your desire in that circumstance is to stay as close as you can, but you know you have to spread out so you don't create a target. I happened to be pulling rear security on the convoy, and we're there for some weirdly long period of time or what seemed like a long period of time. I must have looked scared because I remember a man in one of the vehicles kind of making eye contact with me and kind of waving at me, as if saying, like, "It's cool." I'm trying not to look afraid, and there are people on foot all over the place.

And out of nowhere this Iraqi guy comes up to me. . . . I made all kinds of mistakes; I let him get too close to me; he could've grabbed my rifle or stabbed me or anything. I let him just run up on me because it's hard to treat somebody like. . . . I wasn't thinking. He says, "You have to come with me; my daughter is hurt, and you have to come help me." I was like, "Look." I mean I couldn't do that. The first thing you want to do is to figure out a way where you can do something, but there was no way you could. Even if it were legitimate, there was nothing I could do, but I strongly suspect that it wasn't legitimate. So I'm like, "I'm really sorry. There's nothing I can do about it. It's out of my jurisdiction." He keeps trying to tug at me to get me to go along with him, and I have to push him off of me. There's an Iraqi police officer, and I'm like, "Look, go talk to him; there's nothing I can do." He's like, "I need help; you have to come with me." And I was somewhere between really feeling sorry for the guy and being completely terrified when a car convoy of MPs came up the other side of the road and cleared out a way for us to get across the median. Soon as he saw the MPs, he took off, which makes me think it wasn't legitimate because if he could ask me for help, he could ask the MPs.

They cleared out a way for us to get over the median and get onto our destination. What they discovered was that the wire itself wasn't actually an explosive; they think it was a timing device. They think that the idea was that someone was watching when the HMMWV would hit the wire; they would count 1–2–3 and detonate. But the traffic jam made it impossible. That was intense. The reason I always remember that is that there was all this dead time. There was nothing that happened, but for about twenty minutes, you're waiting out there for the other shoe to drop. That was the time I really thought I'm going to die today; this is my time; this is my place. It had a kind of elongated feeling. Mostly, it just happened so fast: you'd see the remains of a convoy that's been destroyed and the medic. You're going by, but you're seeing out of the corner of your eye. You're seeing an utterly destroyed vehicle, and you know people are badly, badly injured, and that's the road that you're on all the time.

• • •

We had another rocket attack the night we were leaving the country. We were due to fly out the next morning. If there's any time you're gonna die, it's that. . . . So everyone has that sick mind:

we're so close. Everyone's planning their vacations; you just know you're jinxing it. At midnight all of a sudden the sirens go off, bunch of rounds coming in. So you have this rocket coming in, the battery going off, and the first couple hit before they track on it. This was a fifteen round made of, probably, multiple rocket rails, kind of set up on the field somewhere. So you had the first rounds coming in before the thing starts tracking on them. It's called a phalanx weapon system, so it's a counter-artillery gun; basically just fires a tremendous volume of lead up in the air—BOOM! BOOM!—and slowly the rockets start kind of walking toward us, so you hear the phalanx on the far side of the base sort of going off—one a little bit closer, closer. And then one went off that was a hundred meters behind us. And they are *loud*. I mean, more terrifying than the rocket exploding because all of a sudden, it's just this tremendous ripping sound. . . . It's terrifying but also reassuring. And it locked on to two rockets; it dispersed them so close that we were tense. Granted, there are T-walls surrounding it, but if one of those rockets would have landed in the T-wall, it would have easily been twelve or fifteen killed. We were packed to the gills in just canvas tents. They had no protection. It detonated so close that a little bit of shrapnel fell down and bounced off the tent. Okay, that was uncomfortably, uncomfortably close. But it was hilarious because you had the people who were on bases who were just, "Yeah, that's a gun," and then you have the people who have never had anything like that happen anywhere near them and who were just shaking and terrified. Post-break cigarette and it's, "Oh. Still alive. Might as well take five minutes off."

• • •

We were inside the little tin shed, just a little set off. All of a sudden it's, "Incoming! Incoming! Incoming!" I'm, "Okay, whatever." I just kind of crouched down a little bit. Everyone else hit the floor, but I'm, "I do this every day." When they overshoot, they hit our area. Whatever. And then all of a sudden, the first one goes off, and it's a lot louder and a lot closer, and the whole thing starts to sway. And I'm, "Oh! Oh, right, I'm not in a concrete building right now. This is corrugated steel that would be punched through in a heartbeat by a piece of shrapnel." It was one of the moments where, even though you adjust your base-line, you forget to take into account certain variables. And then it's, "Oh, right. Yeah! I've got to follow everyone else's lead and get down on the ground and probably put my helmet on too."

• • •

I can only remember images. When I saw a dead body, it was from a vehicle and not necessarily going by at ninety miles an hour. When there was a convoy hit, you'd often go by very slowly. I can't say that I saw it, and I was shocked. Going by in a vehicle and you see a convoy that's been hit, and there's someone in the road who is obviously dead—whether Iraqi or whether American or whether coalition—there's a certain degree of shock, but there's so much adrenalin going through your system at the time that I don't think I really thought about it until later. It kind of hits you, and the brain tags it as significant, but I think the real thinking about it is deferred until later.

9

Combat

There is a military cliché, as one veteran reminded us, that war is 95 percent boredom and 5 percent action. This chapter is about that 5 percent. In the civilian imagination, fueled by movies and television, the gold standard is the firefight, direct engagement with a visible enemy, even hand-to-hand combat. While some combatants have those stories to tell, for the most part they encountered mortars fired onto a base from a distance and countered by huge artillery from inside the wire, or roadside bombs detonated by a distant mobile phone. Some soldiers encountered insurgent attacks on patrol and fired in the direction of a muzzle flash through a palm grove, an agricultural crop, or a chaotic cityscape. For the veterans of Iraq and Afghanistan, war was both abstract and extremely visceral. Their memories of combat are both crystal clear and confusing, ordered and chaotic, logical and surreal. As such, these events make great stories and are often the stories told with the most relish and enthusiasm, viscerally detailed, shaped by a satisfying narrative arc, and at the same time haunted by uncertainty. The way a soldier feels in the midst of battle is unexpected even by the person trained to engage. To describe those reactions afterward, at home or among civilians, is challenging because it sounds wrong, perhaps even callous. Yet the feelings veterans describe here are as ubiquitous in the war zone as they are unexpected and unacceptable at home.

I WAS NEVER IN a vehicle that exploded. Again, the litany of things I wasn't involved in. . . . That's pretty common. You hear these stories on the news: *Wow!* He's dragging bodies from the mud and throwing them on the helicopter! Those are really powerful images of things that lots of people did and are still doing today.

• • •

In the initial invasion we went all the way through what I think they call Highway 1, Route 1. We drove all the way up to Mosul to come through, but it took us about a day and a half to get to Baghdad—day and half to two because we weren't the initial push, the very first people through. They had a lot of the mechanized equipment go through, and we came behind it, but you still have, y'know, the fedayeen and other different forces coming at you in different ways. We were driving a convoy, and it was your typical cloverleaf on a highway coming off; we were coming off this, and an RPG round came and struck about twenty feet in front of my HMMWV. I was in the second vehicle in the convoy; the other one had already passed, and that thing's hitting just POW!, and you're like, "Whoa!" Everything just sparks, and there's just this big firework. And then my gunner just starts unloading. I was driving, and my gunner's just unloading his two-four-nine out the back, and you just hear *tu-tu-tu-tu-tu, tu-tu-tu-tu-tu, tu-tu-tu-tu-tu*. As I was driving—and I'll never forget this—as I'm driving under the overpass, I looked up, and you could see where the bullets had been—were—hitting, and it was actually making a spark where the bullet was hitting things, just *ting-ting-ting*. Then you hear *ting-ting-ting*, and you're like, "Oh. That was a metallic 'ting-ting,' and we're the only metal around." So that's hitting *me*; in fact, it's hitting *us*! So, "Oh! My God!" You book it. Just hit pedal to the metal and get out of there.

We got about a mile up the road, and my tire's flat because we got shot out. And—ah, man—we don't wanna stop, but we have to stop. We pull over. You get a huge area, and you circle around. And as I climbed out of the vehicle to go quickly change the tire, as we're keeping an eye out . . . I remember coming around. . . . There's a roll bar that comes over the back that's less about being a roll bar and more about keeping the canvas up off of you at that point, but it's a piece of aluminum. I was driving unprotected, and this is before we put the sheet metal on. We were given flak vests that are a solid, single piece of Kevlar that your typical police officer would wear. They're about yea thick; they're very light, and they're very flimsy, and we would take them and strap them to the door because that was where anything was coming in, through that door, usually. You had your Kevlar for the rest of you, but that door was where things would come in. So it had the Kevlar vest on—had it strapped to my door. And when I got out, I saw that—I mean literally—you could reach back and touch it. There was a bullet hole right there. Right there . . . where it had come . . . and the angle was just right of that roll bar. If the guy had aimed that way or that way, we wouldn't be having this conversation now because it would have hit me somewhere.

We didn't get a lot of fire back, and I think that ended up being kind of more typical than what we wanted. I mean, we had a few firefights where we were able to fire back, or we were able to engage the enemy like we were taught to, y'know. It was part of your creed: "I will close with and destroy the enemies of the United States in close combat." And so the typical combat experience wasn't what we wanted it to be. They're saying, y'know, "You don't want any of it" coming in. Later you're like, "Well, actually I didn't want any of it." But when you're there, you do. It's what you want. That's what I trained for. I want to do this. Don't train me to do all this stuff and then make me police call and everything. I wanted to put them in my sights.

• • •

The initial invasion plan got scrapped about fourteen days before we went in. So my duty assignment at the time was. . . . I was a battalion sniper for our scout platoon. Every light infantry battalion has a scout platoon that's assigned to the headquarters company. They do recruitment of sorts, I guess, from everybody in the battalion. They try and pull the people they think will be the best. To go back and clarify, I'm not a school-trained sniper. I don't have a Bravo 4 identifier. Basically, I happened to be really good at certain things—specifically moving into places without people noticing very well. They put me in a sniper element, and . . . I don't wanna say I got really lucky. . . . The saving grace for me and that duty position was our sniper squad leader was a prior Delta Force sniper who had gotten in some trouble in Delta Force and was basically told, "Hey, you're gonna go play in the regular

Army for a little while, and then maybe you can come back." The guy was a veteran of Mogadishu and a number of other places and was very, very good at his job. He was always making fun of me and telling me, "Well, you can't shoot for shit, but you don't have to 'cause you can get so close to people." He spent a lot of time training us. . . .

Anyway, the initial invasion plan called for 3rd ID to come out of Kuwait, through the desert; 4th ID was supposed to come out of Turkey. So we were gonna come from the north, and 24th MEU—that's Marine Expeditionary Unit—I think, was gonna come basically out of the Persian Gulf up through Basra. The 82nd, 101st, and one of the regular battalions, I can't remember which one off the top of my head. . . . Initially, the Ranger battalion, immediately followed by the 82nd, were gonna jump on Baghdad International Airport, which is not just an airport. It's a huge complex of palaces, and basically the intent was to seize the entire Ba'ath Party leadership, just grab 'em. The 101st was supposed to come in behind us, air assault. We were basically gonna put 2.5 brigades of light infantry on Baghdad and attempt to clamp it down until the armored units could get there. Really, right up the doctrine. The doctrine says you can put these light units in, these airborne units, and drop them in, and they can hold for seventy-two hours, or a little longer if you have an airfield—that's what we were grabbing—until the heavy units get there. Basically, as they were looking at these plans, Turkey said no; Turkey wasn't going to let us use them as a staging point. And then the higher-ups started getting pretty nervous. . . . The question was what happens if 3rd ID gets stuck? Now we have ten thousand troops in Baghdad, and nobody's gonna get to them to back them up. The other thing I think made people nervous was that the casualty estimates for that operation to jump and seize Baghdad were really high. Now, I think they were pessimistic to an extreme. But they were running between a 15 and 25 percent casualty operation. And I think that was really flustering some people.

They scrapped the whole plan, right? 3rd ID went and did their drive through the desert; I don't know what they did—their "thunder run." The MEU did its split up through the east, and the 82nd and the 101st went up the two different supply routes and essentially went town to town, house to house, and cleared these towns out of the fedayeen. What the fedayeen were. . . . Saddam had learned a very valuable lesson from '91 and said, "We're gonna lose. Badly." So he took a lot of his better-trained military forces and put 'em in civilian clothes and said, "Go start an insurgency." Essentially. And so we would go through, and it was this real pick and move; you know, the units would go through, and basically what they were doing was they were moving—looking for a contact, looking for the three guys they wanted to ambush, the five guys they wanted to ambush, or whatever, and just clearing them out.

As a battalion sniper, my job, usually, was to try and find a position where I could cover these movements. Everybody thinks a sniper is all about engaging people. It's actually mostly about calling up on the radio and getting the information back. Calling in mortar fire, calling in artillery fire. I think I called an air strike one time; that was cool. Not nearly as glamorous as the movies would want you to believe. It's a long, long time sitting in places, not moving at all. Covered in sweat and bugs and all kinds of stuff, things we're not going to talk about. . . . Very long, tedious work. So I would say for a large part—despite almost constant engagements with these little two- or three-man groups—it was annoying. You just wanted to swat them like a fly because they'd pop out and stick around a corner and just spray an AK in the air. Right? And then one of two things would happen: either they'd run away before someone could engage them or some soldier happened to be looking, like Johnny-on-the-spot, and he'd tag a bullet, and it was done. It was very, very extreme . . . but extremely ineffective.

The first major—really the only major—engagement that we had, a real kinetic engagement, and this was a real extreme. . . . We got to this town called Samawah. Samawah was divided in half by the Euphrates, and they've actually built up a river wall there on either side of the river. So you have the river, a fifteen- or twenty-foot concrete wall, and three bridges crossing it. Now

Samawah—in spite of being in the desert, and there's nothing really around it—for some reason, it's very condensed. It has packed, narrow streets; it's a really small city; if there's no traffic, you could drive through in two minutes. But when you're right in the middle of it, all the buildings are six stories tall and almost touching each other, literally almost touching each other. You moved from building to building by taking a stretcher from our kit and laying it across two windows and then crawling across it; we moved across buildings on upper floors doing that. Seven feet apart, something like that. Completely divided in half by this river. So our scout elements get up there—the first scout element that showed itself on the river; I don't know how they ever got back out. The entire other side of the river—every window, doorway, nook, cranny, I think—had an AK or an RPG or something. It was like something out of a World War II movie. They're trying to get across the river, and it's like. . . . I was on a spotting scope; it's like, "Holy shit, man! Did you see that?" It took us two days to get across because they tell you that the best way to take a river is from both sides, but you weren't going across that river with that wall. We were light, so we didn't have any armor assets to push us across at all. We took a couple injuries; somebody got a HMMWV too close, and, of course, it was just a bullet magnet. Our HMMWVs, they didn't have any armor.

Me and my spotter spent two, three days on the sixth floor of a building on top of some desks we piled up. We gave strafes until we ran out of match grade. I mean, it was busy. It wasn't like it was tense or anything like that; it was literally like being on the range because they didn't know where we were; we were a couple hundred meters back from the river, tucked up in a room. We didn't have to worry about moving because the area was secure. Usually as a sniper you take a shot, and then you're moving. We didn't have to worry about any of that. Eventually the MEU dispatched us a company of tanks, just three tanks; three tanks show up, roll across the river with some infantry support to give us the foothold we needed; that's all we needed. Then the fedayeen just flushed. That actually was interesting too because then I spent the

rest of the day calling in mortar strikes. They were literally load-
ing up buses and trying to drive to the next town, and we were
calling in mortar strikes on the buses.

Pretty uneventful after that; went on to Baghdad.

• • •

This was probably my favorite firefight. It was just super sweet.
We were walking through a pot field on the way back. I remember we were coming back to the COP; we were done with our
mission for the day. We were walking back; at this time, this
was toward the end of the deployment, so we were all seasoned.
I was the RTO—Radio Telephone Operator—at this point, so I
was in the center of the formation. I really enjoyed being the
RTO because I like telling people what was going on. Especially
since I like land navigation so much, I had a very good sense of
direction, and I could tell them. When we were walking through
a big field that obscured us, rather than have my antenna sticking up, I pulled it down over my shoulder. I don't know if the
guy behind me was doing that. I remember getting a call over
the net, like frantic, from our platoon sergeant—I don't know
why he wasn't out with us that day, but he was in the Tactical
Operations Center—TOC—and he was using the eye in the sky,
and he called me frantically over the net; he was like, "We've
got three guys over to the northeast. One of them has got an AK
or something like that." I was like, "Hey, sir, we're about to get
ambushed." Right then a bunch of shots fired; the RTO behind me
drops. He didn't get shot; his radio had gotten hit, and shrapnel
had gone into his arm and lodged in his arm, and he was bleeding from that. It might have been a bullet fragment, shrapnel; I
don't know what it was, but he was bleeding. I remember I was
on the net, and I was saying we're taking contact from two to
three men to our northeast. I don't know what weapons they're
carrying. It sounds like AKs. I called the Medevac for the other
RTO, whose radio was shot, so I had the only radio. Everybody
had small radios, but. . . . When we moved like that, you set up a
support-by-fire position with one of the big guns. They're on the
gun, and they just start tearing into the area that they had shot

at us from. The LT and I just hunkered down. Everybody gets down; you try to figure out where you're getting shot at from.

• • •

We were a simple patrol. We were at the checkpoints, and we were surrounding the city; we had our main hub that we were out of, and we were tasked to go, I believe, pick up what is called a HET team (I think it's Human Exploitation Team). I believe he had a meeting with a local sheik or whoever, so we were tasked to go and pick him up and come back. The sun was coming down, and I just remember my vehicle commander and I, at the time—and we still joke about this, that he jinxed us—he goes, "Oh, great; we're gonna get blown up," because it was nighttime, so we were dealing with a lot of. . . . We were scared of IEDs or attacks on our route back and forth just because it wasn't being patrolled because our main focus was the checkpoints. So on our route back we hit a pressure-plate IED. I just remember we were actually in the middle of an argument when, the next thing I know, he's shaking me and yelling, and it's pitch dark because the sun had fallen. I just remember feeling kind of wet, and I didn't know why. . . . Dazed, and there's steam everywhere. I remember him just pulling me up. I was confused, and I fell off the vehicle; I just hear screaming and I guess some gunfire, and then I just hear him yelling to pull out my driver, and I'm not really sure what was going on. I was so dazed that all I could remember was, "I need my rifle; I need my helmet." So I kept going into the vehicle, and they kept pulling me out, still feeling just wet, and it's pitch dark, and finally our corpsman, who was on another vehicle, came running over. He had a flashlight, and it turns out I had broken my nose, and I guess I felt wet from all the blood that was coming down; I just remember him making me sit down. The adrenaline is pumping too much, so I couldn't sit down, and they're trying to work on. . . . I guess when it blew up, this giant diesel engine came through the vehicle and landed on my driver, so they were trying to rock the engine to pull him out. I remember that. I guess they knew where the pressure plate was because mortar started falling on us, and then I remember glimpses of the helicopters and Medevacs coming and taking us away. And then it was probably about a month to six weeks of in and out of different hospitals, surgeries, and then going back to my unit eventually.

• • •

When we'd get attacked, it was always when you least expected it. You're trained to fight, but you're never 100 percent ready for that first bullet or the v-beid—vehicle-borne ied—that blows up the post. In my area it was dump trucks. They liked to put three thousand pounds of explosives in dump trucks and drive them into posts. It was very surreal. It just seemed like a movie that's playing out; I was just an actor in it. Even when the marines came in that had been hit by the v-beid, and they're all mangled up, it doesn't feel real until you sit down afterwards. Your training kicks in, and, you know, you remember little things that most people mostly wouldn't. . . . Like in a movie; when you see a movie, everybody remembers the main scenes, like a specific movie. . . . It's, like, different because I would remember the color socks someone was wearing, something minute and small. Everything kind of slows down; noises are pretty much muffled, and it's very surreal. It's not something I would ever want to enjoy constantly doing. But it had its fun moments. When you were the person that was ambushing them, it was the best part.

• • •

The first big experience, you find out what you're truly made of because a lot of guys talk a big game, and when stuff actually happens, they're cowering and crying, and some guys who you never would have thought of just rise to the top. That's a very defining moment for an individual.

• • •

I was only present on the scene for an amputation once. It was a double amputation. We were south in the green zone, and this was actually our first firefight. All of us new guys were still pretty green. We had taken over this compound. It was an abandoned village; it was called Killawall. (I've got a shirt at home that says "Kill 'em all in Killawall.") The Taliban had driven out the families that lived there, and it was their central base of operations for that whole green zone. It's where they operated out of. It's where they fled from us to. It was a den of IEDs. This was our first mission: to go down there and push them out. So naturally it was a big mission; it was an entire company effort, plus support from two other companies on either side of us. I probably couldn't give you an accurate number for the whole company; our platoon was always hovering around thirty-one guys, but we were always under strength, never got enough people.

We were running a patrol out to the north, toward the highway, because we couldn't get resupplied with water. It was like 130 degrees that day, and we'd been running around, and you just can't carry enough water to stay hydrated. I have a picture of my buddy and me when we were operating the detecting equipment, and we had to take a break; you can see our sweat has soaked through the Kevlar, around the ceramic plate. Our armor on the outside is just soaking wet. It is a gross picture; you can just see the exhaustion. He's just sucking on his camelback hose; his helmet's askew; he looks miserable. We had requested an air drop of water, but that wasn't going to work. So what they did was, they just filled a bunch of duffel bags full of water bottles. The unit was going to come along the highway, park along the highway, and walk south. We were—I want to say—three clicks south of the highway in the green zone. One squad was tasked with going up there to meet them. They left the compound, went north, and most of the platoon stayed in the compound. I wasn't there when it happened. I was on the wall of the compound suffering from heat stroke, as was everybody else. Everybody had stopped sweating and had blurred vision. . . . We needed water; I mean that's why they went out.

All of a sudden, there was a huge explosion. We think it was an old artillery round, a 155 round, which is a pretty big artillery round. There was a chink in one of the orchard walls; their walls are made out of mud, and there was a chink in the wall, and it was just on the other side, and my buddy hopped over the wall, landed on the pressure plate, and immediately had a double amputation. I just remember hearing the explosion and being like, "Oh, fuck!" Immediately we hear, "Medic! Medic!" Someone is hysterically screaming, "Get doc! Get doc!" Our medic hadn't gone out there with them. So that's when my squad comes in. We got doc to him, and I pulled security while they were working on him right next to me. I just remember everybody—I thought it was stupid—everybody was huddled around him. Not everybody, but all the sergeants were. I think he asked somebody to shoot him. I'm pretty sure he asked that. Of course, they said no. They were like, "Your dick and balls are still there; you're fine. You're fine. You're good." He was in shock. He kept saying he couldn't breathe. We were like, "You're talking. You can breathe. You're talking. Just stay calm." His blood pressure was so low that they had to run an iv into his chest, into the sternum, I guess. We had two docs on him at this point, and everybody was like, "What do you want me to do?" I remember doc was kind of getting frustrated. He was like, "Just open bandages. Just open bandages." Everybody wanted to do something, and nobody could just open bandages, you know. We thought there could probably be a couple IEDS in that orchard or at least one. We found his leg. We felt like he'd probably lost some body parts over the wall and into the orchard area. It was also above the bank of the river. The river was really low, but we were probably ten or fifteen meters above the surface of the water. So maybe he lost it into the river; I don't know. His leg was, like, lying on the ground, like back behind me. The boot was still . . . it was weird. It wasn't his whole leg; it was below the knee. We couldn't find any other parts of him. But he lost both legs: one leg at the mid-thigh and the other leg at the hip. It tore all the meat between the two bones of his left arm. . . . It's weird. We bagged up his leg and put it on the helicopter with him in case. . . . But, I mean, obviously they couldn't. . . . There was about a foot and a half of leg missing between the part we found and the part that was missing.

· · ·

There was a time where I was sitting outside with two Iraqi guards; it was downtown Baghdad, and one of them handed me a cell phone with a video on it, and he was, "Cool! Cool!" And I'm looking at it: it's marines assaulting Fallujah, blowing the shit out of the place. I mean, I'm looking at that, and I'm, "Well, I mean, obviously tactical victory, but there's like civilian casualties; this is, like, Big Bad Army, like actual combat-combat-combat." The marines that I know who are in Fallujah—well, I didn't learn until years after, and then it's many, many beers in and starting to get down to the real core stuff and nothing I saw—I mean, that is just a magnitude of order different. And then looking at that video, and to them that was *awesome*. Like that is power; that is force; that is something that they respected the hell out of, and they wanted to be associated with it. That video made them proud to stand beside me. Because they had that force; that was aligned. But then we're kinda, like, insecure and saying, "Well, yeah . . . mmmm . . . well, we're not allowed to do this, and you can't treat your detainees that way." I'm not saying we should do that, but that's where that disconnect starts to arise. You have this idea that we really had after Desert Storm, and then amplified by the Balkans, that you can have this international interventionist policy with a light footprint and with clean, surgical strikes and tactical weapons and Special Forces teams coming in. And then not have to deal with the day-to-day. And now you have several hundreds of detainees that you don't know what to do with. And now you're dealing with people who are frustrated with what's going on and who are not perfect.

• • •

There was one time where we were leaving and it was in the day, which is always something you want to avoid, extracting or infil-trating during the day. We were just marching, kind of like on the ridge line. You don't ever want to go on top of the hill because then you silhouette yourself, and you don't ever want to be at the bottom because then if somebody does come up, you don't have the advantage of being uphill. And we were walking on this ridge line and somebody came on the other side. We didn't even know that there were people over there. So it caught us completely off guard. That was pretty terrifying. There were twelve of us, and there were only four of them, and they had AKs. I can attest that they were actual combatants, but, I mean, most people over there have AKs. We didn't even know until they started firing. . . . Then, well, crap. I turned. I don't know what the hell anyone else did in the first couple of moments, but I turned, and I started firing and got down in the prone position. There was a little rock, not much bigger than a stack of papers, but I kind of felt a little bit protected by it. I started seeing them kneeling or getting down. I couldn't tell if they were hit or if they were being suppressed. Either way, I was much more comfortable at that time. Then I looked to my buddy Dave to see what's going on, and he said that G—this guy that I didn't know that well; no one could pronounce his last name; he was Polynesian; we called him G—he had been hit, and I remem-ber thinking I don't know what the hell that means. It's vague. You're hit in the head? Or you're hit so it grazed you? Or what? And he got hit; the bullet came down in here. So the AK-47 762 just goes straight through. Our 556, it hits, and it's designed to tumble inside. So he was very fortunate. Then I got scared again after hearing that he got hit because, again, I didn't know what it meant at the time. We're waiting for commands: What to do? Flank or what? I just kept shooting, and then in that moment, I saw that we had guys who had apparently already started flanking, and I didn't hear the command for that, so I ceased fire, and they swept across. At that point, we wanted to get the heck out of there. I called higher command at that time. I switched my radios from Apache to that, to Higher, and called for immediate extract. The other side of the hill was actually deserted at that point, and then the helicopters came and picked us up, and we got out of there. The whole thing went like twenty or thirty minutes. I went through two magazines, which is thirty apiece, and then started going through my third. So people ask me, "Have you ever killed anyone?" I have no idea. We were all shooting at the same four people. I don't know if it was my bullet or his bullet. I'm just happy that they're not shooting at me any more. After every instance I never felt bad; I never felt good. I was just kind of indifferent to it, really. Aside from going with the high-value targets. Unless you're in close quarters, more often than not, you have no idea. The only people I know that I "took out" were when I called for an air strike, which I still don't feel horrible about. I know that's kind of insensitive, I guess. I wasn't happy, like, "Oh! Take that!" I wasn't disgusted either. Just coming back to the fact that everything is good with me and my guys. G's good. He got sent to Germany, and he actually got orders to come back, but at that point we were about a month from leaving, so he got to go home after that.

• • •

We went on this one mission to Ghundi Gar; it was this other unit's AO, and we had never been there before. I guess because our battalion were like the combat vets of our deployment, our brigade commander volunteered us to go help a different battalion in the brigade with their stuff. Two of our guys died because of that. We did an air assault into an AO that we didn't know. It took us months and months and months of IED denial missions and going down twice a day into the green zone and learning where the IEDs are and where they're not—and people were stepping on them in the meantime—and he volunteered us to go to this other AO. It was a two-day firefight; it went into day three, I think. It was a colossal failure of a mission. It was the biggest failure. We took way too many casualties. It was on that mission that my lieutenant lost his leg. Two guys died. Somebody else lost a leg, but he wasn't in our company, so I don't know him. It was a really complex maneuver; there were different pieces moving all the time, in theory. It was such a failure that our entire battalion lined up in ranger file and walked out of there single file. I'm talking about two or three hundred men in line just sheepishly shuffling out and trying to get out of there just because the casualties were too high.

We didn't accomplish any of our mission objectives; it was just a failure. We felt so betrayed and so pissed off at the brigade command that they did that because it was so obvious with the pictures they were taking the whole time. It was a resume builder for them, to get their star. I mean that's our speculation as privates and specialists, but we felt that we were used to get them their star. After that mission, we didn't have any respect for pretty much our entire brigade staff. There were IEDs in various places, but everybody who died got shot. One of my buddies got shot eleven times. He just regained the ability to walk in this past year. He was just riddled with holes. Helicopters were going to pick us up. It was an air assault out of Chinook helicopters, and basically we were going back to a somewhat secure landing zone for the Chinooks to pick us up. Tactical withdrawal. It was so stupid, and it was definitely a retreat. No infantryman wants to do that, first of all, so there was another layer of aggression or hatred toward the higher command who made us do that, put us in this situation where it was impossible to come out winners. . . . There was nothing we could do. We didn't know the AO. I don't even really know what we were doing. We were supposed to help them clear the Taliban out of this village. What does that even mean? What does that mean? The guy who got shot eleven times, he swears up and down that it was an ANP that shot him. I believe him. He says it was a police officer that shot him at point blank range and then just disappeared. Taliban can't shoot at all. They're horrible shots. They've got the worst aim (just like the infantry, just like us), but they hit him, and they hit Sergeant Smith, and Smith died.

• • •

The strangest thing to me is how bullets fly. We were on one operation. We were in civilian vehicles at this time—definitely for the first two deployments we were always in civilian vehicles; we were really driving intelligence, and I was dressed in Iraqi garb. We were blending, yeah, absolutely. So we actually received information that a kidnapping was about to happen. There were a lot of kidnappings happening at the time in Baghdad. We got the call: "Hey, you guys, go stake out the place and wait for something to happen." Well, something happened. They were five feet in front of us. The entire truck is riddled with bullets, and the captain was shot in the nose, but other than that—one, two, three, four, five people in a bongo-style truck. I mean, those Toyotas (you've seen them overseas in the Philippines, places like that)—but we had it set up, and the entire truck's just riddled with bullets. The captain is the only one who gets shot, and it goes right through his nose, so that is the strangest thing when I think about what happened to me. Just the way bullets fly. We called him Bull afterwards. You could stick your finger right there, right through it. But to me, I mean, combat is very slow.

• • •

In Baghdad we had one actual small-arms firefight. We were posted up somewhere for the night; we had to stop, and we got our convoy all set up, and I guess infantry was doing some maneuvers, and they had been backing some people up; they were actually turning and coming our way, so we had to, y'know, engage and keep them off, and it was more of a defensive thing at that point than it was a "Let's go get the bad guy" kind of thing. They were fleeing infantry, and we were in the way, so they're gonna take us if they can. We didn't . . . nobody got injured on our side during that firefight. And the entire time we were there in Mosul, nobody got severely wounded. We had wounds—we had injuries—most of them from explosive devices. It wasn't your typical . . . it wasn't

PHOTO BY MICHAEL GIBLER.

like Band of Brothers, where you're sitting in the foxhole shooting, like you're thinking it's gonna be. Most of combat experience was driving down the road and waiting for the next explosive device to go off.

• • •

Fourth of July is really, really, really tough. Really hard. In the first deployment, in Mosul, normally your convoy's three or four vehicles because you're agile. You get in, you get out; they don't notice you coming. But we needed to be at a certain place for certain training, and there were probably about fifteen vehicles returning back to a satellite camp. The rule at that point was you don't drive at night. Because at night was when they were able to slip in and set up IEDs, get out, set them off, and never get caught because that was their method at the time. So you don't drive at night. We didn't have a choice. It had just turned dark. It was just after dusk when we started out, so we get on the road and are maybe gone about five minutes down the road, and about 30–40 yards in front of my vehicle that I was driving this time . . . was just this *huge* explosion, and the sparks went easily 150 feet in the air; just this massive explosion that caught the left side of the HMMWV that it was geared toward. And the HMMWV came off the ground and landed on its side; the gunner on the back was wearing one of the newer body armors that had a plate, so he skidded twenty feet. We ended up calling him Ninja Turtle later because he skidded on his back. And . . . you've got a HMMWV on its side on fire on one side because of the explosions. We ended up cordoning off the areas—one of the steps that you have to do. So you've got the vehicle that got hit in the middle, and you've got a few on either side, and then there's us making a roadblock across. Nobody comes in; nobody comes out. In the city areas, where that one happened, people would come out to see. Only when they saw it was us and what had happened, the crowd started getting a little bit riled up. And you could see it: we had two hundred civilians on the other side of the HMMWV, and I'm sitting there with an M-16, and I only have 210 rounds, and there's at least two hundred people over there. First off, we're like, "This isn't a good idea! We can't keep these people out." What we ended up being able to do was . . . they brought in an OH58. It's a small, agile helicopter that kind of skimmed over the crowd a few times and scared them back, and no civilians were shot at or hurt at that point. We were able to do that. But the thing that just never goes away is that explosion. . . . I mean, it was so big. It was so close. It was so loud. It was so *real*. And the driver was. . . . I mean, he came away from it, but he came away worse for the wear big time. He didn't lose his leg, but I think he lost a lot of movement in his leg. I don't remember a lot of what ended up happening because you kind of lose track. . . . He wasn't in my battery. . . . So I never got to follow up on him as a person, but I know that he took some serious injuries in the hip and leg area and had hearing loss. Hearing loss, hearing loss, and more hearing loss is the order of the day for artillery men anyway, and he just . . . nothing out of that ear for a long time.

• • •

Smells are always the thing that really brings it back to me. The smell of rotting eggs. In Iraq we got hit by a lot of V-BIEDS. This one particular night it was a busy market day, but they drove a v-BIED into the side of a police station. No marines got killed, no marines got really injured, but twenty-six Iraqis were obliterated, and there's pieces everywhere. And we were the first unit to respond. We had to set up the HMMWVs on the main thoroughfare. There were no people allowed, and you just smelled the smell all night and all day. I was out there for twelve hours, and it was smelling . . . just like burned eggs . . . rotten eggs. Then at night you'd hear the dogs come out, and they'd be on the roofs eating and stuff, and it'd finally click when you started walking around, and you'd see the body parts and stuff like that.

• • •

I was shot in the side plate. We can't decide if it's dumb luck or bad luck. We were setting up the machine gun nest, and we were setting up so that I had the greatest field of fire on a particular road. I decided the machine gun, if it was moved, like, three inches to the right would've been more effective. The gun's very heavy, and I had to get up to move it. When I got propped up on a knee to move it, I got a round to the side plate: sniper fire. We didn't know what happened to me. With adrenaline running and stuff like that, you can't always tell how badly wounded you are. Rule is: machine gunner gets away from the gun if he's wounded. So I rolled away from the machine gun. My loader has to ignore me and get on the machine gun. The 240 represents 70 percent of a scout's firepower. When it goes quiet, the scouts die. So he told me—we had a drunk conversation like a year later—he was all pissed off because he wanted to help me, but he couldn't. It turns out, when I popped up on a knee, the round that caught me in the side plate would have gone through his neck. So when I popped up on a knee, I ended up saving his life. We didn't know it until afterwards. So we can't decide if it's dumb luck or bad luck. Couldn't decide. But we caught the number two bomb maker in Iraq. We knew he was operating in a certain area. So the machine gun nest I was setting up was to provide cover for the scout teams that were going out looking for him, essentially is what it was. And so we were trying to do it as stealthily as possible. In retrospect, I think that's why we started getting shot at, because we were in the right area. But it ended up—because of what happened—I had to go get new plates. So I had to go back to our main base. Two days later they ended up catching him. They caught him in the middle of the night, planting one of the IEDs I told you about. He was planting one of those.

• • •

We were on patrol. We were walking around COS Warrior, essentially checking the perimeter security. What we would do when we would show up to a base is we would take control of their perimeter security while they closed everything down on the inside; we'd protect them. So we were on one of these missions. We had been mortared earlier that day, so we just assumed that it was going to be eventually followed up by ground fire because that's what they normally did. So we were patrolling. We were walking between two of the guard towers because . . . I don't even remember why. We were just walking. Or probably bored was probably it. And then we got hit by incoming fire. They led the attack with IRAMs, which is a shoulder-mounted, Iranian-made missile. Kinda like an RPG, a rocket-propelled grenade. It went through . . . that's the wall it went through. It's twelve feet high, six inches thick, and steel-reinforced. Yeah. It was not a good day. Pretty much the explosion was close enough to me and my loader that it knocked my loader out. And it decided to send me flying, and I was lucky enough to stay conscious. I went through the wall, and the wall kinda collapsed into rubble. Very pleasant experience. Since I was the machine gunner, when I blew up, the first thing I did was tuck the machine gun into my chest because, as I was saying, the machine gun represents 70 percent of a scout's firepower. So the first thing I have to do is secure the gun; that's the gunner's job. If it's his life or the gun, he's supposed to protect the gun because if the gun goes down, the rest of the scouts can die. So I tucked the machine gun, and one of the sergeants comes up to get the machine gun; that's essentially what he was doing, and he saw me getting up and trying to climb back over the rubble. The first thing he asked me was, "Is the machine gun okay?" I said some not nice things back.

...

I'm there, and I'm surrounded by an extremely experienced group of operators. I very rarely felt fear, if I'm going to be honest. We'd get into a firefight almost every mission. Yes, I shot my weapon. Do I think any of my rounds resulted in a kill, as we say? No, I don't. I was shooting in the same direction that everyone else was shooting. We were ambushed one time. Usually if we were in a firefight, it was the result of someone inside of the compound trying to shoot their way out or trying to take us down before we were able to get in there. There was one time where we were ambushed, and I actually didn't even feel fear then. It's not what I thought it would be. I thought it would be high adrenaline because of what you see in the movies. It wasn't like that, maybe because I felt protected almost, even though it wasn't my job to be protected; it was my job to help them in the event of a firefight. But I didn't feel like it was my responsibility to kill the bad guy, to put it in simple terms. My job out there was to be culturally sensitive and to gather intel on women and children and to make sure there weren't any weapons or anything we were looking for on those women and children.

...

I remember the mass casualty when the rocket came over and hit the compound. Me and this firefighter, we brought so many guys on that rickshaw. We were just covered in sweat. It was like 110 degrees, and we were just chugging Gatorade. We would triage them and bring them all in there. I remember just going around with a staple gun to control hemorrhage, you know, because controlling hemorrhage on the battlefield is what saves lives, and we know that. And that's why so many people with extremities are surviving: tourniquets and closing head wounds. I was going around just closing wounds and just stapling with my staple gun. Head wounds don't hurt that bad, so the guy was just like, "Yeah, please!" The other detainees would hold the wound closed, and I would staple it. The detainees were helping each other, and I was helping the detainees, putting tourniquets on their limbs and trying to control the blood flow. Then one of them had severe pain, just screaming and crying. I remember going to him, and I illegally took him medicine, you know, morphine.

• • •

There is a very visceral kind of thrill, like directly injected adrenalin. I've never done cocaine, but I imagine it must feel something like this. When you are going ninety miles an hour through Baghdad in a HMMWV with virtually no protection, for like five months almost daily, that starts to affect you physiologically. There's this sense . . . I can remember this feeling, certain images, like driving past the Iraqi tomb of the unknown, and there's big crossed swords and stuff like that, and feeling like I was never so alive as at that moment. I remember after the five months when we added a driver to the unit and I didn't have to do it anymore, I was thrilled. I didn't have to risk my life. Intellectually, in every objective way I understood that that was a good thing for me. Not only did I not have to worry about dying, I didn't have to worry about having to kill anyone else. And, man, it was almost like trying to come off of the worst addiction you've ever had. The horrible thing about it is—and it's not intellectual; it's purely physical—I miss that. I suspect it probably is just endorphins and adrenaline that you don't have any more. It's like trying to get off alcohol; your body wants it even though you know it's bad.

• • •

A lot of times we were just walking through the poppy fields; the poppy plants are four or five feet high. You'd just hear *snap snap snap snap*. A lot of times you didn't even know where it was coming from. You'd take a few rounds, and then someone would say, "North. Three hundred yards." We'd shoot back, and it pretty much subsided. A lot of the contact we took was when we were in the compound. I remember those ones a lot more vividly, I guess. The Taliban had a well-coordinated five-point attack on a bunch of our positions. It came across at about nine in the morning. And we heard it on their radios, and we knew to prepare. Their radios, we intercepted them, and our translators were like, "Yeah, they're getting ready to shoot." So everyone was on post. We built up posts with sandbags in someone's house and all that. You get pretty antsy anticipating them, I guess, because we're hearing on the radio: "We're going to shoot in five minutes." So you're just sitting up there, kind of waiting, and looking to see if you can see anything. When the time came around, they just opened up machine guns and mortars on us. We had about a thirty-minute firefight, and we got air on station, and they started dropping bombs from helicopters and stuff, but for that day, the fighting lasted probably for about six or seven hours of intermittent fighting and shooting.

Sometimes you could see the people you were shooting at. But they don't want to get shot as much as we don't want to get shot. So a lot of times they'd do a really quick-like peek around the corner, pull the trigger, and hide back around the corner. Sometimes you could see the person, but the majority of the time, no, you couldn't.

To me it was exhilarating, I guess; it gets your blood pumping. It's what we signed up to do: test yourself in battle and see if you'll be a coward or if you'll stand up to the challenge. It was scary, definitely scary. But it was fun too, I guess. I don't know if that makes sense. You don't really think about it; you just think about each other's safety during it. What you're shooting at or where you're getting shot from. That was pretty much all I thought about: "Hey, are you okay?" or "Did you see that guy shoot that way?" Your job. Afterwards, you talk about it and laugh, and it's fun. If someone gets hurt, you're like, "Damn, fuck them."

There was a time at the end of the deployment. It was like our last month, but we were still out in the field. We took over a compound, and this guy threw over two grenades while we were in there. We were getting ready to go on patrol, and they landed fifteen feet away from me, and they blew up, and I took shrapnel to my hand and leg and to my side a little bit, but it was nothing too serious; I was able to stay out there. But that got me kind of depressed for two or three days, or I guess scared, because it was the last month, and I was, like, "I really could have died right there, or anybody could have died, and we were so close to going home." It was kind of overwhelming for me. I guess I was lost in my thoughts, like, how would my family deal with it and all that. The next mission, I was a little hesitant to go out; I felt bad because of that because I was almost, like, scared to go out and take over another compound. But I talked to my team leader, and we talked through it, and I went out on it. That was the only time I was, I guess, depressed for a few days. It was embedded; one stayed in my leg for a little while, and I, like, pulled it out months later. One took off part of my finger, but the shrapnel is gone; there's a dent now. It took it all the way down to the bone. It grew back really well. I don't know. It didn't hurt. It just happened. We thought we were getting mortared; no one even saw the grenades because we were changing guard at the time, and they timed it pretty well. So the grenades landed and blew up; there were like ten of us, and I was the only one who got hit, and everyone was like, "Hey is everyone okay?" I ran inside, and I looked down; I was bleeding out my hand and my leg, and I was like, "Oh, man, I got hit." And my doc was like, "Are you all right, man?" And they undressed me and made sure I didn't get hit in any vital organs or anything. I was fine; they just bandaged me up, and it was like, "I don't know; should we call a helicopter for him or not?" And I was like, "No. No helicopter or like that." So we stayed out there another two days and then walked back.

• • •

But to me, I mean, combat is very slow. You know, the first time I got out and engaged, we were coming out of Rāwah; the first time I was actually in a firefight. So the RPG just rushes in front of the truck; we had Jordanians with us this time, and we're trying to control the Jordanians, and everything is just moving slowly. They wanted to duck, and they wanted to fire up in the air. "You know, what are you doing? Keep your bullets; we don't know how long we're going to be here; we don't know if anyone is hurt." In the background you can hear little potshots coming at us. To me, everything is really slow, and I guess I took a pause; I'm looking at my buddy, and I'm like, "Wow, this is it." You always think you're going to be ready and be able to bound forward without hesitation, but it's like, "No, whoa, hey, that just happened, and these bullets are actually flying." So kind of making eye contact, like, "Well, we have to do something. We can't sit here." So then we're getting the Jordanians going; we're pointing out at least the right direction, trying to get them not to shoot just sporadically but to find out where it's coming from and shoot, but that's not how they do it, you know. Somebody's shooting; they don't care where; they're just sporadically sending fire in any direction. We tried to do it the best way. I mean, I think that's what separates Special Forces from a regular Army combat unit or a soft-skill unit that gets caught in combat. We had the responsibility to identify and cause the least amount of destruction possible. But it is slow, even when you're running and gunning. You may be in a five-minute firefight, but it felt like it was forty-five minutes. You're doing so much, and maybe you're moving quickly, but everything is happening slowly.

10

Comrades

Esprit de corps, a term that comes from the military and describes the ties among comrades in arms, has no equivalent in civilian life; it is a bond that emerges from mortal conditions, that is sustained across a lifetime, that demands complete trust, and that returns absolute obligation. Friendships, marriages, and family may come and go, but these friends are always there for each other. For many veterans those ties make war endurable, evoke deployment nostalgia, and are life-sustaining and permanent. Not every veteran, however, is sustained by comrades in the field or upon returning home. The close quarters and sustained contact can also engender rancor, suspicion, and raw alienation. For some the "band of brothers" is a cynical myth that crumbles in the face of experience.

I MISS THE CAMARADERIE more than anything. Deployment is kind of nice. Your only job is to stay alive. You're with your best friends. The only way it could possibly get better is if you got to have a beer before you went to bed. It was kind of nice, as messed up as people might think that is. They're my best friends; I lived with them, I ate with them, and I slept with them. (Not like that!) I mean, everything you did, you did together, and it was nice. You didn't care about what you looked like. You didn't care about anything. You didn't care about having the newest iPhone or paying your bills. . . . We did start a nine-hole golf course. It was all sand trap. It was a skills course. Somehow somebody had gotten hold of a full set of clubs. They were pieces of crap, but someone had gotten a full set, so we just built a nine-hole golf course right around base and played. We built a hammock out of cots that swung. You could just lay back and smoke. Nobody cared if you smoked there. . . . There was a big hill on base. It was all dirt, obviously, and it was our comm hill. We had gotten wood, and if you iron a trash bag, it makes a slick surface; we put it on the bottom of the wood so that it was like a snowboard almost, and we slid down it. It was actually pretty cool. Nobody made it all the way down without falling. We weren't the first ones at that base, so there was a whole collection of random stuff. It wasn't all in one spot, just randomly around base. There was a stereo, which was nice. Somebody had a scale to weigh themselves, which I don't know why you'd care about that.

• • •

When we got together for this funeral last month, one of the guys had broken his wrist semi-recently. He's had to have surgeries on his wrist. He hasn't been able to work out very well, so he's put a little weight on. And we were more than happy to let him know that he's looking a little cuddly. It was funny; he wrote on Facebook the other day: "To all my so-called friends who've been letting me know that I've been putting on weight, I'm going to get super fit to spite you, and I'm going to fuck somebody who you love." The responses he got were really funny; everyone was like, "Chubby bunny." Comments like: "Dude, just embrace the dad bod." Some people might have taken offense, but if I know this individual, he was laughing his butt off reading the comments.

• • •

Last weekend I took my kids and wife and went out of town for my friend's baby's baptism. I would do anything for him. We were together there. He's about the only person from that experience that I can talk to about it because I have to talk about the failures, those experiences. When I talk to the soldiers, they're always shocked that I had any problems because I was the caregiver. I was always there for them. So I'm ashamed when I talk about my own failures. And he understands that because he felt the same way; he was a signal officer, and, you know, just dealt with it over there and is dealing with it still. And to me that's the closest relationship I've had in my life and probably ever will. I get emotional when I think about it. I'm married now, and she knows it too. She jokes about it, but she's also serious about it because that's real. I think that's the thing about war: there are all these things that happen that I wasn't aware were happening, and one is that the strength of the relationship was forming; I had no idea that would be the case. Being in the military, I thought, "I'll see these guys, then I'll go to another unit, make more friends." But that experience is just unalterable and gets stronger. It's the same with the bad stuff. There are low-level things that are happening that I didn't realize would be the things that would stick and become the things that make life troublesome in the present.

• • •

Me and my loader are very close. After the incident we spoke about earlier, I was put on suicide watch because they were all afraid I was gonna go crazy. It was a distinct possibility. Well, my loader never left my side throughout all of that. I started having nightmares, and what he would do is he would sit in my room. And whenever I woke up from a nightmare, he'd make me do stuff with my machine gun. Because the busy stuff with the hands distracted the mind. Me and him grew really close during that. I think it was a week before I was back to normal. Well, my loader had his first child while we were deployed. They didn't let him go back home to see his wife. It made all of us very angry because we wanted him to go home. So what we did was we locked him in his room, gave him a laptop, and set him up on Skype with his wife. And we posted two guards in the door. I was there, and I was standing outside that door. We would get him food, water, whatever he needed. If we were attacked, the two guards were to escort him and the laptop to a bunker so he could stay on Skype with his wife. It was the best we could do.

• • •

It's because you're fighting for the guy on the other side of you. All of these ideals and the flag and jingoistic whatever just kind of goes out the window. I think there's some truth to that. I think that's the piece that's missing. If I go to a veteran's tailgate and meet you at your daughter's wedding, find out someone's a veteran, there's immediately a connection; there's immediately a brotherhood. No disrespect to Colonel Gibler, but he's the type of guy that I probably would have butted heads with my whole military career because I was that kind of . . . that wild NCO that was really good at my job, but I'm not a very PC person. . . . That's what I went through my whole military career, officers being like, "Yes, I understand, I understand, but. . . ." So there's a brotherhood there nonetheless. Maybe he and I don't see eye to eye on what the best way to finish out the war in Afghanistan is, right? But it doesn't matter. Immediately we can share a drink, a beer. . . . So I think the brotherhood is what transcends those difficulties.

• • •

I would love to know about the prosthetist that came out of Baghdad to help me build prosthetics for the detainees. I would love to know about him and his little girls. We had a fond relationship. My wife would send baked cookies that I would send on to his wife and kids, and we developed a very nice relationship. The prosthetist was always in fear of his life because he had a government contract with us making prosthetics for the detainees, so he was always moving and fearing for his life and also his daughter's ability to go to school or not go to school. So they were both very stressed about what would happen to them upon our departure, and I suspect both of them are dead now. If you had to ask me, if I had to bet, especially now that we've pulled out, they're probably dead by now because we pulled out so prematurely in my opinion.

• • •

From my experience in Afghanistan, when I find out someone else is a veteran, I look down on them. Initially. I'm like, "Ugh. You were in the military?" It's very snooty. . . . From that moment I want to know what they did. Obviously, every combat veteran only cares about other people who were in combat. I definitely care about that. I don't want to act like I'm above that. If you weren't an infantry man or at least a combat MOS, I really don't care. I feel kind of bad about that. If you were in a firefight sure, but. . . . That exists across the military: if you have a CIB or a CAB, it's a lot different than not having one. When I find out somebody was enlisted in the military, I immediately switch into a different mode. It's like detective mode, trying to figure out, "Which kind of soldier were you?" I care less initially about whether they were in combat than what kind of soldier they were. "Were you an idiot and the reason that I got out of the Army? Did you get out because it was not what you thought it was?"

• • •

When I was there, those were my brothers. That's who I spent my holidays with and every moment. I hated them some days. I loved them other days. I was sad to see them go. Excited to see new people come.

• • •

I spent a lot of time in those towers: four hours at a time, just talking with my buddies. Two people. For the first eight months or so, we went up in twos. And then they were trying to transfer responsibility to an Afghan private security firm. So we were up there for the last four months in a tower with an Afghan who didn't speak English, and sometimes it was a little . . . not scary, but you're just wary of that guy. Some of them were the nicest people I've ever met. I worked real hard, and I learned a little bit of Dari and Pashto while I was in those towers, but I've forgotten it all now. I ordered a book while I was over there and studied, but I was the only one who made an effort to do that.

• • •

There's a couple of bazaars; there's one that's open once a week, and there's one that's open every day between certain hours, and every time I'd come, he would offer me a drink; he would offer me food and ask how I was doing and ask about family, small talk, talk about home, just talk about different things, very friendly guy. I never saw him as a threat in any way. I'd bring my friends to shop with him, and, of course, when I would bring them, he'd give them a good discount. There was a gun I got my dad for Christmas, and it was cool. It was a really cool gun, and I listened to him quote a price for a guy, and I would ask how much is that for me, and it was like half off; it was a deal. I gave him the money. I have to back up because that's surreal too. They're selling guns on a base. So they are camel guns, is what they're known as. His is cool; his is shorter. It's a wooden barrel, and it has actual camel bone that's been carved out and put inside. It has six cylinders, so it looks like a revolver, but it's not like you click and change the chamber; you turn the whole thing, and so there's six barrels, and you shoot each one, and then you turn it. Mine's longer, and there's just one barrel. They're supposed to be authentic, and they're not. They totally scam us while we're out there, which is fine. I would not expect to pay a hundred dollars for a seventeenth-century. . . . But it was something cool to bring home. It's hanging on my wall at home. I couldn't even figure out how to work this thing. These have no firing capacity whatsoever.

• • •

Our xo went to usc and I went to Texas, and usc and Texas are rivals in football, and he and I had a kind of rivalry about it. He managed to get our data center lined up to where they could patch a version of the game in the middle of the night. So we stayed up that night and watched it. It was really weird to be there in Afghanistan, and, of course, I was exhausted because I had worked all day, and then I was staying up to watch this game, and we got killed. It was like the worst game. And then he gave me a bunch of crap about it for the rest of the deployment.

• • •

One of my favorite interpreters while I was in Iraq was named Hassan; he had been a helicopter pilot for Saddam Hussein and his regime. He gave me a gift; we exchanged gifts. We got to talk. I had so many questions about his culture, and he had a wealth of information, so I really developed a close relationship with him. So, yeah, I have this gift on my desk at home, and I look at it all the time. It's a little lighter that has the Iraqi flag on it. He had it in his pocket, and he flipped it all the time. He had it for months while we were there, and he smoked. And one day I was just like, "Man, I really like that lighter." I loved seeing it. "I don't know why. It just cheers me up when I see you pull that lighter out." And he wanted to give it to me, and I was like, "No, no, no; I can't take that." And he explained to me, "No, you have to take it." In their culture, if you don't, it's an insult. And I was like, "Aw, I'm so sorry, I didn't know." So he was able to explain it clearly to me. I still keep that, and I think of him all the time, all the time; great relationship with him. He was able eventually to come to the States. Yeah, he was wonderful.

• • •

Everybody has their own motives for doing what they do. But in combat, your motives don't matter really. As bad as it sounds, you don't fight for what you believe in. You fight for the person next to you.

11

Chain of Command

Everyone can relate to having a bad boss. Poor leadership or inept management can make every day on the job a trial and every evening at home a temptation to fixate or complain. But during a deployment, you don't go home. You don't get away and mull things over. Every aspect of a soldier's life during deployment is under the control and management of the leader. Poor leadership can be a mere annoyance and a chance to bond with comrades, but the daily grind of incompetence or bullying can become a source of stress and a threat to mental health. An inept commander can also get you killed. In contrast, there are leaders who know how to make a group cohere through some combination of excellence, discipline, and fun; there are men and women who inspire their troops to push their limits for the greater good, who protect the men and women who serve under them, who make just the right call to pull the unit back from the brink.

I REMEMBER THE COMMANDER. When he ran PT with us, he looked like a fricking gazelle; I mean he did a mile . . . I don't even know what his mile was. It looked like he was just galloping off into the distance, and then he passed us all, and we weren't even a fourth of the way done.

• • •

We had our colonel relieved nine months into a ten-month deployment for cause. The most scarring thing from that experience was realizing that my greatest threat to my safety is not the people who are trying to kill me; it's the guy that's gonna shoot me in the back because he's tying my hands, and he's preventing me from doing the things I need to do to protect my safety and security and everyone I'm representing, which is the whole reason I deployed.

• • •

Take the worst marriage in the world. The problem that makes it bad is that you have to live together. It's like that in war. You live with these people. You're with them all the time, and they have so much power over you. Usually it was a hierarchical relationship that was bad. All the anxiety that this guy's feeling is taken out on that guy. And the shit just rolls downhill, as they say; it just rolls down. It was usually really close: it was a sergeant and a specialist, like one rank away. People you had to spend all day and all night with. So many complaints, grievances, counseling I did; so many mental health issues were related to that happening.

• • •

I just thought the whole military was supposed to be elite. When I first got to my unit, my first squad leader was a joke. I couldn't believe that this guy was in charge of me, that he was E-6. He was really an E-6 only because he'd deployed three times. I don't exactly know what he did on those deployments. Maybe he just sat back on the FOB. But I was not impressed. In my opinion, he just never got out of the Army because he couldn't do anything else. I remember it was one of the first training exercises we did as a platoon when I got there. He took our squad out and got us lost. That's the proverbial joke about the lieutenant; but this guy is a squad leader, and he should not be getting us lost. He's got three deployments; he doesn't know how to use a map and a compass. I was astonished; I couldn't believe it. He couldn't do PT, and he was very inconsistent during training. He couldn't get his hand signals right. Every time we did a certain battle drill, he'd want it done a different way. I was terrified, actually, to deploy with him; I had about three months before we deployed, and I was really scared. He was the butt of the first sergeant's jokes for a long time. First sergeant hated him. I don't know why he let him keep training with us. He got removed to some staff position eventually, which I'm very thankful for. But I wish it hadn't been one week before we deployed. We just got some new squad leader a week or two before we deployed; didn't know him.

• • •

CHAIN OF COMMAND

We got in trouble, and I forget what we did. I'm sure it was justified. But what they made us do is they made us clean our HMMWVs free of sand. In a desert. Which isn't physically possible. But they were just doing it to keep us busy. Well, to do this, they kept us awake. They didn't let us sleep for two days. Why they did that, I don't know. It was, like, three a.m. one morning, and one of my nicknames was Mudflap. There was three of us out there, and we were cleaning out the HMMWV. And one of us was like, "Wanna know what would be funny?" And we're, like, at the point of lack of sleep to the point of delirium. So his idea was for me to roll around in the mud and then chase him back to the compound that we were in. So we did this. There was two of them come sprinting into the compound, and I'm following them, and they're like, "Oh, my God, it's Mudflap!" The sergeant just kind of looked at us and was like, "Okay, everybody needs to go to bed. Everybody go to bed right now."

• • •

The captain I had, he was an infantry captain. He was a former enlisted. He was a Somalia veteran and a Desert Storm veteran, just kind of an older, more mature captain than most. He was good because he would stick up for us to the higher officers if they were putting down bad orders. We were having this training mission. The battalion CO or someone was saying you need all these vehicles to conduct this mission. I was in charge of all the maintenance and everything, as just an extra thing for me to do. I was getting all these vehicles ready, and there just weren't enough vehicles; there weren't enough parts. There was no way we could sort it out to have enough. The higher-up CO was like, "It doesn't matter; just do what you have to do." So I had our mechanics disassemble another vehicle partially and cannibalize—it's call cannibalizing and it's illegal; you take the parts off and put them on another vehicle that you need. So we had everything we needed for the mission, and we were going to come back and put it all back on, and no one would be the wiser. And I got caught. My CO kept me from basically being completely demolished by the higher command just by sticking up for me. Actually he stood up for us on some other things, and he was not well liked for that reason and was forced to retire. Being a good CO isn't always going to get you promoted, unfortunately.

• • •

You think people should be able to shoot in the infantry. People can't shoot. They can't aim. You're supposed to be able to go onto a firing range and qualify in one try with forty rounds. People stuff their pockets with ammunition so that they can get extra rounds in the mags so that they can get two or three shots at a target. People go up multiple times until they hit expert. You're supposed to go up once, and what you get is what you get. There was one time—it might have been the last exercise I did before I got out of the Army. We had just gotten a new platoon sergeant, and he was everything a platoon sergeant should be. He was a hard ass. We hated him. But he knew what he was talking about, and he didn't jerk us around. He was awesome. So we had already zeroed our weapons the night before or the day before, and we were qualifying. When you qualify on paper targets, it's a paper target with all these silhouettes that's supposed to simulate the sizes you see at the distances they're at. And what you do is you shoot at each and every target. You're supposed to shoot in the order you would shoot outdoors or on the range. They're encouraging us to cheat. You start prone/supported. Then you go to prone/unsupported. Then you go to kneeling. They encourage you to hit all the small targets while you're prone/supported. Basically, at the end of the qualification, you have to have four rounds on each target for a forty out of forty; there're ten targets. And they encourage you to hit all the small targets while you're in the prone/supported position, where in reality you're supposed to go through all of them. I remember just scoffing at that. The platoon sergeant came up to me because I wasn't doing too hot; I wasn't shooting very well. The ground was very dusty, very fine powder, and as soon as everybody started shooting, the dust came into the air. I couldn't see. Excuses. Excuses. I wasn't shooting as well as I could. So he asked me, "Are you shooting all the targets?" I was like, "Yes, Sergeant." "Why are you doing that?" "I have integrity, Sergeant." I just remember the look on his face. I could tell from the look on his face; he was like, "Fuck, yeah." Nobody else was doing it. I mean, I just had a lot of respect for him.

• • •

My team leader, he ended up being one of our psych-eval casualties. He ended up going crazy and started not following orders. Sort of just rebelling against our commanders. While his complaints may have been justified, that can't happen in a combat unit. It compromises the unit and makes us less effective. Greater chance for us to die, so we can't do that. He left and then came back. He was separated from our unit because of what they considered most of our troubles to be. . . . The human body is supposed to be able to operate on four hours of sleep. However, four hours of sleep is not an easy task.

• • •

I had gotten on the bad side of my first battery commander. When I first showed up as a second lieutenant, he was making lieutenants buy him breakfast and bring him coffee in the morning, which totally goes against the Marine Corps ethos that a senior person would ever expect a junior officer to ever pay for him. It really burned me because I'd just gotten out of training. I got there, and I was like, "This is completely wrong." I just didn't do it for a while. The other junior lieutenants were doing it, so he called all the company officers together, and he was like, "What's the deal? Why do you have a problem with our unit?" I told him that I thought that what he was doing was bullshit. He kind of acted like it was a joke all along, like it wasn't real, because he knew I was right. But after that, he tried to send me on a deployment: individual augment to Iraq for a year right after that. I had just gotten back from my first deployment. I was home for like two weeks. Someone in the headquarters unit, some officer, was like, "Yeah, you've got orders to go to Iraq." Right after coming home. So I went home, and I told my wife, "I got deployed again. I just got home, and they're sending me to Iraq, this time for a year by myself." She was so upset, and I was upset. I knew it was because I had crossed my co, and he was kind of trying to get me out of the unit. I happened to be neighbors with the regimental adjutant who is in charge of the administration for the regiment. He was a captain, and he was a friend. His wife and mine were good friends. I told him, and he basically got me out of it by finding some legal loophole.

12

Did You Kill Anyone?

Dear Reader: Did you begin reading this book by skipping to this chapter? We thought you might. It is natural to want to know this most intimate of details. Or at least it must be "natural," given the number of people who ask veterans questions about killing. One man to whom we talked shot an enemy combatant at long range. His unit then navigated a drone over the pile that dropped where the man once stood. They needed the drone to confirm the kill; that is how far away it was—a pretty abstract experience of killing and yet one that is not uncommon in contemporary combat. In the opening line of *An Intimate History of Killing: Face-to-Face Killing in Twentieth-Century Warfare* (New York: Basic Books, 2000), historian Joanna Bourke writes the following: "The characteristic act of men at war is not dying, but killing. Politicians and military historians may gloss over human slaughter, emphasizing the defense of national honor, but for men in active service, warfare means being—or becoming—efficient killers." There are few veterans who would readily agree with these statements, though Bourke devotes five hundred pages to backing up her seemingly obvious, yet actually bold, claim. It may be the characteristic act of a soldier to kill, but it is not for the experience of killing that men and women go to war. "People think it's like '*Call of Duty*,'" one veteran remarked, or that "It'd be cool to do that." But for the veterans themselves, killing was not the central fact of war but a deeply private fact, a border crossing that comes with having killed. Some veterans believe it separates them from the rest of humanity. Some veterans are sanguine about death in combat, but one veteran sees the face of a killer in the mirror every day and has to convince himself that he's not "a monster." But go ahead; we understand that this question is pressing. We just hope this chapter will lead you backward and forward to others, that you will get to know the veterans who speak in this chapter by reading about why they enlisted or what they learned from an Afghani farmer or a Takfiri detainee.

WHEN WE WERE FIRST going into Iraq, we crossed this huge mound that engineers set up between Kuwait and Iraq. We lined all the trucks up—got a battalion worth of people lined up, practically. I was a specialist, newly promoted to E-4, driving this huge truck, and my chief came up to me and says, "Okay, now here's the deal." They didn't normally give you . . . mission obstacles; I guess I'm at a loss for what the word is right now—things that you're likely to run into, you know. Some of the things that they're gonna do. But this particular thing, they just came up, and he said, "Hey, uhm. I know you're a Christian, so I don't want you to think that anybody's going to think less of you for backing down off this and wanting someone else to drive, but—uh—one of the tactics that they're using right now is to—uh—to line the kids up across the road and hold hands, and they make them. . . . So you stop, and they climb on, and they take everything off of you." And I had—I had our MREs. I had our food. And he said, "You don't stop. You're not going to stop." We didn't have anybody line up all the way across, but there was this one young man who, uh—I say young man; he was probably about twelve or fourteen—he was like reaching up and touching every. . . . I could see: he's jumping up in front of every vehicle and jumping out of the way and taking a little bit longer, and some of the guys are weaving around him, but I'm in this six-wheeled, three-axle vehicle that doesn't do that. It's not a HMMWV. There was a Howitzer—a towed Howitzer in front of me; it's a big cannon—and that's what's being towed in front of me, so it's a truck and the Howitzer. The kid had a lot of room, and he steps out behind the wheel, and there's all the tube of the gun that has to go past, and he's standing there, and he's trying to get me to stop, and that was the point. I hit the gas and, uhm. . . . I don't know what happened to him. I know he tried to step out of the way, but I know that he didn't get out of the way completely. Uhm . . . and I remember I almost did take him up on that. . . . I almost did

take him up on that, on not driving. And, . . . I mean, what do you do with that? That's the one we don't talk about. My wife, I've talked to her, and I think that changes everything, since I was able to talk to her. I've spoken about these stories before, just not to anybody besides my wife.

• • •

One of the things I was responsible for was picking targets or helping to pick targets for long-range artillery. There's a kind of abstraction that comes from that. One time we found a Scud. They were driving these things all over the place and trying to hide them, constantly in motion. Some poor Iraqi conscript driving these. . . . I don't remember if I was the one who found the value target. But I remember somebody got the bright idea. . . . You know, they had UAVCS on it so you could watch the target when we fired on it. We got to watch the effects of that on video. On the one hand . . . I'm embarrassed to say this. . . . On the one hand, you feel good about it because that could have had chemical weapons that are pointed at you. On the other hand, you're freaking, watching somebody die. And the guy was terrified. I mean he knew; he saw the aerial. He knew he was about to die. . . . But people were happy about it, somewhat. I mean that's the kind of stuff that haunts you. A lot of stuff that I did wasn't the personal, face-to-face stuff. A lot of the stuff that I carry with me is that. I helped. I may well not have killed a single person with my rifle. I was a bad shot. But I helped kill a lot of people with artillery. And probably, almost certainly, people who had no business dying, if anybody had business dying. I had a sergeant who was a devout Catholic, who honestly believed he was going to hell because of it. It may seem silly to me, but that's the thought.

• • •

I've been asked, "Have you ever killed anyone in war? Are you messed up at all?" The stereotypical questions—"Were you scared?"—stuff like that. I don't take offense to any of that because I realize we went somewhere, we were gone for a couple years, and now we're back, and now no one knows how to talk to a person.

• • •

I only drove twice, down and back to this one base that was pretty far away on Route Tampa. We had a machine gun on the roof, and we were part of a convoy. So I was pretty amped up about that. And I was ready for anything. One of the things you have to be ready for in driving is to run somebody over. We were going through towns and villages along the way. You have to be ready to just step on it when you see somebody, even a child. This is the trauma of war: you make a choice between doing the right thing (which is to run somebody over) or chickening out (or whatever it is not to hit the person). So I was kinda ready for that. We were all ready. It was in the air, so I didn't notice that that was an odd thing to be part of because this is what we talked about all the time; this is what we knew was the truth. And the truth in war is not the truth anywhere else in life. It's this one truth though. It's real pure and simple.

• • •

The one that kind of haunts me, the biggest regret I have about deployment: one night we showed up in this town, and we were in the wrong compound. Intelligence told us to go to this place because the bad guy was supposed to be there, and he wasn't there. It was actually a school, a madrasa, a religious school for boys, all young, all somewhere between the ages of six and twelve. The only adult there was the imam, the head of the school. My job was to search and question women and children, mostly for cultural reasons. There were all these little boys. I don't know why, but nobody helped me; it was just me, and I had to search all of them and question all of them myself because everyone else was just pulling security because at the time the political climate was such that they didn't want any of the men rough-handling any of the children. I realized we have a very limited amount of time before the helicopters come back to pick us up.

You have to kind of triage the situation, figure out who you think is going to give you the information that you need, so I couldn't possibly question every single little boy; I had maybe fifteen minutes. So I went over to the group of boys. I let down my hair; I took off my helmet; I pulled the card that I thought would work with this group of particular people, little boys: "Which one of you is the bravest?" I don't have an interpreter, by the way, and I don't know how to speak Pashto. All the little boys start jumping up and down; they're waving their little arms, and they want to be the one to talk to me. So I pull one over to the side, and I start trying to figure out where the bad guy really is. We know he's in the village; we just don't know which compound, and we don't have enough people to search the entire village-worth of Afghan compounds. So he starts talking to me, and I can tell he's scared, so I know we're kind of on the right track. I can tell that the closer I get to asking questions about this man that we're trying to get, the more he doesn't want to talk to me, and I don't have the time to deal with him, so I bring him back to the group. I tell the whole group of little boys that this little boy's a coward and that I need someone who is really a man, the one who is the bravest, the true man in this group, to talk to me.

So another one volunteers; I bring him over, and he agrees to lead me to the insurgent we are looking for (who happened to be a high-level Taliban commander), to the compound he was in. It was a small Afghan village, and everyone knew everything that was happening, so he knew exactly where to take me. So I sheath my weapon; I'm not actually holding my weapon; I hold his hand, and I lead the entire strike force of Rangers through an Afghan town in the middle of the night to the right compound. Once we got there, the little boy wanted to leave; he was scared. He didn't want to stick around. But I wouldn't let him leave; he kept asking to leave; I wouldn't let him leave because I wanted to be able to use him for more information; if the people that were in that compound were lying, that little boy could verify their story or tell the real truth.

In the fog of that whole situation, the Rangers are pulling all the men out of the rooms; they're searching the house. I'm searching the women and children who were in that house. The little boy is sitting up against a wall, and he's got his shirt over his face. This is all in hindsight, but I realize he didn't want anybody to see that he was the one that narced, that he was the one that tattletaled. But I was too high off the thrill of being the one that brought this entire strike force to the right place, and I was just too busy with all the other things I was doing to pay attention to how he was feeling. So the women and children in that compound start yelling things to the little boy across the compound. I just told them to shut up, and I just kept doing my job. It was obvious that everything that was coming out of their mouths was a lie, and I tried to get the little boy to talk to me and help with this intelligence as I'm trying to figure out what was true and what was a lie, and he just completely shut down, completely didn't talk.

We actually didn't find the guy. We found out later that he was hiding in the well. He had jumped into the well. . . . It was such a deep well—maybe fifty feet; I don't know exactly how deep it was—but our dogs didn't find him; we didn't find him. We walked out empty-handed that night. We came to find out that he was in that well later. The way the Taliban works is after the Americans come to a compound and do something like we did, higher-level leaders or the Taliban for the town come around to that compound the next day, and they ask basically, "What did the Americans want? Why were they here? What did they say to you? What did they take?" We found out that the family that was living there told the Taliban that that little boy ratted them out. I found this out two days later: they executed the little boy that I chose to bring into that compound.

When it comes to trauma, that would be my trauma, living with that situation, knowing that I could have affected the situation had I really been thinking of him as a person and not just as an intelligence asset. What I realize now is how easily people stop looking at other people as humans, especially if they're from a really different culture, like the Afghans are. There's nothing familiar about that culture; there's just nothing that seems even remotely similar to ours. I think night after night of going out there and being lied to by these women and children and dealing with them. I just think I stopped caring about them, really, about their well-being. They're not just intelligence-collection assets, obviously. I think what I've learned is just how easily you can get sucked into that dehumanization. It's not just cool, gun-slinging soldiers that are a little bloodthirsty. It's really just so easy. I never thought I would be someone who would be capable of forgetting someone's humanity. You have to constantly be on guard and watch yourself. So as I continue my career in the military, I'm doing so by looking out for signs of that in myself and in other people.

• • •

I'd much rather have someone come out and ask what might seem like a rude question: "Did you shoot anybody?" I'd much rather they just ask me that if that's what they want. I don't know if I ever shot anyone; I sure as hell tried. But I don't know if I ever hit someone. I was a driver, so my job was to keep the vehicle going. But I did fire, and I guess I'm blessed with the lack of knowledge about that. What action I saw was behind the wheel of a HMMWV. What would generally happen is—you're not talking about pitched battles here. That's not the kind of situation I was in. You're talking about insurgents taking potshots at you from locations. Our job was just to return that fire and make sure we could get where we were going. Really, if all we accomplished was to get them to duck without being able to fire anything off, that's good enough. So if we were stopped, whenever the vehicle stopped, my hand came off the wheel, I picked up my M-16, and I was looking through the area I was responsible for, for the report of a rifle. If that happened, I fired back. But I also had eyes on the road because as soon as we could move, we needed to move; that was my job. So I do not know. I was never in a situation where a clear silhouette was somewhere firing at me and I put the bead on my rifle and saw, "Man, I got them." When I was firing, I was firing back at a wisp of something—somebody that came out through a window, fired a couple shots, and then ducked down, and I fired back at the window. So I don't know.

• • •

The first five or ten times somebody asks you a really dumb-ass question, it's just annoying. After that it starts to really piss you off. First time some kid asks you, "Well, did you ever kill anybody?," you're, like, going, "Really? Is that what you're going to ask me?" And then somebody maybe is being even more insensitive, and they ask, "What's it like to kill somebody?" And then my gut response is, "Well, do you want to find out?"

I was working recruiting; we were in Austin, and we were staying at a hotel there on I35 and eating at Pappasito's. (Favorite restaurant, honestly; favorite restaurant anywhere.) This lady comes up to our table, looks kinda like a used-up hippie. I mean, I don't know, never grew out of the '60s or something like that. We were all in ACUS. So she comes up; she's obviously a little bit drunk, very loud, and she walks up to me, and she's almost like spitting words at me, right? She's like, "Have you been to Iraq?" I was like, "Yes, ma'am, I have." "How can you do that?" And I was like, "Do what?" And she goes, "Burn babies!" And I was like. . . . You know those times you start thinking about a whole lot of different options and different things. Pappasito's is generally a very loud restaurant; it got very quiet. Right? In the back of my head I'm going, "You know there is nothing I could ever say to this woman to convince her that I don't burn babies, right?" So I said, "Well, ma'am, have you ever tried to eat them raw?"

• • •

I don't know if I've every killed anyone, but I know that I've saved lives, and that was the reason I joined the military; that was the purpose I was aiming for. I think a lot of people, when they look at the military, don't look at it that way, but I know I have. I helped find untreated leukemia in a marine, a mess sergeant who was just checking into our unit. It was just the doctor and me there that day. I checked in most people anyway. I took him back. First off, he stuck out like a sore thumb because I'm used to healthy individuals, and he looked kind of sickly. He was a lively guy, very exuberant, but he was telling me that he used to run a lot. . . . I started looking at his records, and he had all this inexplicable weight loss over the course of a year and abnormal vital signs, and he was getting pushed around by these health-care providers who were supposed to be taking care of him. His vital signs, to me, were abnormal. He just gave me a bad feeling. So I talked to the doctor and told him I thought we needed to order some tests on him because I felt like he was actually sick. Sure enough, his blood tests came back, and he had leukemia. He was immediately flown back to the States to get treated. I don't know what ever actually happened to him. He wasn't treated for a year, a whole year. That was my goal in getting into the military, to practice medicine and, yes, participate in the war. Yes, I wanted to be at the fight, but my ultimate goal was to bring people home.

• • •

We were at a checkpoint—an Iraqi traffic control point. Actually, what they do is they search vehicles as they go through the gate, I guess. We were caught in the line. Even though we could have gone around, we decided to wait in the lines. And there was a car. . . . I was the rear gunner of the convoy. The vehicles we had at this particular point in time were called HMMWVS, which are up-armored, and we had M1131s. The gunner himself is exposed, though, because he has a turret around him, like if you cut a hole open in the cab of a pickup truck. There was a car that was approaching our convoy at a really high rate of speed, so I go through the escalation of force that we were given, which is "Shout, Shove, Show, Shoot, Shoot." I waved my arms and yelled, but he was in a car, so he didn't hear me. I can't shove him because I'm in a vehicle. Show: I racked back the 50-cal, and when he didn't respond to that, I put three rounds through his hood, trying to disable his engine. But the odds of that are not very good. Since he didn't slow down, I got clearance to engage, so I put three rounds through his windshield. And then we dismounted—my team. Since I was the dismounted machine gunner, they rotated me off the gun. So I dismount. My team took point. We approached the vehicle. We had to check the vehicle to see if there were any explosives on the inside, to basically justify the reason why we fired. In the rear of his vehicle, he had what we call a . . . I'm trying to remember the name. I think they're called EFPS. (I don't remember what the acronym stands for.) But they're essentially paint cans with a copper plating on top and C-4 stacked underneath. And the purpose of these IEDS is . . . there's not a single bit of armor in the U.S. arsenal that can stop this. They shotgun through tank armor, just straight through. Because when the C-4 explodes, it secretes the copper. And it goes straight through uranium. He had, I think, six of them, but I can't remember the exact number. I think it was six. So, I mean, the firing was justified, but the car wasn't a car bomb, which is what I thought it was. As we approached the vehicle, I heard a sound from the inside. When I opened the door . . . I had killed the driver. I had splattered his head all over his child. Six years old. He was sitting in the passenger seat. The 50-caliber does a number on the human body. The man's head was just gone. It was everywhere. My first kill. Most of it was on the back windshield, but some wasn't. We secured the body because that's what we're trained to do. And we brought the child out and handed him over to the Iraqi police who were at the checkpoint because we didn't know what else to do with him really. We secured the armaments in the car and then blew up the car. That's pretty much it.

• • •

We called him baby Hussein; his name was Hussein. When we had beds, if Iraqi civilians wanted to present themselves to our gate, they would be triaged. If we could, if we had the resources at the time, we would care for them. And this young couple with their twenty-eight-day-old baby presented to our gate and came to my unit. He apparently was seen at some other facility—I think it was an Iraqi facility—and he suffered an infection at an IV site. Anyway, he came in, and this whole cascade of events occurred. We tried to work him up for some sort of immune problem, but, I mean, what a cascade of medical events. He tried to die several times on me. I had an incident of not being sure if I should obey my Hippocratic Oath or my officer's oath. It was at night, I was on call, and he looked like he was decompensating. We had just taken out his breathing tube that morning, and he really didn't look good to me. I felt like he needed to be intubated, and I'm not that comfortable making that decision because I'm a geriatrician; I'm not a pediatrician. Normally, if he were older, I would have intubated without a guess, but because he was such a young child, I went and found my colonel, who had great experience in trauma. I figured, all right, he's higher up in the food chain as my commanding officer, and I felt he might have more experience. Well, to make a very long story short, he came in, looked at the baby, and said not to intubate. I didn't intubate him right off the bat; this sort of was drawn out, and I was really freaking out. . . . I went back a couple times . . . and said, "I really want to intubate him," and he said, "No" because you want to be thoughtful to avoid frequent intubations if you can. Anyway, I ended up calling Germany, trying to talk to a pediatric trauma surgeon there because I needed to get this kid to be intubated, but I had asked the question of my commanding officer, and I was told not to. Fortunately another team member was a trauma surgeon who wasn't on that night but happened to stop by the hospital, and he had been trained in pediatric trauma. I dragged him into the ICU and said, "I want to intubate him." And he freaked out and intubated the child. It really disturbed me because I was really angry with myself for not doing what I thought was the right thing medically for my patient. My commanding officer ended up apologizing to me. He said, "I'm really sorry I put you in that position, but frankly I don't know how to treat this child." So that was a very difficult case; I almost let him die because I didn't follow my gut. And that was actually the only day I took off in the war. I told them that I needed time because I was just. . . . I think it was not just baby Hussein. I think he was sort of a vehicle that allowed me to mourn the loss of a variety of people.

• • •

I had a soldier who killed himself. I'd known him for about a year and a half before we deployed. I didn't know him that well; he was real quiet. He was really into the *Fast and Furious* movies. Real quiet. The platoon he was supporting was working on clearing the roadside stuff. He was a mechanic, so he would stay on the base and wait for them to come back; he'd fix the vehicles during the day. And this is right next to Sadr City, where there was a big mess. He'd gotten caught up with an ultra-fundamentalist Bible church, really a cult where they all lived there at the dorm and gave their money to the church. His two buddies were gone when he killed himself. They were on leave. They'd been gone for probably two weeks at that time. He had nothing. He had lots of resources; there were people everywhere, but no one he could trust. I prayed with the convoy before they left. I was even talking to him, just small talk. He was sitting on the bumper of the vehicle. The story is he went to the Internet café, got an email, I think from his fiancée, saying that they were breaking up or something. I've never seen the email or what it said. That's what I was told later. He goes right back to the. . . . They were all staying in a room with cots because they weren't permanent on that base. That was just the guest lodging for people that were there. I guess he was

DID YOU KILL ANYONE?

just there by himself, and he came back and shot himself in the head with his M-16. His sergeant came in. He came in and saw him sleeping there—because people slept whenever they could— and kind of knew. They saw the blood, and he'd shot himself in the head. It was pretty late at night, ten o'clock or something like that. I was at the main base.

And then it was just confusing. I was in such a weird state of mind even when I talked to the platoon or the company that was gathered. I didn't do a very good job of it because I was the one who was in charge of suicide prevention for the unit. I gave the briefings. Of course, after that everyone had to have an individual meeting where we talked about things. But, I mean, everyone was suicidal there. That was the shocking thing. There were just people killing themselves. Suicide was in the air. Most of the platoons had people on suicide watch. They would take the bolt out of their rifle. So they'd walk around with their rifle with no bolt in it. I always said if the enemy comes over the fence, nobody's going to be able to shoot.

They had constant people on suicide watch. I think it was the hopelessness of it. For the people who were suicidal there, it really was about relationships back home and the powerlessness of being able to do anything about your wife or your girlfriend or boyfriend or husband back home. It was the powerlessness, and suicide is one of the ways of getting power back. Suddenly you're in control again; you can do something. His friends were really devastated and still are. It's so unthinkable why anyone would kill themselves in the middle of a war. Part of it is that they see violence as a solution. It's just obvious that that's what you do. Ajax and all those plays that are so good. . . . Sophocles, I think, was a general. He understood this despair.

• • •

It was during a mass casualty situation; I was in the ER, and we were triaging a bunch of young men from our coalition forces. And he had suffered a high spinal injury in the cervical spine, and I knew that it was going to be permanent because it had severed the cord, so it wasn't just swelling. (Once swelling goes down, you'll regain some of your neurologic function.) I remembered looking down at him; he was on a wheeled gurney, and he was wearing these ridiculous glasses, and he looked so young and silly in this outfit, and yet here he was, naked and couldn't move. And he asked me, "It's bad isn't it?" And I said, "Yes." You know, I told him the truth. And he said, "I don't want to live. I want you to kill me. Can you kill me?" And I said, "No, I can't," which I couldn't. And I certainly personally don't think I would have. But it really just grabbed at my heartstrings to have somebody suffering so much. You hope; I mean you read the data that 9.9 out of ten people who suffer devastating injury like that, a year out—if you interview them—have adjusted to their lives and the change in circumstances. So I just tell myself that maybe he'll get there, and I told him that. I said, "You'll feel differently once you're back with your family in Germany and things get better." I think back to this particular case, and I just hope that this young man is all right. I was there for him at a very horrible point in his life, and I really hope that I said the right things or at least didn't say the wrong thing to him.

• • •

We had our own mortar tubes, and we'd drop IDF—Indirect Fire—or mortars on them. We would get live feeds from the jets or the helicopters, and we would see them drop bombs on them as well. After firefights we have to do BDAs—battle damage assessments: go out and see how many people you did kill or whatever and try to estimate the number. See if anyone is alive, what guns they had. So we'd go walking around, and we would find bodies, so we knew that people did get hit. . . . We had long guns and . . . designated marksmanship rifles . . . so those guys definitely know whenever they shot someone because they saw someone go down. I was a machine gunner, so my job was to basically put down suppressing fire, to keep their heads down, so they wouldn't pop out.

• • •

We're supposed to pat everybody on the back if they kill somebody. I had a soldier who shot somebody. My soldiers didn't shoot many people. They were doing their job; they had security around them, usually to protect them while they worked. But this guy was doing guard duty in a guard shack. Somebody shot from a house; he reacted; he just put his rifle up and pulled the trigger. They went out there and found this guy dead. He had a rifle and everything; he had shot at him. I was pretty excited about this. I would go visit these guys in their guard towers; they couldn't really do anything; they couldn't read; they had to stay focused on looking at what was going on. It was really boring. Once in a while a car would drive by or a donkey or something. And they knew what everything was; they knew that was the university, right near Baghdad University, so people would come and go there a little bit. But they were just so bored. So I was just like, "Wow! We're actually doing something out there."

I talked to him, and he was just so broken; I could see that something had changed in him. The thing that stuck with him, he said, was that "Everybody congratulated me." For him, that seemed like the craziest thing to do. And from my perspective, I was like, "Well, yeah! You did exactly what you're supposed to do, you know. Somebody shot at you, and you shot back at him, and you hit him! That's even more amazing!" But I kept quiet; I just listened. I realized he had crossed a line; there's something different about him, and he doesn't understand. I just really listened to him about his feeling about what he had done. I didn't try to take it away. We were always focused on how you help people recover from trauma that was done to them, the victim stuff. But the perpetrator stuff is a whole other. . . . I wasn't even aware that that was an issue for people. Now, looking back, I can see that he was not ready to go back to normal life and maybe isn't now. I don't even know where he is now. I don't even know if I remember his name. I probably could if I talked with someone from his company. I remember seeing him; I can picture him sitting there, but it was just one more thing. Every day there were these things that I'd never heard of before just happening. But now, looking back, . . . he needed some kind of sacrament of reconciliation. And that's moral injury; the idea is that you have to work it out some other way.

···

What I have to live with is that for money, for about sixty thousand dollars in student loan repayment, I sold my soul. I guess I hadn't thought this way for a while. For everything I enjoy now—I have a nice job, I have a great wife, a car, all the luxury that comes with middle-class American existence—I bought that; there was a price tag on that for me, and I was willing to kill people for it. I mean it wasn't like . . . the contract wasn't written in that way. It wasn't quite that direct, but. . . . It's an extreme way to put it; it's not entirely true put that way, but it's not entirely false either.

13

Enemies

There's a well-known story about the Great War: during the Christmas of 1914 soldiers on both sides of the conflict left their trenches and played a rousing game of soccer in no-man's-land. The story is told to illustrate a sense that the enlisted men had more in common with each other than with the officers who led them or the civilian leaders who sent them into battle. At the beginning of the war they had no particular quarrel with each other. By the end the situation was a little different. The Christmas soccer story illustrates an ideal by which there is no strife between nations that could not be resolved by some healthy competition played by universal rules or that soldiers in general have no dispute with each other, that it is not always clear that the man in your rifle sites is your enemy. At least in trench warfare those lines should have been or could have been clear. In the wars fought a hundred years later, the division between enemy and ally is unclear in new ways when the map is ideological as much as topographical. There are still games of soccer being played: American GIs are photographed with children, winning hearts and minds. But those same children or their peers might also be seen throwing rocks at incoming troops, the enmity entrenched before children can grow beards or factor integers. Men of the same backgrounds have worked as civilian contractors for the U.S. military and volunteered for Al Qaeda or the Islamic State. Or both. Or neither. The high-value targets seemed more and more like ordinary men before the Islamic State brought new impetus to the fading forces of Al Qaeda. Your troop might occupy a family's compound, and if you were the new guy, you might be assigned to watch over the adorable grandchild. And what is that grandchild thinking as she reaches out to try to touch the gun holstered by your thigh? Were you allowed to play with toy guns at her age? In a war fought over the course of a generation, is today's grandchild tomorrow's refugee, last week's terror suspect, next month's sympathetic member of parliament? So who is our enemy in Iraq or Afghanistan?

THERE WERE A COUPLE guys that we had been chasing after for a long time, these two brothers, and we finally knew where they lived, but they were never home for obvious reasons. They were wanted for some kind of brutal killings and murders of other people. I guess whatever had happened, happened a long time before I was actually there—in fact probably before our unit was even there. Some people had pointed these two guys out as horrible gang killers or militia killers or something. We knew where their parents were. So we actually went and spoke with their mother, and their house was strange. They had an ice cream stand, which is a strange but kind of awesome thing to have in the middle of Iraq, and it's really good too. It was just a weird sense. They offered it to us and, like, it's typical hospitality; that's what they do. We sat down, and the mother was pleading for them, and we said, "Look, we just want to talk to them; we need to figure out what's going on. Have them come here because we know that you know where they are; they're probably close by. Just get them; let us talk to them for a few minutes; we promise we will not detain them." And after a while they actually showed up. They really did. And my sense of these two guys was the same: these guys looked weak, like children. I mean, they were probably in their—I would say—early twenties, both of them. Maybe the other one was a little bit older, but it's difficult to judge age there because everyone ages kind of differently. . . . Somebody you might think is in their forties might be twenty-six. Or something like that. But both the brothers were sitting there, and they looked almost pathetic in their way of pleading for mercy and things like that, and we didn't detain them. We let them go. . . . That was my commander's call, and I think he made the right decision. He caught a lot of hell for it later because these guys were on our list of people we needed to detain, and they said, "How come you didn't take them?" And he said, "Well, the only way to get them there was to promise we wouldn't and to see their faces. So now we know what they look like; if we really want to get them later, we can. But we would lose all credibility in the entire area if we said we won't detain them and then we do. That would be it; we would never get anybody to ever talk to us ever again." I don't remember what happened to them later, but just the sense that I got, the description of what these guys had supposedly done, did not fit the type of person that you would expect to do that. And maybe that's the way it is for everybody. I mean, you look at pictures of Adam Lanza, and these guys don't look like killers. So nobody looks like a killer, and the ones who do look like killers . . . it's hard. I don't know how to make a distinction between those two things.

• • •

Have you seen the movie *The Patriot* with Mel Gibson? There's this evil British dragoon, and he kills Mel Gibson's son, and then Mel Gibson goes on a rampage and joins the Continental Army. . . . There were civilians that got killed, and I can totally imagine one of those kids' or a person's relative just picking up a rifle because we killed their son. I understand there's collateral damage, but to be honest, I really don't think we should have been there in the first place. A lot of people died on both sides of it, and I don't think there was really any reason for it at all. I don't. Seeing people's legs get blown off, then seeing people get shot a bunch, and then seeing Afghans crying over their relatives that we had brought to the COP, and they had to identify them. . . . I mean everybody's human.

• • •

I took my job very seriously. The way I look at it, for every innocent person that dies, that's five more terrorists. And so the further away they are. . . . I can't see the whole space; I don't know who else is in the building, if there is anyone else in the building. Who is in the truck? I can't always see that, so . . . I need to get this right. The other aspect of it is I know that they're bad if they're shooting at me. When they're further away, they're not shooting at me, so maybe they're just on their way to dinner, and they happen to have some AKs. Nine times out of ten, I knew for a fact that that wasn't the case, but the intimacy . . . to know they want to kill me.

• • •

It was extremely bizarre. I guess I only really thought about it afterwards, and I didn't really consciously look at a patient and think, "Oh, my God, that could happen to me." I'm sure that was going on in my mind on an emotional level, but I just did my job, so I saw the patients as patients. And the only time that I really was kind of jarred out of that and was made aware, "Oh my God, we're at war," would be. . . . There was one time that stands out where we had a VIP; I can't remember who it was. At the time, we were the place to be in Iraq because we were the hub hospital, so we always had four-stars coming through and whoever else—you know, people from the media. We surmised that intel got out that somebody important was on our base because we were mortared extensively, and I was really scared. I mean, it's funny; I never thought I'd ever have degrees of fear, but my fear was very, very, very palpable. All of us were scared, and I remember they finally put an end to it because they took the predator out, and a predator, mind you, had artillery that takes out tanks, so the fact that they took a predator out to get these guys, I found intriguing. So all of a sudden the mortars stopped, we heard that the predator had gone out, and then about an hour later they drag in one of the combatants. And he was spitting and yelling and screaming, you know, in his language. He was upset; he was what you would expect, I guess, from an enemy. He came in with the security forces, and the only reason why I thought about it is because one of the nurses that I worked with kind of freaked out and was like, "What the hell? I can't believe we're treating this person; he tried to kill us." And I remember thinking, "I don't understand why he's alive." I didn't understand that. That's when I had my first taste of military law, and I guess some of the strategy behind the war, and that's why I thought twice about it. The predator went out and got most of these guys, except he survived. So I was confused. I was like, "Well, I don't understand; he was trying to kill us. Why did we leave him to be alive?" So that was a little bit bizarre. We ended up treating him, and then he left with security forces, and I'm sure they wanted to gather intel from this individual. So incidents like that would kind of remind me that we're at war. I look around at my military colleagues who are in the direct line of combat, and I feel like, "Well, I don't understand why you guys didn't kill this person. I kind of thought that's what war was about?" But it's not; it's far more complicated than that, so I just did my job and took care of him.

$\bullet\ \bullet\ \bullet$

They told us that just prior to that day they had arrested a man who was a local working in our dining facility. They went to his house, and they found he had plans in his house to set off a bomb in the dining facility. He had worked there for years, but his family was taken hostage by the Taliban. That wasn't something he wanted to do; I mean, he liked his job. Even after—from what I understand, from the intel reports later—even after they arrested him and stopped him, they murdered his family. They no longer had any use for him.

$\bullet\ \bullet\ \bullet$

The thing about the Taliban is, there was maybe one Taliban point of contact in a five-, ten-mile radius, and in my opinion all the farmers that are pissed off at us for ruining their lives or bulldozing their crop fields or killing their children are coming to that guy and saying, "Hey, give me an AK." I could be totally wrong. But what I gathered from everything—from the intel we got, the briefings we had, people we were looking for—we were mostly looking for two or three people in our whole AO, and there were more than two or three people shooting at us. And who were those people? They were nobodies. A lot of them were Pakistani hired guns, obviously. I think a lot of people were just pissed off that we were there. When one sovereign nation fights another sovereign nation . . . I don't know if it's just or right, but I would feel more proud of myself for defending against an entity that means to hurt the United States in a more geopolitical way: the way wars have been fought between nations forever. I would definitely be more proud of that than some nebulous undefined group of people, some of whom may be hired guns, mercenaries, and some of whom may be people who are just upset that we won't leave them alone.

• • •

Once I moved to the reconnaissance, it was about establishing who was a high-value target, so I saw it from both sides. Whenever you go to get them, at my rank anyway, I didn't know shit but their name, what they looked like, and occasionally there'd be, like, "He's making IDs" or "He's doing this."

• • •

One thing we talked about a lot was that we think the Afghan people kind of understood that whether it was the Taliban or insurgents or Al Qaeda, someone would be there after the American military was gone. So they were very hesitant to believe that we were going to be able to protect them long term. So sometimes they would accept help, and sometimes they would get killed for doing that. Like people got killed over the voting for one, and sometimes I would think they were trying to use us. I didn't blame them because they were living in abject poverty. But they take corn and then say that we didn't give them any so that they could get more; they would have a dead animal, livestock, and they would say that it got blown up by something that we did, and we would know that that wasn't true, but they just wanted us to pay them. Frequently they would bring in their people who were sick or injured and want us to fly them up to one of the bigger bases to get medical help. That was the biggest thing that they wanted. And we tried to do that because that's one of the best ways we could help them because they don't have any kind of hospitals. I mean, I'm sure they do in Kabul or Kandahar, but where we were, they didn't have anything like that. I don't know how well the civil affairs thing really worked after all. I didn't see the big picture either, you know.

• • •

An Afghan national was killed somehow. I don't really remember how he was killed. I'm pretty sure he wasn't Taliban. A lot of people were like, "They're all Taliban." But I don't really think we had any reason to suspect him of being Taliban. His brother came in.

I mean, they were not old, old men. Not old men. I mean you age very quickly over there. They were probably in their fifties, maybe forties. He was in the medical tent, but I could hear him wailing. We were just kind of hanging out and doing something stupid. I don't remember what we were doing, but I remember hearing him wailing and watching him come out of the tent, and the tears were streaming down his face. Their culture, they're not downers. They use a lot of euphemisms for death. They're not a very direct culture as much as we are, I guess. It's definitely enhanced when they're around Americans. But I'd never seen an Afghan cry except then. It was really sad, you know. You could just tell that it was somebody that he loved. Everybody was just making jokes about how they were gay. Stupid. It pissed me off.

• • •

We knew when we were getting contact because you'd see the women and children, like a caravan, leaving. . . . These ICOM radios you could buy at Radio Shack; you could hear what they're saying, and the interpreter's sitting there telling you, "Yeah they're looking at us right now," or "They're getting ready for the big assault." And a lot of that is just them talking to each other, and we call it "dicking" with us. You'd see a guy standing there with the radio. . . . In Iraq you'd kill a guy if you saw that; if you saw him with a radio or a video camera and you were getting attacked, you could kill him. But in Afghanistan . . . they would dick with you. The British would call it that, so we started calling it that, and they would just stand there and look at you. They'd look at you with the binoculars, and they'd say things like, "Mohammad, why aren't you attacking? You're such a coward."

14

Homecoming

During a deployment there is a date on the calendar when everyone in the unit will return home, and you count down the days to that golden moment. If a tour is extended and ninety days are suddenly added to that date, the unit frays from that feeling of delay before beginning to count down again. Leaving the din and danger of the war zone is an unspeakable relief. Freed from bureaucracy, red tape, and onerous command structures, you as an individual can once again reconnect with your sweetheart, siblings, parents, pets, and pizza. All the arbitrariness, drudgery, fear, and exhaustion drop away. You are celebrated for your service, congratulated, and thanked. You eat favorite meals; sleep on your own schedule; and wake to a world of safety, prosperity, and convenience. Yet you are also separated from the people with whom you spent every waking moment for many months, the people who gave you an obnoxious nickname, who were there when the funny thing actually happened, who ate the same food and lived through the same adrenaline rushes. Yes, you are an individual again, and you don't miss anything about deployments except the people and the clarity, maybe, of knowing your purpose every day, of pursuing the same goals with a unit committed to the same aims, of serving a purpose higher than yourself with skills you have honed through hard labor and raw talent. And then people assume you returned home traumatized. It is not that you have post-traumatic stress exactly, but it is hard not to scan the debris on the side of the highway. Last month you dropped from a helicopter or stopped the bleeding or delivered food and water to an isolated outpost. But you can't exactly admit you've changed for the better by going to war. Yet now people who have never even seen an open abdominal wound or heard incoming mortar fire are offering to help you or trying to start up a political conversation where you're either the expert on war or an unrepentant hawk, and you are not sure which direction they are about to take it. And you don't want anyone's help; you want to serve a larger purpose, and you have mad skills with communication equipment and navigation gear. Every day you have to see to your own basic needs in a bewilderingly banal menu of luxurious options and plan your day carefully to complete basic tasks and get to know the people you were once closest to, apart from those who know you as you are now, even though the way they breathed was starting to irritate you. This is the country, these are the people, those are the freedoms you risked your life to protect. Everything about this world is loved and precious, of course, and now you have the rest of your life to find your way in it. But maybe it would make more sense to just redeploy. Or maybe your whole career will be with the military, and this last tour opened up real possibilities to make things happen if you could only figure out all the passwords and user IDs for your bank account and insurance plan and credit card and electricity and mortgage.

THE PREMISE OF COMBAT changing me, it kind of presupposes that there was a stable identity beforehand that was then changed as a result, but I was clay that was fired in the kiln.

• • •

I remember when I got to fly out of there; that was an awesome feeling; that was an *awesome* feeling. Getting to look down from a C-130, out the little window at the Hindu Kush mountains, was beautiful. I'd never seen mountains like that before. Just chains and chains of mountains capped with snow.

• • •

When you're in a combat situation, you know what to expect and how to do it. You know when you're supposed to be where. Every part of life is arranged; it's organized; it's set. You do what those above you tell you, and you tell those below you what to do. If it's not done, that's the exception, and it's a major problem that you address vehemently. You come home, and you've got your wife, who you don't outrank, and she doesn't outrank you, so how do you work that? And then you've got your kids; your mind says you outrank them, but there's not a rank structure. They're not your troops. You know, you don't come in and bang the trash can

PHOTO BY DAVID EISLER.

at them and pull drill sergeant stuff on them. You can't. And you think about this equal who's been running things for a year without you, and now you come in, and they almost don't need you, it seems. They don't—you're not even necessary. You're extraneous. So you sit there going, "Well, what's my role?" And you're upset because, well, the kids are doing what she says, and they're not doing what I'm saying, and that's just disrespectful. And how do I manage them? How do I become "Dad" instead of "Sergeant"? How do I become a husband again who listens and cares and is concerned, instead of the combatant who has a mission, achieves his mission, and that makes him a good person? You know, when you get your mission done, the rest of your time is yours to do what you need to. To do what you want to. When I got that administrative position last time I was in Iraq, I was able to use the computer. I did schoolwork; I did college. And so I'm doing online classes during my free time, focusing on schoolwork and me, me, me, me. And then doing my mission during the daytime. And then I get home, and I'm thinking, "You gotta spend time with the kids and read the little book with your daughter." Y'know, son's going to have a little bit of an attitude problem, but you can't just scream at him every time. Y'know, there's most of the family integration. That's the hard part. Just getting back into, "What is my role? What does it mean to be 'Dad'? What does it mean to be a husband?"

• • •

Sometimes in war, there's no one you can call. There's no one who is going to help you. And that's not a good thing, but I think it can be good to experience because it makes you a little more self-reliant.

• • •

The weirdest thing is coming back from those countries and realizing how rich we are and how green this country is. You're just overwhelmed by how green everything is in this country compared to the desert where we are during deployment. It's just a sensory overload—not just of colors—but you go to the grocery store, and you have a million options for what kind of pasta. . . . You're like, "Really? I have fifty noodle options right now?"

• • •

I had lost something, but I didn't know what it was. I really thought I'd be injured or dead or somehow put on a pedestal. I thought one of those three things would happen; I'd win some big award or be shot or killed.

• • •

I've had to become different. We did a lot of marriage counseling right when I got out of the Marine Corps. I had been gone for the first year and a half of our marriage, and the whole time I was in, we were like, "Oh well. If we were just around each other, we'd be a lot happier." Then when we were around each other every day, it was just too much. I wasn't ready for it. I don't think I was a very compassionate or patient husband. I had to learn that, I think. Marriage counseling helped us quite a lot. I would recommend it to anyone but especially someone coming out of the Marine Corps or the military.

• • •

HOMECOMING

The best thing about coming home was seeing my dog.

. . .

No, the best thing about coming home was having a great family there to support me and seeing them. The second best thing about coming home was having a girlfriend who waited for me. And then the third best thing about coming home was realizing the dream about finally getting into graduate school.

. . .

"If you didn't die, we don't know what to do with you now. If you gave your life, oh, we know what to do: we make a statue in your honor, and you live forever and gave everything." But it's, "You came back; now what good are you? We don't need your ability to kill people. We don't need your ability to withstand struggles. We don't need your abilities to face fear, danger, and adversity." Nobody needs me to jump out of a helicopter for them. I'm really good at it. I can rappel out of a helicopter. It's one of my favorite things I ever did. Air assault was so much fun. Helicopters are a blast. But, y'know, nobody needs that out of me. So what is my purpose? And that's true, I think, of a lot of vets: they come out of the service, and, okay, so they go back to school, but what in and why and how and where, and what am I going to do? They stay in for twenty years, because the only people who think they're valuable any more is the military. You're valuable to the military because you can contribute strategies. But what we need is a way to show veterans, "What you did over there can still be valuable now in the real world."

. . .

It didn't seem exceptionally horrible over there, so it didn't seem to me exceptionally great coming back. It was just something I signed up to do, and I just did it. I didn't put a huge emphasis on being home. To me it was just matter of fact: that's what was going on.

. . .

Dave and I were getting out at the same time. We were going to open up a gym in Austin, Texas. I'd never been to Austin, but I knew it was in Texas, and it was the capital, so everyone was going to have a gun and cowboy hats and everything. His mom ended up dying, so he had to go take care of his mentally challenged sister. So I was in Austin by myself with no game plan, and I thought about suicide on a regular basis. I thought, "I gotta do something." So I went to college. It's been a huge blessing or extreme luck, whatever you want to call it, but it has definitely helped me. I just went to the third funeral of one of my buddies who had just killed himself. I really think it's just a feeling of loneliness. I think once you experience being that close emotionally with another human being, it's hard. . . . If you fall in love with someone, that doesn't even compare with how in love with your friends you are. And you lose that.

• • •

I haven't shared that story in a long time, actually. I haven't shared a lot of the stories outside our circle, now that I think about it. My girlfriend doesn't really know, and I've known her through both my deployments. I haven't told my girlfriend, and we're about to celebrate four years.

• • •

I could say probably close to 70 percent of my unit came back divorced, separated, or single. We had a colonel—my director, my DO—his wife just got up one day, cleaned the house, took the kids, and was gone—just disappeared. He had to call his family to figure out where she was, and nobody had any idea. It wasn't until he got home and could start to search that he found out where his wife had left and taken the kids and everything he owned.

• • •

I think working at the veterinary hospital, working in the anesthesia department, we have dogs that will code, and it can be kind of frantic when they start CPR. I think that's why I've stayed there over the years, because it's a little bit of adrenaline. And yet I like to evaluate myself on whether or not I was calm in that situation. I don't know if it's one of those "let's-see-if-I've-still-got-it" things or not, but I think it keeps me there, as far as finding another part of the hospital or employment somewhere else.

• • •

The best thing about being home is being able to let your guard down. It's learning not to be on all the time. Because it really, really drains you. It drains you not just physically, but it drains you emotionally. You start compartmentalizing everything with the combat setup, and there's a place for every aspect of your life, and they don't overlap, and you don't let them. You don't open the door from one to the other. And it really starts to feel robotic. You stop feeling human, and so being able to come home, sit on the couch, realize it's Saturday morning, and you don't have to do anything. And that's okay. Nobody's going to be mad at me. I can just sit here, and it's quiet, and I can turn off. And that was hard—it was really, really hard—but it was really good. Just the ability to say, "Okay, it's not my responsibility." There's somebody else protecting me. I can stop.

· · ·

One of the shocks that I faced first getting out: I'm an infantryman; there's not a lot of need for infantrymen, you know, coming out. Some of the mechanics and stuff, they had it made; they have pretty nice careers with these car companies. My trade doesn't transfer well. I think that where it does transfer, I'd be back overseas in a private sector doing embassy security. I've got a lot of friends doing that. Or being a police officer or something.

· · ·

I'm happy people aren't trying to kill me any more. That's always a bonus.

· · ·

I met my wife two days after I came back from Iraq. So that was the best thing about coming back the first time, and the best thing about coming back the second time was that a few weeks later I got married. So I cannot separate all of those things. Coming back the first time, the worst thing about it was I was alone. There was no one; I had to beg for a ride home; there was nobody even to pick me up because at that point, they hadn't thought about it. There were single soldiers that were just like, "How do I get out of here?" And they wouldn't give us our cars back the first day because—I don't know—that was part of one of the rules of reintegration: you couldn't get your car until, like, day two or something. So I was just like, "I don't have anyone to take me home." My wife cries when she hears that story; she's like, "I wish I would have been there!" But the second time coming back and getting to see her again for the first time; I can't separate that; that was the best. And then shortly thereafter it was basically vacation, and then my family came to visit. I was in Germany, so they came out, and my friends came out for the wedding, and we were still essentially on leave from the tour. So that was just like one of the best months of my life. Germany, you know, in the summer is the best. And basically my day was: wake up, walk down into the square, meet my family, have breakfast, sit at the same table for a few hours until it was lunchtime, order beer, order sausage.

• • •

My own wife at the time fell in love with her neighbor at home. And I came back to that. So the whole year just seemed false to me when I came back. All the phone calls I had made to my wife were a big lie. I mean, I thought they were real, but they weren't. Maybe they were. Hard to say. The fact that she had a boyfriend that I didn't know about for months when I got back. . . . Finally I found out about it, and we got divorced. It just cast the whole experience in a different light. I had no idea what I was doing. I thought I'd been okay. I'd been there for all the events. I hadn't slacked off. I'd done everything that I could do. And yet it was all upside down. So that made me question everything.

• • •

This is going to sound harsh, but I was DJ'ing a wedding one time, and we did an anniversary dance and found the oldest married couple and asked for advice. And this crotchety old man, I asked him what his advice was for the married couple, and he looked right at the groom and said, "Say 'Yes, ma'am,' and do whatever the fuck you want." That's a funny moment, right? But there's an element of truth there. So when you come back and you're not ready to do things the way that she wants, one of the things you learn how to do is say, "Oh yeah. Yeah." But no. No. Little tricks like that allow you to reintegrate without the conflict. It's better to

ask forgiveness than permission. I'm not saying that every decision is like that, but there is an element of that, an element of just
kind of doing your thing, finding your quiet spot. My wife knows
that I have a spot; my garage is mine; if I go out in the garage,
leave me alone. I'll just go out and tinker on the car because I can,
because there's always something that needs to be fixed. That's my
routine. I found that I couldn't go to sleep for six months after I
came back unless I went out; I'm kind of a night owl, so it's usually like midnight or one in the morning, and I just walk up and
down the street. That's what I missed there, because in Baghdad,
I would go up on the roof every night and just get that feel for
the city, feel for what is. So I'd just go ahead and get a feel for the
neighborhood and what's going on: who's up, who's not, who's
having a party (I don't really care), just so long as I know what's
going on; then I just go back in and sleep like a baby.

• • •

I just subconsciously change lanes when there's a broken-down
car, and I count the number of vehicles. We drove from Wash-
ington State to Pennsylvania. We got to Pennsylvania (it took us
several days), and my daughter asked me, "How many cars were
broken down on the side of the road?" And I said, "Forty-two."
And that was five days' worth of driving. I knew generally where
they were. My mind thinks it's a threat, but I'm here in my home
town. When's the last time an IED went off in my home town? I
have a tremendously strong family, and every reintegration has
gotten better because I've learned in every reintegration not to
walk back in the house and then take the checkbook over and
then screw up the first month of freaking bills.

• • •

Learning to drive again is tough. Not that you don't know how to
drive, but you drive so aggressively. You have road rage, like beating on the steering wheel and cussing at everybody. A semi right
next to me blew up, a retread just exploded, rubber all over the car
and everything like that. I mean, I was pedal on the floor, weaving
in and out of traffic, yelling out commands to people who weren't
in the car. I'm out on the road doing a hundred miles an hour,

and my wife's like, "Could you pull over?" I was coming down the highway about the same time period—I'd been home a month—and the group that was out there that picks up the trash had been out there that morning. So there were trash bags on either side of the road in the same spot, and I literally locked up all four tires, came to a screeching halt, sitting in the middle of the highway, and I had to make myself—like *make* myself—drive through.

• • •

My wife and I spent the first ten years we were married under the same roof for four. Okay? It seems like a logistic that makes a lot of sense on the surface, but you probably never thought about it. If you're married, the first time you move in with somebody, for the first month everything's fantastic, okay? And then the little things start to irritate you: the way she does this and the way I do this, right? By six months into it you're at each other's throats, right? And you do this little roller coaster thing; you get some things worked out, and it comes back, and you get some things worked out. But that roller coaster, it's a decreasing return. Eventually you find that even keel. And then you go to Kosovo for six months, and then you come back, and you do it again. Then you go to the Sinai for three months, and you come back, and you do it again. And then you go to Iraq for eight months, and you come back, and you do it again. It teaches you how to do it. So going on a six-month training or flying to Kosovo and then coming back teaches you how to reintegrate with people. I think without my wife and her skills at putting up with me, which are pretty impressive, then reintegration isn't something I ever really would have learned. If I was an NCO evaluating my soldiers coming back, that'd be the first thing I'd be looking at: who is this guy reintegrating with? Because if he's just reintegrating into the barracks, is he actually reintegrating, or is he just back and gets to go to a bar every night? So how many times has he done it? Because people act like the more deployments you have, the more prone you are. No, I think it's a skill, a learned skill, because you've done it over and over and over again.

• • •

You'd think I'd be relieved to be safe, and I am, so that is number one, to not have to worry about dying. But that aside, I'm happy to have a bathroom and that I don't have to put on all my flak gear and walk, you know, six city blocks to get to the bathroom in the middle of the night.

• • •

I couldn't engage with other people. I mean, after you've been through an experience like that, it's not just, "Oh, gee, they don't understand." I remember when I first got off the plane. The next day after I had slept, I was wearing civilian gear, and I drove myself to an outdoor mall, and I remember just being really dazed and confused. I really felt like I could not connect. I was so confused; I couldn't believe that just thirty-six hours prior to that I was in a war. And I still feel that way, you know, five years out. So I guess coming back is just not being able to reengage with your old life. I haven't been the same since I've been back. Even though I am me, I'm just very different.

• • •

A lot of guys can't find a job when they get home, and that makes it even worse. It took me, like, two months to find a job, and it felt like an eternity. I was so miserable. I had free time for the first time. I was around all my friends, and I was completely miserable. I just felt lazy, like I'm not doing anything. I don't know how to handle those interviews. People ask, "What did you do in Afghanistan that prepared you to do customer support?" I'm just like . . . I have no idea . . . nothing. It actually is really beneficial to work, but it's hard to explain that. So I just took the first job that I got. Actually it was a marine who hired me, a Desert Storm vet who I'm now very good friends with. Luckily he saw my resume and saw Marine Corps on there. He interviewed me, and that was it.

• • •

I really feel like I speak two languages. I feel like there's a duality to my nature now that I'm not entirely able to reconcile. A friend once described me as a chameleon, in a positive way. I think it was in a positive way. I'm really good at adapting to a situation. I feel like I kind of lost my center in a way and never really got it back.

I mean, even in close relationships like with my wife, I'm aware of all these aspects that I can't communicate because there's not a unified center there. That's probably true of everybody; I think it just made me more aware of it.

• • •

We go to war to preserve our independence and our safety, I guess. I have to tell myself that. Although after looking at the paper about the Boston Marathon today, with some explosion that went off at the finish line, . . . it makes you wonder. I feel like, "Are we really that safe in this city?" But, you know, times have changed; for the most part we are so privileged. I start to feel sorry for myself that my life has changed so dramatically; I just try to take it in stride with perspective because I think back to the people who live in Iraq and what they don't have, let alone what they're still dealing with— war and violence and all that. I just am happy that I'm not them.

• • •

I don't like to have the military define who I am.

• • •

I remember the first night we got back. We all went out. Someone's mom rented out a bakery. We all went there and had beers and stuff in the middle of the night by the water. It was in North Carolina. It was right on the ocean. We all got blackout drunk and ran in the ocean and stuff. There was a point there when I went out to have a cigarette and a drink, and I saw all the cars driving by, and I thought of Dave, and it made me tear up. I started crying. We're all back here, counting our blessings. We made it home safe, and some of our brothers didn't. Some of us are in the hospital right now without a leg, but they're still alive. That was very hard for the first couple days because you kind of felt survivor's guilt, being able to appreciate all these things and being alive and knowing that others didn't make it.

• • •

The hardest thing about coming home was coming home different than when I left. Physically I did great, but mentally and emotionally, I was just distraught. That's not to say that good things don't happen. When I was headed back, my dad and I got to leave together, and everywhere we went, people saw that father-son rela-tionship. He was caring for me; he looked after me; he went where I went. So people saw that, and we were allowed to be of use, to be a blessing to people wherever we went. When I finally got home, I was one of the first amputees where my hand was amputated, so there was this expectation on me to be that poster boy, so to speak, to succeed in whatever I did. So what I did was I pushed down in my mind that I wasn't okay. I didn't really deal with my injury the way that I should have. That was probably the biggest part of my recovery, realizing that I'm not going to get it back, and it's okay. I left with two hands, with pretty good self-esteem, self-confidence, self-image. And I came back with just none of that. I struggled with, "How could people love someone that's injured like me? How could people meet me, when I can't. . . ." So all these things. And I was searching for my identity. That was probably the hardest part: accepting that people just genuinely cared for me.

• • •

I think I'm relieved to be finished with feeling like I can't have my own voice, so to speak, because the morals and the values that I have now would not have been accepted in the military. So I feel like I have that freedom to share the story, to share what I've seen and not feel like I'm being silenced while doing it. It's not to say that that's a bad reflection of the Army; it's just the Army has different morals and values.

• • •

I would love to work with HALO Trust. Actually, that's what I'm hoping to do.

• • •

I often think about the fact that it just seemed like kind of a big waste—not necessarily a waste of my life; I'm glad I went in and just saw that part of the world and everything—but I just wonder what the point of it was. How we could be in Afghanistan for so long, and I could be there for seven months, and what came of my time there and our experience and the casualties? What ben-efit came from that? It's hard to think of any real benefit. There's just kind of this level of absurdity about it.

I'm glad I went because I just appreciate my life so much more now because life while you're deployed is really lousy. It was for me. It was lonely. Even though I had friends, I felt lonely a lot of the time. I was overworked; I was stressed out; I had nothing to look forward to. That was probably the worst. Here at home, I could work or I could be doing something, but I'm always looking forward to seeing my wife at the end of the day, or I have something fun planned with friends. But there it's just nothing. There's nothing to look forward to, and that kind of grates on you. So I think experiencing real suffering, real hardship, makes me appreciate my life here with friends and family. The wealth of our society is really special, actually.

• • •

War is kind of a failed enterprise to begin with. You're going to experience failure because the standards are so high: life and death. To embrace that a little bit is probably a good step. Since the trauma was not verbal trauma, it was experiential trauma; very little can be done to undo it verbally, I think. Experiences are the things that heal, with people, with organizations and community. I think the meaning of the past can change. It changes the experience a little bit when you see it differently.

• • •

I'm so glad to be out because they own you. They own your whole life. They can take you away from your life and send you to Iraq for a year because you pissed someone off. They can recall you.

• • •

I never really took the time to appreciate little things, which is why I found my way into yoga. I feel like so much of it has drawn me in my yoga practice, and I love sharing my experiences in my yoga classes just to help people feel emotions they generally turn off and don't understand. I'm thankful that I have a home to go to. I'm thankful that I have friends and family. The more I try to learn about myself and the world, the more I study, the more I appreciate those moments of being in Afghanistan, not just because of the scenery and the exposure. . . . I mean, people talk about poverty; they've never seen poverty. Poverty in the U.S. is a joke when you go overseas.

• • •

I would definitely do it again. I would dread it. Now that I know what it would be like to reenlist, I would dread it with every fiber of my being, but I would do it absolutely again in a heartbeat just because of what I got out of it. It was just so amazing. I hate crediting the Army with that. I hate it.

15

Loss

A sense of helpless responsibility accompanies loss in a combat zone. Sometimes there is a tiny protocol that was not followed, one that is occasionally circumvented with no problem, but this time it is fatal. Then there are the fatalities that take place just where you were yesterday, and you are left with the feeling that it could or should have been you that died. You may have actually been replaced by a soldier who is killed on the mission you missed. It is not that veterans feel survival guilt in the face of loss. Rather the extensive training and preparation bring with them a sense that every problem ought to be solved and every eventuality anticipated. Some deployments are riddled with loss; medics, physical therapists, and physicians face loss as a job requirement. Infantry and marines endure tours steeped in danger. Some veterans wear black metal bands on their wrists with the names of those they have lost to war. The bands fit only so many names, so some rotate their bands daily. With every loss of a friend, there is a little loss of the person you were with that friend, the person you were before being faced with your own mortality in the form of another's death.

WE HAD JUST FORMED a new platoon, and he took us on top of a hill, and he gave us a big speech about complacency, about watching out for the IEDs. And while we were sitting on this hill, I remember watching the bomb-sweeping squad come through on the highway. And they were so slow. We spent so much time outside of the wire, being QRFS, that a hot meal was something that, you know, at the time, we cherished quite a bit. So we got on the highway and were following behind the bomb squad, and there was a separate road that looped around, and we could get around them, so they made the call to go around them, and probably about two hundred yards after we passed them an IED went off. And he got hit, I guess, in the helmet, and it went through, and we had to . . . and we responded to that . . . and that was pretty rough because he was a well-liked sergeant. So we lost him.

• • •

We were starting our last few patrols, and his vehicle blew up on an IED strike. That one was a rough one, and I still deal with it today. But I had just talked to him; we had just settled our plans for our girlfriends to come and meet us in North Carolina, and we were all going to spend the weekend. Just over a month we'd been working out plans. I believe from what I understand, he was the only one that died in the vehicle because he was the vehicle commander; vehicle commanders are usually popped up probably about waist-high outside of the vehicle.

• • •

One of my best friends stepped on an IED. He was on a mission; he was in a different platoon, so we sometimes did different missions away from each other and sometime did them together. At that point he went out at, like, two o'clock in the morning with a group of others, and he stepped on an IED, and he lost both his legs and ended up bleeding out because of that, and he died. A few days earlier I'd seen him and talked to him. Even before the deployment, he was like, "I don't think I'm going to make it back from this one." I don't know. It was just really hard to lose a really good friend. He's a really good person. He's very driven and funny and fun to hang out with. He was one of the most popular guys. We would always run together, and that was the thing: we went to boot camp together. When I first saw him, I thought he was a drill instructor because he was a body builder before he joined, and his arms were, like, as big as my head. So they put him in charge, and I didn't even know who he was. Then we went through all our training together. And he started to lose weight because you need more cardio than muscle, I guess. So he started slimming down but was in super shape. I was always a really fast runner. So we'd, like, run together and stuff, and his goal was to beat me in a run. I never let him, but one day he told me he ran a fifteen-something three-mile. My best was 15:33. I didn't run it with him, but he said he beat me, and I guess I believe him. He was just very smart; he was on point; he knew what he was doing and was just a good kid. What happened was: the night previous they had gone out, and they went through a wadi and checked on something and came back. And then the next night, they followed the same path. And the first guy stepped over the IED, and he was the second guy, and he stepped on it. It was, like, in the wadi; there was no way they could have known it was there. But they followed the same path, which is something we were taught to never do. There was a lot of anger and a lot of blame going around. He died within forty-five minutes of hitting it; he wasn't able to get to the hospital or anything. He wasn't the first person we lost. We knew it was definitely a possibility. But whenever it's one of your closer friends, it doesn't feel the same.

• • •

I got really dehydrated, and I went to the emergency room. We were doing one last training thing. After I got back from Afghanistan, we had one last training event, and then I was going to go; I was going to leave. For some reason I got sick; I ate something, and then I couldn't stop throwing up. So I was at the base emergency room, and I was fine; they gave me an IV or whatever. A man from my first deployment came in. He told me, "Did you hear about so-and-so?" He just got killed two days before. He was the marine I was kind of close to on the first deployment. I was a platoon commander. He was in my platoon. He was a combat engineer. Anyway, he was like, "Yeah, he just died." And I was just sitting there. He died where our unit had just come back from. Someone from my first deployment. I had just gotten home. He was where I was for my second deployment. It was just really devastating. It was weird being home and people were dying, almost more than while I was there. That was probably the saddest thing, I would say. I hadn't felt sad at all up to that point, not through my whole deployment or anything, but that experience brought it all home. I went into the bathroom and locked myself in there at the hospital. For some reason I didn't want my wife to see me.

She was with me, and for some reason—I wasn't thinking about it, but I just knew I didn't want her to see it. So I just went in the bathroom. Then I came back, and she was like, "What are you doing in there?" And I told her about it later. She was sad for me, but I think she was worried that I was hiding it from her. I don't do that any more, not that I get sad a lot any more.

• • •

I just had a guy who was out there with us; he actually just died last month. Between transitioning out of the military, getting back into drugs, and having a string of bad days, it was just a lot. I don't think he was any less of a person. He was a free-fall qualified sniper. He was one of the best guys on our deployment; he definitely saved two of our guys' lives; two people are alive today because of him. There's nothing short in character there. It was just circumstance.

16

Nostalgia

We know that the transition back home can be difficult, but what some cannot fathom is that veterans sometimes experience a kind of homesickness for their time at war. What makes a war zone a home for someone who might yearn for it? There are actually many strong forces at work here. First, there is the sense of purpose a deployment brings. Then there is the sense of community that comes with sharing both that purpose and the arduous process of serving it. The bonds formed under these conditions are unique and primary. Then there is the routine in a war zone: a person may work long hours and make life-and-death decision while sleep deprived, but if daily life is arduous and dangerous, it is also shared. Back home, life is organized around individual effort and personal responsibility; it can be exhilarating, but it is also deeply alienating after the shared experience of war. Not everyone, of course, is nostalgic for deployment, and not everyone shares in the deep connection of camaraderie. It is possible to be completely isolated in conditions of war if one is the only woman in a unit of one hundred, an officer among enlisted, an introvert, or the only person of color. But for those who experience the ineffable ties of the brotherhood, the memory of deployment is pierced by a sharp pang of yearning for "home."

COMING HOME, I VOLUNTEERED every day for a month and a half: "Please send me back over there. I do not want to be home. Please send me back over there." I missed it. I missed the structure. I missed the environment. I missed the brotherhood. I missed knowing what I was going to do every day. I didn't have anything to worry about when I was over there. My stuff was in a storage unit that was paid for; I didn't have any bills; I didn't have to worry about whether or not I was gonna eat. I had a gym. I had a bed.

PHOTO BY MICHAEL GIBLER.

It's all I needed to worry about. Other than that lurking thought—
"Okay, could today be the day?"—I had no worries. And, I'd say,
that's probably the most de-stressed I've ever been was being in
theater. And I was amped up the entire time. I am more stressed
now, coming home, than I was over there.

• • •

I miss the excitement. I miss the feeling of purpose. You're out
there, and you're doing it.

• • •

Before I joined the Army, I was kinda anti-guns even. I didn't
hunt; I didn't do any of those things. I thought them kind of primal. Beneath me. And when I got out, one of the first things that
I found I really, really, really wanted was the sensation of shooting. I picked up hunting. I hunt hogs whenever I have the time
to do it, not because I love to hunt but because I almost absolutely need the feel of the trigger again. I need the sensation. . . .
It's almost a drug, the ability to pull the trigger and see the result
at the other end of the tube. To see it pop. It's a control. It's an
adrenaline rush. It's strength. Despite all my injuries, despite the

fact that I'm not a fit soldier any more—I'm fifty pounds heavier than I was when I was at my peak—but I can sit there and say, "I fit." I miss those moments of clarity that come with it. There is no argument about what's going to be right and what's going to be wrong. The right thing to do is preservation of your comrades. Preservation of your battle buddies. It's "Get everybody back alive that is wearing the same uniform as you are." You know who's on your side; you know who's not. Y'know, I miss the . . . black and white of it.

• • •

I also enjoyed just having time where I can justifiably spend it on myself as opposed to feeling like I need to cut myself off from something and just be, "I'm here, and there's nowhere else I can be; it's not my fault." Or just being able to excuse things away in the name of emergency: "Oh, mmm, I forgot that person's birth-day." It's, "Sorry, oh yeah. I'm terrible. There's like this war going on. . . ." But, I mean, it got to the point where you felt like this is the only thing that really matters.

• • •

I've only been out since last fall, so there are only a few times when I kind of miss putting on the uniform and going in and standing in a formation and just feeling that sense of camarade-rie and belonging. Only a few times. . . . More often than not I'm happy I got out because it was the right decision for me; it's not the right decision for everyone. But it is something to be proud of, and I think most people who serve are proud of what they've done, even if they don't necessarily agree with it.

• • •

I miss having twenty-four hours a day to do my job. I had a real purpose in life, and everyone thought I had a purpose. I could see that every day. People were glad to see me coming by every day to talk to them. I really was there for them unless I was going on another mission. I was there, even though there was always more I could have done; I could have gone to more visits. My own internal dialogue was always going, "I could have done more." I also was trying to preserve my own psyche. I remember after four months there I was hunched over. I could see everybody else too; other chaplains, other workers, everyone walked with a bent-over shuffle; it was a kind of depression that descended on everybody.

• • •

The noble sense of purpose that my life had . . . I mean, that's why I wanted to go to Iraq because for me that was the epitome of being a physician: to serve those who truly need you. And I'm not even going to say politically if it matters whether I agree with the war. The bottom line is that we were at war, and my skill set could help victims of war. And in general I really miss that; I miss that teamwork; I miss feeling like I was doing something good and noble and that all of my skills and efforts and life experience up to that point were what brought me there to help others. So I miss that; I do. Ever since Iraq, to practice medicine, at least in my field, has not been very satisfying.

• • •

It was easy; it was simpler. No distractions. You knew your job and what to do and how to do it. You did guard at night, and then you went to sleep, and you woke up, and you did what you were told. There's no complications. No bathing. No shower. I miss the brotherhood, the camaraderie. Some of my best friends are people I met in the military. I miss the actual firefights, shooting guns. I miss seeing explosions or bombs dropped. There's nothing cooler. There's a plane called the A-10 Warthog that, I think, has a 20-millimeter machine gun on it. When it flies down and shoots, it sounds like thunder ripping through the air. It's one of the coolest sounds ever.

• • •

I miss the unit I was sent to by mistake because they really wanted me to stay. They demonstrated what it was like to be a band of brothers, that camaraderie. They're like, "Hey, we need you on our team."

17

Struggling

The direct engagement with an opposing force, for which soldiers are amply prepared, is alarming and adrenaline-charged, even frightening, but it is not frequently the source of difficult memories or revisited regrets. The sources of post-combat stress are usually subtler. When a child's death is the unintended consequence of proper procedure, memories haunt and isolate the veteran on returning home. Yet we have heard so many stories of children dying in these war zones; it is hard to see an individual carrying the responsibility of a life lost in a context where children's lives are commonly and even structurally fragile or worse, fungible, or where the moral convictions about the sanctity of a child's life are used as a tactical advantage. The loss of a friend can lead to feelings of helplessness, hours spent running alternative scenarios in which the other guy survives, someone saves the patient, or intervenes before the suicide. Perhaps a veteran should feel grateful to survive into ordinary days when so many have died, when so many are condemned to live out their years in a war zone of unspeakable brutality. But there is another kind of grinding brutality in the isolated days when a veteran is trying to rebuild a sense of purpose, fending off offers of help or expressions of gratitude, when the real need is for a new form of service he or she can provide.

I HAVE TO TRY every day to remind myself that I'm not a monster. I did what I was trained to do. I did everything right.

• • •

It comes up every year. The mind just won't let go of that. Anywhere you're at where there's fireworks, and it seems so petty to even talk about. I gotta say that bringing it up like it's some kind of PTSD issue, which obviously it probably is, feels rather silly. "Oh, get over yourself. It's Fourth of July; nobody cares. It's not that serious. So don't light off fireworks, and you'll be fine." But it's amazing how real it comes back. I'll walk around every day, and I don't have any issues with anything. I sleep fine at night; I don't have any moral ambiguities about what we did. I don't really concern myself. It's not, like, y'know, I don't drink heavily from it. There's no negative effects; it's just the dang Fourth of July will come along, and I feel like crawling into a hole. I don't wanna see any of that any more.

• • •

I chose to kind of bottle it up for—April, May, June, July, August, September, October, November, December, January—for about ten months before it finally got to the point where I had to talk to somebody about it. When I came home, initially, I did not sleep. I slept maybe an hour or two a night. It was a rough transition. I slept an hour or two a night every night. Until my body just forced me to collapse. Nightmares. Reliving particular events. Particular images. Stories. I didn't want to sleep. I didn't want to deal with it because I knew exactly where my mind would go, and I hated it. So I didn't sleep. I found ways to keep myself up. Take, like, an hour power nap to avoid the REM. And I just did hour power naps about every 14–15 hours. An hour nap. Maybe a two-hour nap. And then one day, because I hadn't been sleeping, I crashed. I was supposed to show up for work for the shift changeover at seven. For about five hours nobody knew where I was. Couldn't get a hold of me. I was so crashed, I was sleeping through my alarms, sleeping through phone calls. Nothing. They ended up calling the police. They called hospitals; they called pretty much anybody and everybody they could to try to figure out where I was. I woke up to my cell phone; I had 117 missed phone calls because nobody knew. I woke up; I called into the office, and I was like, "I'm here. I overslept. I'm sorry; I'll be there as soon as I can." And they're like, "All right; when you get here, let somebody know." So I showed up to base, and my superintendent was waiting for me at the front door. He grabbed me by the back of the neck, walked me right into his office, sat me down, and goes, "You've changed. Spill." And that was the first door that opened. That's the first time that I started talking about it. I told him I hadn't been sleeping, I'd been having blackouts, excessive amounts of nightmares. I wasn't eating. I'd lost close to thirty pounds since I got home. I was eating maybe a meal a day, if that. I didn't want to go out. I didn't want to socialize with anybody. I just wanted to lock myself in my room. I was waking up in places I wasn't falling asleep at. I'd wake up under tables. Under couches. In corners of rooms. Just sitting there. I wasn't talking to anybody, and I wasn't coping with it, and I wasn't looking for help because I didn't want to get tagged with anything. I never talked to my family. I pushed them away. I was like, "Stop talking to me. I don't wanna talk to y'all." It got to the point where I couldn't be in crowds. I can't do crowds.

• • •

Even to this day, I have to sit where I can see doors. And it's not because I was shot at or I was in combat. I mean, I'll sit there and tell everybody, "I didn't go door to door; I didn't clear rooms; I wasn't shot. I wasn't anything." But if I'm not in an environment I can control, I get paranoid beyond all reason. . . . I'll make sure that I'm sitting on that first row so I can turn around and see the crowds. . . . I just . . . even thinking about it right now, I'm starting to get antsy, get anxious; it's starting to make me nervous. I remember the first time I heard an explosion at home; I actually hit the deck in full uniform. Oh, it was hilarious because everyone else kind of laughed, and I thought, "Oh, ha, ha, y'know, I slipped and fell," and I just kinda blew it off. I mean some of the guys kinda poked at me a little bit, "You okay?" They could kinda tell, but I continued to go downhill.

• • •

I feel a sense of shame and failure for not suffering more. I've noticed that theme in a lot of people I've talked to. There are the concentric circles of the military. You go into it to have an experience of war because it's so fascinating for everybody, I think, to some degree. Then you go into it and realize there's a smaller circle of the real soldiers, so you try to get into that circle. Then you deploy, so you're in another circle, but inside that circle there's another one. Maybe the Special Forces are in the very inner part of the circle. But even they are very different than the young infantry people. War is never as bad as people thought. Most people imagine it to be just sheer panic, running for your life, being chased by a pack of wild dogs in your underwear. It's not like that; you actually have a huge amount of power that you can exert on others. I miss that power so much; I miss that control over the universe that I felt riding a HMMWV around. There's something about that unchecked power that is really addictive and never comes again. There's never another experience of that, at least in my life, and I think for most people. That's part of the feeling of failure; if we had all this power, why couldn't we do more?

• • •

Special Operations provided for all of us after we got back. . . . It was actually a mandatory session with some type of therapist; we had to go.

• • •

Because of the cadence of the mass casualty situation, I just couldn't be engaged, so I feel like there're so many lost stories. And I go back and I find myself re-guessing and wondering about the decisions I've made, and I hope I didn't do more harm than good. I mean, I try not to get hung up on that because it was so cloudy; there were a lot of ethical issues that surfaced. You know, if you treat this person and then discharge them only to be shot in a Sunni hospital (if they're Shia). . . . Well, is that the right thing to do, to have intervened in the first place?

• • •

I get this letter from the VA. I'd just spent time with my kids, so I got to see my ex-wife, got to see her husband, got to see my kids. I got through all that; I come home, and I get this letter from the VA: "You failed to show up for an appointment last Friday." And I had canceled the appointment a long time before, but this generated a letter. I saw the words "you failed," and I just lost it. I was supposed to go to a birthday party next door for one of my friends, who is leaving for good. I didn't go; I stayed home; "I'm going to bed," I said. I lay down, and I couldn't talk about it. You know, that word, "failed." So I told the psychiatrist, "I got this letter that I failed. And I didn't fail." I couldn't blow it off. People get letters like that all the time. Because it's from an authority source, I just get like I can't handle it, can't handle authority telling me I'm not doing a good job. That's my childhood stuff coming back: authoritarian childhood, looking for it other places, found it in the military. As long as they like me, I'm okay. I've got to be aware of that new identity, of the fragility, that I'm emotionally fragile.

• • •

I woke up in my bathroom, covered in my own blood. And that's when everybody knew. I could count on one hand the number of friends I had when that came up. I lost them all. They all said, y'know, "Best of luck to you. I don't wanna deal with it." I had someone literally tell me, "I don't wanna deal with it." That was probably the lowest point I'd ever been at. One guy put it as a "ticking time bomb." Sometimes anger, sometimes depression. Sometimes solitude. They didn't want to deal with the mood swings. The attitude shifts. The paranoia, almost, in some cases. They didn't want to deal with it. And I lost almost everybody. Everybody that wasn't a veteran, everybody that wasn't affiliated with the military—gone. Family? Gone. They pushed me away even further. Of course I had to tell my unit. Of course, y'know, it's kind of hard to hide scars. Very obvious ones too; nonetheless, I have no recollection of doing it. And that's what I told them; I was like, "I have no recollection of hurting myself. I just remember waking up, and I was bleeding." In fact, my roommate found me that way. And that's when I started seeing a counselor. I finally got to the doctor, and they started getting me on medication. They put me on a medical hold, which is probably the best thing they ever did for me because that took all that stress away. . . . It's been difficult to deal with that kind of a diagnosis. The media hype. The ticking time bomb. When am I gonna set off? If anything, my PTSD has made me more focused. I get blackouts about once a month. They cluster, about three or four within the day or day-and-a-half period. A significant period of events—negative events, if they happen in sequence—can cause some high stress. But with the stress-management techniques

I have, with the things that I can deal with, they don't happen as often. They still come around, but they're not as often, and they're not what was described as "violent" or "aggressive." Like, I'm not waking up and moving. I'm not hurting anything; I'm not hurting anybody. I'm not, y'know, falling asleep in my bed and waking up under the table. Now they're more concentrated at night because that's usually when the medication kinda . . . y'know, take it in the morning, and by the nighttime it's kind of tapering off. I'll usually wake up, and it'll take me two minutes to figure out where I am because I have no idea because my nightmare was so real. I don't know where I'm at, and I have to figure it out, and that's the only thing that still comes around, that kind of freaks me out. I'll wake up sweating, confused, disoriented, nauseated. And until I can get a light on and figure out where I'm at, I'm stumbling around trying to figure things out. When I get stressed, if it's during the day, I can feel the headache start to build. And once that headache starts to build, I can start to note the physiological changes, and I can kind of sit there and go, "Okay, I need a hit," because I have my regular medication, which is Paxil, and then I have the Ativan for the quick-reacting. Like, you feel it coming, and I can sit there and start to shake; I'm starting to have problems concentrating. I can feel it kinda building to where my vision is starting to blur. And I've got, y'know, the breathing exercises. It's amazing what just sitting down and deep breathing, closing my eyes and deep breathing, will do. Sometimes it looks kinda odd 'cause it'll come in the middle of the daytime. It's very rare. It used to be really often in the daytime. The last daytime was probably two months ago, where I could really just feel it coming around, which is good. It means I'm improving, and that makes me happy.

• • •

Some of these memories are still kind of painful. I mean even the ones that I haven't talked about. Still thinking about them.

• • •

Suicides, I don't think, are connected to PTSD. PTSD has become a badge of honor these days. The VA just gives it to you because, number one, you get more disability money for it, and number two, if I am talking to someone who is a vet, they'll ask if you have PTSD, and if I say "No," they'll just instantly assume I didn't see shit or I didn't do anything, because it's like a badge. Anyone who joined post-9/11 knew what they were joining for. The two legitimate cases that have PTSD are people who stayed in after that and they didn't know, they didn't sign up with that intent, and people who signed up to be a food guy, a cook, but ended up seeing it but they weren't expecting it. . . . When your expectations don't line up with the realities, there's something wrong. I, and everyone I know, joined up with the expectation of war.

The people that I know that committed suicide, I know they didn't have PTSD. When we got back, they were fine. It's associated with leaving your friends and not associated with war. When we were all together, they were happy, always having a good time when we got back from Iraq. Everything was fine, and nothing was different. You'll have like two weeks where you think about stuff in detail, but they were perfectly fine. One of them started working in a post office. I mean, there's no one working in a post office that you can talk to. I told him. I call everyone at least once a month. Now I try to call them more frequently. I told him to join the VFW or go to a bar where you know veterans hang out. But, I don't know; he never felt that connection again. If you're with vets and you're just with them for one night a week, I don't think that really does it justice. I know I didn't even want to go to the VFW. I didn't want to see anybody or hang out with anybody that wasn't my friend. I felt like that, and I still kind of feel this way with a lot of veterans. A lot of veterans have seen a lot more than I have, so why would they feel bad for me? They're just going to tell me to man up. I think that mentality from the military kind of transfers over into civilian life. And I don't mean this is just veterans. It's true of African Americans, for example. How do you communicate your reality to someone when it's so foreign to somebody else? How do you translate it? You have an expectation of what their reaction should be, and then their reaction isn't that.

• • •

Fortunately, I never had an MRI done after the blast. I guess they didn't feel I need it. That's just one of the things that I deal with. I have times when I have dizzy spells quite a bit. Running's a thing that I used to enjoy, and it's kind of something that's hard for me to do, just because I feel dizzy quite a bit. I think PTSD and traumatic brain injury symptoms can be so related. . . . You know, . . . do I have PTSD or is it traumatic brain injury? Some of these symptoms . . . it's something that I've always wondered about because of my understanding of class three concussions, the highest concussion you can receive. That always interested me, but I guess that I don't clinically show neurological signs that would make them do an MRI.

• • •

We're having a hard time realizing you can't just tell people what to do. And we're having to learn as confrontational people who deal with problems: there's the military way to do this, there's the civilian way to do it, and you've got to kind of find the in-between. That's one of the things that we talk about. And then we share training. . . . We mostly, we really only talk about training. Nobody really talks about where they were or what they did in Afghanistan and Iraq.

• • •

The hardest thing about coming home was I felt that I started to establish myself in the military; I started to pick up rank; I had billets beyond my rank; I had responsibilities; I was doing well; I was going on boards, winning boards. They have "Marine of the Quarter": you know, you stand before a panel, and you go against people within the battalion and you do general knowledge, your PFT scores and stuff. So I was doing well, and . . . I felt I was established within the military, and when I got out, I felt like I was eighteen, nineteen again. . . . I felt like I stepped back, you know; I felt like my life was on pause, and I just ended up coming back to the same life, without career options at the time. I started working in a dog kennel, just because it was the job that

I could find, and I felt like my duties, my responsibilities, went to zero, and I really didn't have anything.

• • •

The huge sense of entitlement that I felt then lead to disillusionment. I was over there doing all that stuff; I deserve better than this. So any time I have a setback, it's like this huge betrayal. Lowering that has been good; to realize that everybody has hardships in life. Mine just happened to be in this one place, but everybody's got hardships they're working through. I always get this feeling that if people know what I'm like, they're going to fire me. I was pretty good at the Army thing; I was able to function in that environment pretty well. This other environment, I don't know.

• • •

I was in a veterans' writing project when I got back. That was a place where I really started to go into what the meaning of all this stuff was.

• • •

I get maybe three hours of sleep at night, if that. I know some of it is from nightmares. I woke up two weeks straight to the sound of helicopters. There's not a helicopter I know that flies at three a.m. I was pretty sure I was going crazy.

• • •

I haven't really told anyone besides my mom and my best friend this: I have major depression, and for the first time in my life, I actually thought about suicide, and that was a really scary thing for me. I've never thought I would be that person. I fought the VA every inch of the way when they told me that I'm depressed; I'm such a positive person. . . . I was talking to my friend, and I confided in him because I know him like I don't know anyone else. He was my best friend, and I told him that I thought about depression, and he told me a few weeks ago he had a gun in his mouth. And that baffled me because he's such a happy person. I never would have seen it coming. I don't know how many guys out there are experiencing the same thing. Every veteran that I've talked to— and there's a few that will snap out of it faster—but there's quite a few that are, like, "I was on the verge. I tried. It didn't happen." I know guys who pulled the trigger, and it didn't fire.

• • •

We're going to do another pilgrimage in July, a pilgrimage of reconciliation, where they start to go into some of the sacrament of reconciliation, which is confession and then absolution and that ritual. In the Middle Ages, they would go on pilgrimages of penance. We look on that as horrific: making those poor soldiers go on some march so they can come back to church. The thing is they all come to church, and then they don't come back. They walk out because they realize they're different, and "Everybody else around me is real nice, and I'm not." They're going to leave. That's my thing; you can't just welcome them back to church and say, "Come on back; you're fine; start over again." They went to church, and the first thing they did was leave because they felt like they weren't welcome any more. It's really from God; they don't feel welcome from God, whatever that relationship is. So they have to do something to get back to that place. And there's lots of resources for that. The church has had those for years, but nobody's doing them because it sounds offensive to soldiers, like you did something morally wrong when you killed people, which in some sense you did, and in some sense you didn't; that's a question of ethics. The problem is that we have this pacifistic strain in our ethics; I don't know what the word for it is. It's, like, "You guys can do all that for us; don't make me do it." Because you don't have to serve in the military any more, you could not know anyone in the military now. So it's easy to say, "Those people over there can do it, but we're not going to do it because it's wrong." To me, even a Christian ethic can incorporate war into it.

• • •

I lost track of time when I was there; I didn't even know. I would just keep doing everything every day. But when I think back to a memory, I can't pin it down to what time of year it was because it was so hot. Unless it happened in the rainy season; then I'll have a memory where I see a lot of mud. It's almost like my memory is not functioning really well from that time period. I'm trying to work on that a little bit. I have a lot of memories of what happened, of what I saw happen, but they're not in chronological order.

• • •

That's what I missed about the Army so much: the community. It was like instant friends, instant shared experiences. I still get that . . . I-don't-trust-anybody stuff. I go into that. And I go to the VA; I was there this morning talking about some stuff. Those groups are really helpful. On Wednesday one of the doctors described building that safety/comfort zone around yourself that gets smaller and smaller the longer you build it. That's what I was doing in Iraq; that's what I did when I came home. I called it minimalism or downsizing. I was really just trying to make my life so simple, but the problem is it's not simple and stuff happens, and I just got crazy when it did. How to realize that there's a stretch zone that's safe; it's going to be scary, though. Then there's, like, a danger zone that you don't want to go into. But the stretch zone. . . . It all feels like danger. The loss of the illusion of safety. That's a real symptom; there's nothing safe; even though I'm ready for a fight, I also feel threatened by everything . . . one big threat.

• • •

We were exposed to probably the most toxic air our toxicologist had seen in twenty years of working and analyzing air because on the base they burn everything, and there's this huge black cloud of smoke that we took pictures of and that would waft over our tent. And I came back, and not only do I have PTSD, but I came back with asthma; I never had allergies, never had any problems. I have early-onset menopause, so I can't have children. I'm forty-three and in menopause. I now have an autoimmune thyroid problem, and my bone marrow is failing. So I have very real medical problems. I am now starting to go to the VA to try to have them accumulate data because I think it's the burn pit potentially because I don't have any autoimmune problems in my family, no reproductive health issues with my family either, and it's all bizarre that all of this would be happening. I had a friend who developed lymphoma, and she's convinced that it's from the burn pit. I mean, who knows? Maybe it's all a coincidence. I hope it is. But if it's not, I really hope that they are keeping this registry and they can follow people and hopefully treat people. Being on both sides of it—being a physician and also being a patient and being a military person who's had this experience—I understand the mission. I understand, and I'm not saying I agree with it, but I understand that a lot of decisions are made for the composite for the mission as opposed to the individual. I had all these untoward health effects because of this burn pit, because it was the most cost-effective, easy way to get rid of stuff over there, so I was subjected to that toxic air. Yeah, if you're out in the field, you have to have an eighty-pound pack on, not just your flak jacket and your helmet. And mind you, when I went over there I weighed 115 pounds, and I put on fifty pounds on my back. The first time I thought I was going to fall over. I was so strong after that. I even bought a vest to just walk around with because I got into the best shape just by wearing my flak jacket. But, yeah, I'm not surprised that people are having back issues. I'm surprised I don't, but I don't have any muscular or skeletal problems fortunately.

• • •

That's the big lie about war: that there were these good wars like World War II, where people came back fine. "What's wrong with you? Get over it." Well, the truth is they didn't. You read any person who's worked with World War II veterans, and they'll tell you that's not true. Larry Dewey says most of them die within ten years; the seriously mentally injured folks, they die, and you never hear from them. This other group is more resilient, and they look really good. There's a lot of Vietnam veterans who look really good today, and they're doing great, tons of them. And there's a group that isn't. I think the moral injury ramps up when you realize it was all for a bad reason, or you feel like it wasn't worth anything, all these things you did.

• • •

But that was really just the hyperawareness stuff; so much trouble with hyperawareness. You go to the mall with all these people moving around all over the place. The mall is the worst example; that's just the worst location. When you're trying to put out security in a combat zone, you don't have to worry about everything. I worry about my piece of the pie, my little piece of it. Somebody else has got my back, and you've got that trust; somebody on my left, my right. So you walk through the mall with people going different directions. You start trying to keep track of all of it, so my field of view is only so far. You're trusting your ears and different things like that. It starts to . . . for me anyway, it builds. It builds like this frustration that builds as you're trying to track all of this. . . . And what's really frustrating about it is, just like Iraq, you don't know where the threat is; that's what you're looking for—you're trying to identify the threat, but you don't know where it is. Where is the threat from? So the tension just keeps. . . . And for me, it's just like a panic attack; it's like you just want to shut down. . . . You get overwhelmed by all of the pieces of information. I think it's a subconscious thing, but your body in a combat zone learns to take in more than just that peripheral, what you're seeing. I don't want to make it sound like it's a supernatural thing, but you feel like you're trying to pull all of this in, and you're just getting overwhelmed, right? It's really, really scary. I had a lot of problems with that in '05. Once I got over it. . . . You know, I had two incidents with it in 2011. One was really mild, and one was a little bit stronger; it was in a math class, and it was weird. I just got out a notebook and started to write down what I was feeling and never had a problem with it again. One of those weird . . . that's cathartic somehow.

• • •

Most people don't understand, can't even have a way of understanding, what veterans go through. You know, I never really had problems with PTSD. I fought a little bit of hyperawareness stuff when I came back from my second deployment—just trying to keep track of everything, and you can't do it. So it's kind of panicky. But I would say that I came away from my experiences relatively unscathed. With that being said, if you haven't been there, you can't understand the emotional and psychological effects that those types of things have.

• • •

I went from riding pretty high to this plummeting depth—that I had done something wrong, and this was what I got for it. This was payback. It was real strange. I thought I had a good marriage, had done everything right, and all that stuff. I really didn't; it was better than some marriages but not better than others. It lacked . . . I lacked an emotional intimacy and feelings that I think she picked up on. I didn't have any feelings when I got back. I just was glad to be home, and I was just numb and trying to numb even more. I hadn't started drinking yet, but I started shortly after that. I was starting then to numb with drinking, even though I'd never been drunk before. I didn't drink before, but then I started, and that's when I just got better and better at numbing myself.

• • •

I've got a bunch of torn cartilage in my knee; I've got back problems and all sorts of stuff.

• • •

I think that I'm still trying to understand my own PTSD, but as I'm piecing it together, I think it was that constant fear of death, like it would literally drop out of the sky. I think it would have been easier—and again I'm not comparing people's stress or trauma—but to some degree it would be easier if I were in hand-to-hand combat because then I would know my enemy, so to speak. Whereas if you're just busting your ass in a tent trying to put people back together again and you never know when a stray bullet or a mortar's gonna land on you, that's stressful. It's always there, I mean, even though I didn't have it in the forefront of my mind because I had to function, and I had to do my job and survive; that's the problem. I never dealt with the fear, and it's happening now. My PTSD does take me back to the place; I do dissociate, unfortunately, and I do get back to the place where I think I'm dying because of the mortars, and I do think it harkens back to that particular time. I mean the whole time it was an adjustment because we were always being mortared, but that particular day or series of days where we were mortared repeatedly is something I have to work through. It's that threat to life that was constantly there, and then the threat to life that I would see in the injuries, in a composite of all the patients. Again, I didn't think of all of this in a conscious way when I was there, but emotionally, I think, that's what I was needing to process and haven't yet.

• • •

Did it affect me negatively? Yeah. I mean on and off I struggle with alcohol since I got out. I wasn't really aware that I was having much of an issue, but I got out, and I got married not long after I got out. My wife insisted that I go talk to somebody; it was at that point that I realized I was doing crazy stuff. The way you feel good and you feel safe in a combat zone is that you're constantly checking things. Is your rifle clean? Will your rifle work if you have to use it? Is your vehicle good? Everything you can imagine: you're checking, checking, checking, checking, checking. You can never check things enough. And I think that I kind of have an inclination in this way, when I think about OCD stuff in my family, but I find myself walking around our house checking stuff all the time. I would do this several times in the middle of the night. I'd get up and walk the perimeter, go check windows and faucets, burners on the stove, and just over and over and over. It was getting out of control. So I went for a while to a psychologist. I think we had five sessions. That was really good; that helped. She diagnosed me with generalized anxiety disorder. I'm told now that soldiers coming back with that diagnosis are just straight up diagnosed with PTSD. If I had it, I had a very mild case of it. The way insurance worked, I could only see her for five sessions, and I had to talk to a psychiatrist she referred me to, and he was an idiot. He wanted me to take medicine and everything. But I think for the most part I've adapted very well. I have as good a marriage as anybody does. My career is going. Like I said, alcohol has been an issue, but not so much that I've ever gotten into trouble with it.

• • •

We came back a week before the Fourth of July. When I went home to see my parents in Seattle, they were shooting off fireworks. The first couple of days it would wake me up. It never made me scared; it was just like, "Whoa, whoa, something going on." And then I'd realize it was just fireworks, but other than that it hasn't been lasting. Loud noises don't scare me any more. It's just getting your mind to transition back to, "Hey! You don't need to look at the road to see if there's a bomb planted there." Or something like that.

• • •

I talk about everything. I'm really not shell-shocked about anything.

• • •

There's something about the military that leaves a hole in you. As soon you go into basic, it's just a very primal need for love because you were so detached from everyone. That's why I think guys will grab onto the first girl.

• • •

I hadn't dealt with some of the parts that were sad. I hadn't dealt with that while I was in. So when I got out, I was thinking about some stuff from before. The worst was right when we got home. I had to do a suicide investigation on a marine who killed himself right when we got home: interview his girlfriend, interview all his friends. Another marine was going about one hundred miles an hour on his motorcycle and was killed. Another marine had his children taken from him because he and his wife got into it with each other. I had to go with him to Child Protective Services. He was just devastated. He was not ready. . . . It was a sad family situation. He really loved his kids a lot, but I guess he didn't get along with his wife. It was really sad for him to come home and lose his children.

• • •

A lot of us—me and my close friends who were with me or who I met later who were in Iraq and Afghanistan—a lot of us are super cynical. And I think that can be off-putting because a lot have really bad experiences. Whether it's just being in 130-degree heat for too many months or suffering from the bureaucratic nature of the military or just having a lousy co now and then. It makes you cynical, and it beats you down, and it takes a couple years after you get back to kind of even out, to not be so pissed off about it and to start seeing it holistically, I guess.

• • •

I guess the PTSD is really the big elephant in the room for me. I don't really talk about it much. I still am not happy with the fact that I have it, and I don't know if you call it embarrassment or what. It's this complicated relationship I have with my PTSD; it's just I wish it weren't there is the thing. And with any mental health issue, it's always difficult because of stigma. . . . I wish it were something different; I wish it were more tangible. Not that I wish I had cancer or anything, but I wish it were more tangible.

• • •

We had had an argument earlier that day over water or something like that, and I remember I was just, like, . . . I didn't hope that it was him, . . . but when I heard the explosion, he was the one that it happened to in my head. That's something that's really fucked with me really bad. That's something I don't like thinking about actually. I felt so guilty about that for so long. Why did it have to be the guy that I thought of? I didn't want it to be, you know. . . . Obviously we called a Medevac, got him out of there. And then we didn't get the water.

• • •

Having PTSD from that experience has really interfered with my life. So in that regard I'm still carrying it. I'm very annoyed by that because I'm overall proud of my service, and I am really annoyed that I have to be dealing with this problem. So it's changed me because I can't move on with my life until I sort of get to the root of it, I guess. It's horrifying; it's a nightmare. I dissociate, and that's really frightening. It's really hard to explain. I mean, if somebody had explained it to me, I don't think I would've gotten it, but it's kind of like you're in a dream, like you're aware that you're you, but you're doing things, and you're just kind of along for the ride. One person had described it as, like, you're a puppet on a string, and somebody else is pulling the strings. So you react in ways that are very emotional from some experience. And I still don't know my triggers, so it's a mystery when I'm going to dissociate and what triggers that. I've gotten my sleep finally; after four years I am finally able to sleep. It took me a few years. It took me a long time, but now I'm able to sleep. I wasn't able to sleep for so many years, and it was terrible. And occasionally I'll have flashbacks, but those are rare.

Typically for me I have complex PTSD because it's not about one single event; it's sort of an accrual of chronic exposure to the violence of war. So it's not like I can say, "Oh, if I can just face whatever, you know, this traumatic event. . . ." No, it's like the whole war is my event, and it was the state of mind. And so I do have more of the quintessential symptoms that, I guess, women do. From my reading, there's a lot of emotional numbness and apathy and agoraphobia, which is so not me. I mean, I am not this person, but I am now. The me without PTSD is an extremely social, capable, confident, happy person, but the me with PTSD is one who lives in fear, who's afraid to go outside, and that's been tough. I'm trying to get over it in the sense of I'm trying to push through it; I'm trying to acknowledge what's going on. The six months that I was there I just survived and existed and functioned; now I have to feel. I have to feel those six months now, I guess. So it's been a long road. I guess that would be the sum of it; I'm very proud of what I did at the time, but it is pervasive. It's something that has changed my life. Not for the better right now; I mean, I'm going to try and turn it into something good. And I think there's a lot of other vets out there; I mean, I think there's a lot of people out there like me who are quiet and suffering.

18

Thank You for Your Service

For civilians, the proper etiquette when meeting a veteran is to say, "Thank you for your service." Veterans hear this phrasing often, and it has a different ring with each iteration. It almost always sounds sincere, but it may also sound perfunctory, like a closing door rather than an opening to an exchange, the end of a conversation that never got started. Sometimes the tone carries not just dismissal, but also pity, an uncomfortable sentiment to receive from a stranger. Or there may be a little note of relief: not having traveled in those boots, the civilian is relieved not to imagine their heavy gait. Then there is the awkward process of formulating a response. Should it be "You are welcome?" For what? It certainly was not "my pleasure," although that is a routine way to describe a small service. It is not very gracious to admit that I hardly did it for you or even for my country, as such.

I THINK IT WAS *Time* magazine that had an article last year about how the military culture is so separated, and what the people really mean when they say "thank you" is, "Thank you for me not having to do that. That's just such an icky job; I'm glad I didn't have to do that." Very few people, and I don't hold it against them that they don't know, but they don't know what it means when I say, "Yeah. I went to Iraq twice." And I don't want them to know everything about that. I don't want them to know that. That's part of the whole purpose of serving, that selfless sacrifice, that "Yes. I'm doing it so that you don't ever have to, partially because you never could."

• • •

Almost everybody says, "Thank you for serving." Almost everybody doesn't mean it. Almost everybody knows that you're supposed to say that. It's like an atheist saying "Bless you" after you sneeze. And it feels that way. You're like, "Yeah, sure, whatever." You're, "What you really mean. . . ."

• • •

Most people that I know didn't join for God, honor, and country. They joined because they in some capacity wanted to experience war. So thanking you for your service, you feel kind of bad that you didn't join for the reasons that they think you joined.

• • •

The first thing I'll try and do is shift the conversation toward, "Baghdad is a really impressive city." You'd be surprised how many people don't care to know about that. Or you'll tell them about a school you visited and just how cute the kids are. And some people want to hear more, and other people don't. Most people are fishing for, "Tell me about that really cool, badass combat experience that happened." And it's not that I'm frustrated that I don't have that story to tell. I'm perfectly happy that I don't have that story to tell. But there's more to it than just that.

• • •

Most people who ask, I just tell them I did some world traveling. Some people will dig a little deeper and ask, "So where have you been?" I'll tell them, "Oh, you know, the usual places—Japan, South Korea, the Philippines, Germany, Tajikistan, Afghanistan—you know stuff like that."

• • •

I just wish we could have a conversation like regular people, you know. I honestly feel that when you look at military schools, they shoot for a 98–99 percent retention rate. Almost nobody fails out. This is not something that every person can't do. This is something that many people who are well below average can do and be quite successful at. A sergeant of mine who I really liked in the Army used to say, "The Army gives assholes a chance to succeed." And that's really true. The Army turns assholes into heroes. Good people can do good stuff too, but I just kind of wish there wasn't all this pomp and ceremony about having been in a combat zone. It's really not that big a deal. I try not to ever act irritated. I mean, people are just trying to be polite. You have to understand too that maybe a lot of my irritation with this comes from my own particular perspective. . . . I had it a lot easier than a lot of people did. I was not seeing people next to me get killed and stuff like that. Nobody in my unit got killed.

• • •

They feel sorry that I was over there. They feel like they have to apologize for my injury, which I get, I understand. Or they'll simply just ignore the fact that I was injured, and it just becomes really awkward for them. When there's someone who is disabled in a room or in a crowd, . . . a few people will gravitate to them, but more often than not a lot of the people pretend that they're not even there, which is funny because when I meet new people, I shake with my nub. When I stopped seeking the approval of man was when I began to realize that I don't need the approval of man; I have the approval of my heavenly Father. And I no longer seek people to thank me; it just happens. And when it happens, it's an opportunity to share with them what I'm sharing with you. If they want.

I love kids; I love their reaction. I love little toddlers because they'll come up to me, and they'll touch it, and they'll be like, "What happened?" And I get to tell them: "Well, I got a boo-boo while I was fighting, and they had to remove it." And a lot of them will be like, "Well, where did it go?" So then I get to explain to them where it went, and it's an awesome opportunity for me to speak through the kids to the parents. In my mind, I'm a perfect opportunity to tell parents and allow them to explain to their kids about disabilities. So I love kids.

I don't go into extreme detail about the gore and the calamity of the situation.

• • •

I make light of everything, and that's not honest either, but I'm always afraid to be the crazy veteran in the camouflage jacket that's yelling at everybody.

• • •

I believe every person has this innate quality to want to protect that which they love. As a soldier who went to Iraq, the greatest sacrifice and gift is to be able to die for another person. There will be men and women who sacrifice their lives, who sacrifice their limbs, who sacrifice their mental state so that the person walking next to them, who doesn't even know that they've done that, can continue to live that lifestyle. And do we go unrecognized? I mean, yeah, absolutely. . . . It's really weird for me to say this, but it's okay because doing something where nobody will ever know that you did it has such a greater value than millions of people knowing that you did it.

• • •

I didn't fight off the Nazis. Afghanistan was a retaliatory strike. I think I understand where people are coming from when they say that, but I hate hearing it. I just wish that when people found out that I was in the military, they would say, "Oh. Badass." Leave it at that. Sometimes people tell me, "I was going to join." And that irritates me too. I don't want to hear that. I don't care. Especially because it took me so long to figure out.

• • •

I was in Napa with my parents; we were on this wine-tasting deal not long after I had come home from Afghanistan, which is weird: to go from austerity to one of the most comfort-driven places on the earth. We were at this bed and breakfast, and there was this guy who didn't really talk much. His wife was talking a lot. She and my dad were arguing about politics or something. The husband came and talked to me later. My dad had told him that I was in the Marine Corps. And he was like, "Yeah, I was a pilot in Vietnam." He had this whole story about being shot down . . . this really interesting, really sad story. But he had never said a word to anyone else the whole trip. I had that experience a couple of times, usually with older guys. The occasional World War II vet—there are not many of those left around—an older Vietnam or Korean War veteran usually. . . . There's a silent understanding that I appreciate. It's almost like a brotherhood, partly of having been in, partly of knowing what it's like not to talk about it a lot to most people. There's that understanding.

19

True War Stories

Embarking on this project, we were warned to beware of the exaggerated war story told for self-aggrandizing purposes: Everyone is a Navy SEAL. Marine Corps sniper. Special Forces. Space ship door gunner. We found instead that veterans tend to tell stories at their own expense. When there is a story of bravery or valor, it is always about someone else, often someone who has died. Fitting experience into a story line is how we make sense of what has happened. But so much of what happens at war is incomprehensible, so how do you talk about what happened when it is not a story? Telling a true war story, as Tim O'Brien reminds us, is nearly impossible: "In any war story, but especially a true one, it's difficult to separate what happened from what seemed to happen. What seems to happen becomes its own happening and has to be told that way. The angles of vision are skewed. . . . In the end, of course, a true war story is never about war. It's about the special way that dawn spreads out on a river when you know you must cross the river and march into the mountains and do things you are afraid to do."

LIKE MANY VETERANS, I have my kind of war shtick, the stuff I've understood well enough myself to then tell somebody else.

• • •

Do you guys know what an RG33 is? It's like the big, up-armored school bus. They have three hydraulic doors. They're so heavy that they have to be on hydraulics. Then they have hatches on top; if you can't bench press 185 pounds, you can't get the thing up. We were going across the Euphrates, and I'm not claustrophobic, but I'm terrified of a situation I can't get out of. If this thing goes in the water, you can't get out of that situation; you're drowning. So we're going across the Euphrates, and we start getting potshots, which in an up-armored vehicle is not a big deal at all. Somebody's calling it out. Then all of a sudden, there's an RPG that's coming, and it hits the bridge, and all I saw was a big cloud of dust and then more blue than I saw before. I could have sworn I felt the bridge shake, so I scream—it's hard for me to cuss here—"We're gonna effing die! We're gonna effing die! Get the eff out! We're gonna effing die!" So I throw open the hatch; I throw my weapon out; I pop up, and I run 4:40 off this bridge. We get to the end, and I still had my headset on. It took forever, but the gunner finally started shooting at where the RPG came from; it took forever, but they finally catch up to me . . . and everyone was laughing hysterically, and they say, "Go back and see the bridge!" So I go back, and the guardrail was bent; that was it. So we get back to North Carolina. A couple months go by, and we all decide to take a scuba-diving trip to Key West. There's this big bridge. All of a sudden everyone just starts opening up: "We're gonna effing die! We're gonna effing die!"

• • •

I was in intel school at Fort Huachuca, Arizona, when 9/11 happened. I was on a shift where we started out at four in the morning and broke for lunch at noon. And at noon the NCO in charge came in and just kind of said the Pentagon has been attacked and the World Trade Center is on fire. We started laughing; we thought it was some kind of training exercise.

• • •

We saw a man in black pop out, and he had an RPG, and he shot it at us. And, you know, rocket-propelled grenade launchers do not travel very fast. The way I remember it, it was basically watching this slow rocket come at you but not slow enough to react and get out of the way. But there just happened to be a telephone pole with a piece of rebar . . . and the grenade hit the rebar and just shattered and ended up peppering the ground around us. My friend Dave got a couple of burns from it, but nothing. . . . So it just kinda shattered, and it was one of those things; we were terrified but laughing at the same time: "Wow! Did that really happen?" Even though it was a dangerous situation, at the time, I guess, our release was to laugh about things and to experience it that way. I mean, just to see the machines, the bombs being dropped, the helicopters flying over, shooting their guns and stuff. . . . I feel for whoever was on the other side, but at the same time it was the front row to the greatest action movie I've ever seen.

• • •

I was on a plane in Germany when the doctor walked in and said, "You know, I'm going to try it here." So they took me off the plane, and I had surgery there. It was over Christmas, and I don't know if they just try to keep you a little happy; maybe they gave us a little more drugs than they were supposed to, but it was the best Christmas I remember. So they had Christmas carolers and Santa Claus and morphine. I just remember calling home saying, "This is the best Christmas I've ever had." After that I had a second surgery after I got out, through the VA, so I can breathe a little bit better.

• • •

There was a bag. I just remember seeing a scout walk up to it, and he just opened the bag up, looked in it, and I was like, "What is he doing?" And he closed the bag up, tied it back, turned around, and started running. And it was an IED. And we always laugh at him because he took the time to tie it back, like it would help him.

• • •

In Afghanistan there was a time I was asked to come out and be an adviser for another sort of economic development project thing. We just walked, and walking there is not an easy thing to do because it's kind of mountainous and rugged terrain. And the Army combat uniform that I had, it was not the newer one that's, I guess, supposedly better. The one that I had, the gray one, is not known for its durability. So we're walking up these steps to get to the village, and I take a step, and I heard the loudest rip of my life. I ripped the crap out of the front of my pants. . . . It was the seam that goes; . . . see this seam right here? That's what it was. Keep in mind I'm wearing forty pounds' worth of gear and stuff like that, and the lifesaver in this, of course, was we had these Kevlar groin protectors, which hang in front at the bottom of your armor. I've heard stories that it's effective when it needs to be, but nobody thinks that, you know; it's just kind of there, dangling, but it was the only thing that saved my dignity because, of course, . . . we were going to meet with a local elder who was kind of in charge of the area; he was the spiritual guide and leader and wanted to show us the irrigation line that they wanted to do. "Have a seat." "Okay!" And the funny thing is, I was contorting my body into positions to make sure I was covering everything that I possibly could, and it was like, "No, it's fine; I'll stand!" And they were like, "No, sit," and I was like, "Okay." I can't say no, so I sit down, and it's difficult—you're very top-heavy in that case—and for a while I was trying to do this. "So, tell me about your irrigation project." . . . And it's also not comfortable when you're wearing all that stuff. So I'm sitting down cross-legged, with my groin protector maintaining my last shred of dignity. And as we're walking back, it's only getting worse, and there's a group of kids who see it, and they're just laughing.

• • •

They sent letters home to the families, and my parents decided to send me one of these letters. And in the letter. . . . I should lead this with the whole story. First of all, we were given eight HMMWVs to start when we got to theater. We took our HMMWVs apart and put them back together, and we had two working HMMWVs. We had one that couldn't turn; we had one that wouldn't start. We had one that didn't have air-conditioning, . . . that was one of the two that we considered working. I'm in the turret of one of these working HMMWVs, and I'm talking to the guys over the radios, and we're sitting there talking about the letter. And the letter states, "Soldiers have increased morale and confidence in their unit." Which we all thought was hilarious, but as soon as I finished that sentence, they turned on the second HMMWV, and its engine fell out. Yeah. We're all just sitting there. . . . We all just started laughing; our sergeant had to get out of the truck because he was laughing so hard.

• • •

Combat soldiers wear distinct uniforms. We know who each other is, so we all go running behind this bunker. There's, like, eight of

us behind this bunker, and this guy comes out in a normal uniform and gets behind the bunker with us. Our sergeant is like, "Get back inside." That's not the words he used, but I don't feel like cussing. . . . The guy who comes running out looks my sergeant straight in the eye and says, "Don't worry sergeant; I played *Call of Duty*. I'll be okay." All eight soldiers behind that barricade just kind of like stopped everything they were doing.

• • •

I'm scared to death of spiders. Absolutely terrified of spiders. And camel spiders are mean-looking. Me and him were setting up another machine gun nest, and I look up, and I see a camel spider, like, thirty yards away. So I point at him like, "You! You stay over there." He, like, looked at me, raised his leg and did that . . . so I assumed he understood me. So I go back to setting up my nest, and I look up, and he's closer. I'm like, "Hey! You stay over there." And he, like, looks at me again, does the little leg thing, so I'm like, "Okay, we're good." I look down for, like, two minutes, and when I look back up, he's sitting on the sandbag right in front of me. So I have a little heart attack moment, and instead of being smart and slapping it with my hand, I decided to stand up with the machine gun and start firing. My loader was watching all of this, by the way, and he thought it was the most hilarious thing he'd ever seen. Well, I fired, I think it was thirty rounds into the sandbags. The spider was gone. I don't know if I hit it; I don't know if it ran away; I don't know what happened to it. Since I fired the machine gun, everybody was like, "Oh, crap, we're under attack." So everyone comes running out . . . and they're in various states of undress. There's a dude that came out with body armor, and that's all he had on. They all come running out, and I'm just standing there all guilty-looking, looking down, and everybody was like, "What happened?" I was like, "There was a spider. He's gone now." My loader has not let me live that down for, like, two years. My sergeant told me to take off my bra and panties.

• • •

We went through an Iraqi Army checkpoint, and there was this young soldier who looked like he was eighteen talking to this really old man in a long white or brownish robe, an older guy who looked like he was in his seventies or eighties, maybe eighties, and they're talking kinda animatedly. It's very common there for everyone to be right up in each other's face, talking with their hands. The soldier looked over at us as we came slowly through—we were creeping through—and saw my assistant. This is my interpretation of it: he saw a female, an American female. I was always shocked by how the Iraqi men . . . just groped her when we played soccer together; they treated her like a prostitute, kind of. I don't know what the deal was with that psychology about American women . . . maybe because she was wearing pants, dressed like a man. I don't know. Something. That always bothered me. And I always told her, "You know, you can point your gun at somebody if they're doing something to you." There was something going on with that dynamic. So this young guy at the checkpoint looked at her, and then he just punched the guy in the stomach, the old guy. He doubled over, and we were gone. I remember the look in his eye, like, "I'll show you." This juvenile. . . . It resonated with some of the feelings I was having of indestructibility and power. For some reason, that just stuck in my mind. I just think that was when I realized that we were in this power dynamic that was completely off center. And we were part of that too. I was participating in that small act of abuse of power. It was a tiny, little thing in the grand scheme of things, but it was a symbol of all of us.

You know, we would just clear cars away. . . . We had these police lights on our vehicle, so we could drive through with sirens; you know, everyone gets out of the way. I think that did something to me.

There's that idea of fractured narrative: you kind of bounce around to different things, and there are these gaps that are unresolved conflict. So I'm trying to make sense of that. There's something about war and women; Mars and Aphrodite. My chaplain assistant was hit on constantly by everybody, and every female was. They would put notes in the HMMWV, and I'd say, "Are you sure those aren't for me?" I fell in love with people over there because we worked together, and you were having these feelings that were overwhelming. War is mysterious. Now I describe it: to be in a war is like being in a brothel. How would you ever describe that to somebody? The good times and the bad times because there are good times and bad times. There's a certain kind of experience of those kinds of places that everybody's interested in. We're all kind of fascinated by those worlds. Visiting a brothel is not the same as working in one. You can say, "Oh, I visited one." In some ways I visited war; I'm starting to realize that I was a participant in it too. I was part of the machinery of it, and that's that moral injury part . . . just participating in these things. And then when you expand it to America, we're all participating in war. We're all part of it as much as the guy who punched that old guy. We're kind of in on it. I don't know what can be done about that completely.

I stopped telling stories because they didn't make any sense, like the story about the guy who got punched; that story doesn't make any sense as a war story or a story of deployment because it's just like . . . what's going on like that? Why is that a bad story? Why is that the one that sticks in my head? For my own self, I try to use it as a way to interpret the whole experience and my loss of my belief in God at that time. I stopped talking about it when people asked me.

· · ·

We were on a dismounted patrol through Fallujah, and this guy comes running up and starts yelling. So we called the interpreter over. The interpreter walks over, and the guy starts talking to him. And the interpreter just starts laughing. So we're sitting there like, "Tell us! We want to laugh too!" He's like, "He wants to marry that guy for two camels." So we're all sitting there like, "Heh, heh. Wait! What kind of camels are we talking about here?" And the guy's like, "What?" And we're like, "We're negotiating." And we're like, "Are we talking about the white camels or the brown camels because the white camels are worth more." So we're sitting there; we ended up negotiating it to two white camels and two hundred dollars cash. We were negotiating for a good thirty minutes. He was mad at us. He was like, "You guys suck!" We're like, "You're a team player; you need to take one for the team! We're getting camels out of this."

· · ·

I kind of don't really know what to say because I feel like I don't want to burden people with my story. I don't want to expose them to the horrors because I've had people cry when I talk, and I realize, "Oh, my God, this is something beyond what people can tolerate."

· · ·

This is a true story. I'm almost reluctant to say this because, I don't know, I've told other people this, but I've never really been able to explain it. When I left Iraq, the Army had us fill out this questionnaire about things we'd seen. I'm sure the reason they did it is that they're trying to protect themselves from claims of PTSD or whatever later. It was all this different dramatic stuff you'd seen. The one that stands out for me is that one of the questions was, "Did you see a dead body?" You know, I had to think about it. You would think that that would be immediate: yes or no? But it just seemed like if someone had said, "Did you have a cup of coffee for breakfast?" You'd have to think. . . . My tour of duty was very soft by almost any standard, but the answer is "Yes." But I literally had to think about it. And I don't think that means that I was in some conscious way making myself inured to it; it's just after a while it's amazing how you adapt to the circumstances.

• • •

I've always said that if I were to write a book about the experience, it would be about three volumes of nine pages, and almost all of it would be just, "Blah, blah, blah." It would only have about two paragraphs that really had. . . .

• • •

Have you ever seen the movie *Platoon?* Not a very good movie, but there's one line in it. . . . After being in the Army, I saw it late one night on TV, and I was like, "I get this now." Charlie Sheen is out there working with an older black soldier, and the soldier says, "How did a rich white kid like you end up sitting in the Army?" And he says, "Well, I just didn't think only the poor kids should go off and serve, so I signed up." And the guy responds to him: "Hell, you have to be rich in the first place to think that way." I understand that now, and I have a totally new perspective on it. And I think there's this very constructed, ultimately very heavily elitist, way of thinking about the military.

• • •

An Afghani family—it was a grandfather and grandmother, father, and two children—hit an IED driving their vehicle and came to us for medical help. The two children were mobile. They came up to the hill. We actually met them at the bottom of the hill. We brought down all our medical equipment and stuff. The grandfather died in the IED; the grandmother was the least injured; she was walking around. And the two kids were mobile, but they were bleeding out their ears, so they definitely had brain trauma or concussions, but they were able to talk and walk; they were sensitive to light. The dad had a big hole in the back of his shoulder, and his left leg was fractured and fragmented. So he was on the ground, and we worked on him for a while to try to get him to live. He was doing decently well, and then we got the helicopters in and got him evacuated with the kids. I did a lot of medical stuff with that guy. . . . It was kinda hard. He ended up passing away. It happens. He was big, I remember. He was like 220 pounds. He was huge. There were four of us on the stretcher trying to get him to the helicopter, and we had to take, like, five breaks, because he was really big. The kids are fine. They ended up being good. It was a unique thing because we don't usually see that. Usually when someone got hit, they didn't come to us for help.

• • •

One of my contacts in Sadr City when I was in Baghdad was an eighteen-year-old boy, seventeen-year-old boy, and he would meet me. He was poor; he would come from Sadr City, and he did it for free. So it wasn't like the normal contact or source who just wanted money and was part of a cell, you know, operating in Baghdad or Abu Ghraib. He really just would ask for, like, a wheelchair for his brother, stuff for his family, but never monetary. He said, "Hey, if you give me a car, I can get deeper into the city." So I would do stuff like that. And he saved a lot of lives. He would call and say, "Hey, the Mahdi militia is having an L-shaped ambush on this street. I see Americans heading that way." And then I would call command up there in Sadr City and say, "Hey, you gotta watch out; here's the Mahdi militia." They'd call me back an hour later and say, "That was perfect, spot on. We detained and killed someone." I don't know where he is today. He lived through it. Yeah, I think those stories are few and far between. Most of the guys I was dealing with were, you know, doing it for funding. If I could pay him more than Al Qaeda or one of those dudes, then he'd work for me: "Hey, we're set up here; there's about to be an ambush." You know, stuff like that. . . . But that kid, great. And that's how I felt, and I still feel; outside of the government, a lot of Iraqis really wanted us there to get rid of, you know, these militias and Al Qaeda and stuff like that. What I most remember and what I'm most proud of is saving American lives. My Iraqi friend in Sadr City called me daily and sometimes two or three times a day with time-sensitive and life-saving information. I'm positive during that deployment I saved hundreds of lives. I don't think I'm overstating the number.

One thing that I saw was the brutality of the U.S. soldiers to the Iraqi people, which you probably won't hear that much about. That first mission, we secured a home, and basically the occupants of that home were removed. We stayed there for about two or three days. Leading up to that period, I had found a cache, which is a large weapons deposit. I remember we weren't able to find out who it belonged to, so basically what my higher-ups decided was, "Well, we're going to blame it on the people who were in the home." I remember watching them, and the way that they treated the Iraqi people was just not okay. There was pushing; there was taunting. It really gave me a perspective of, like, this is really a war. All else aside, this war is about two cultures, two societies, two types of people who have bad blood toward each other. I learned there's always going to be that as long as there's man because we're not perfect. You know, I get it. I get the fact that we lost men—and I've lost brothers—to the war. But at a point it's, like, how far does humanity take hate and tyranny? Yeah, we're fighting against it, but it's another thing when we demonstrate it to other people. I use that story; I tie it into the Bible and how I've come to love my enemies; I've come to pray for the salvation of the men who tried to kill me. Because it's so contrary to what people want me to be like. If I was among fellow soldiers—and I have been—I've told that story; they look at me like, "Well, they deserve it." And I'm like, "Well, no; they're still human beings, and we need to respect them as such." It's not very popular, but it's the truth.

• • •

We were carrying him to the Medevac helicopter, and he had got shot all in the abdomen. Doc had had to cut his pants off. His genitals were out. You don't get to shower a lot there. I remember I was holding him on the litter, and we were running him to the Medevac helicopter, and I remember the smell that hit me was horrible. I was like, "Oh, my god, dude, your junk stinks!" It actually wasn't his junk. He had defecated on himself because he was full of holes. He kind of laughed and covered himself up. Obviously it was not his junk that was making that smell, but the fact that that's what my mind went to. . . . I feel a lot of guilt about this actually. When he got shot, I went around the corner, and he had short boots (or small feet), and one of my best friends has got small feet also, and I thought it was my best friend, and I remember being like, "Oh fuck! No!" When I found out who it was, there was a little bit of relief.

• • •

This happened in two separate instances. We built this thing; we called it the Flying J, like the truck stops. It got built by our battalion. It was really just a checkpoint to divert cars through; it was on the highway between our COP and the FOB. I remember at the beginning of the year it was flooded; the whole strip between us was flooded. There should have been some engineer in charge of this. I would think if you're using who knows how many dollars of resources to build this fortified truck stop that you're going to turn over to the police, to the ANP, that you would make sure it wasn't in a flood plain. Well, they didn't check that, and as soon as it rained, the entire thing was about four feet under water. I remember we would drive by it on the way to the FOB, and we'd be like, "Well, there it is." We did the same thing toward the end of our deployment. I guess everybody had forgotten that when we first got there, it was funneling all the water from the desert down into the Arghandab River. It was a creek. It was wet. We worked so hard. It was pretty impressive. It was a well-constructed strong point, I guess: very tall walls. Normally, the standard for a COP is two Heskos wide at the base from the outside to the inside and one Hesko on top. That's the standard for a COP. Then our COP had a chain-link fence around that with barbed wire. Strong points don't have the same standard; they're smaller. You put them up quicker; you use two eight-foot sections of Hesko and then a four-foot Hesko on top. But we built it to the standard of a COP; it was very impressive. I remember thinking the whole time, and me and my buddies would talk about it: "Wasn't this a river when we came here?" And then, sure enough, it flooded. It was just so stupid. I feel like it was weird that nobody thought about that, that nobody listened to somebody say, "Hey, isn't this going to be under water?" We got told from Higher that they wanted a strong point down there. They wanted progress; they wanted updates; it had to happen quickly; no time to bring in engineers or anyone who knew anything. So we built it, and it flooded. I'm pretty sure it got abandoned as soon as we left. We forced the ANA—Afghan National Army—to go down there and occupy it. We were like, "No, you have to keep people down there." And they were like, "We're not going to use it unless you come down." So we had to send a platoon down there on rotation to keep them happy. As soon as we left, the guys who replaced us from 82nd Airborne, they didn't care about that. They didn't take it apart. For all we know the Taliban are using it against them. I don't know.

• • •

People want to know about the firefights; they want to know about the action, and mostly I want to talk about the dumb stuff and how miserable we were on a day-to-day basis, how much it sucked. It must feel like I'm beating a dead horse to a lot of people because how much can something suck? The trudging. Those irrigation ditches are about two feet of mud, so you're up to your knees with a hundred pounds on your back; it's horrible, and it sucks. When you're in the pomegranate orchards, it's the mud; but the way they grow them or the way they maintain them, they have really low-lying leaves, so you're bent over the whole time, and it's just physically exhausting, mentally exhausting. That's where I gained the most; it's that perspective. Looking back on it, you don't remember the bad things; you remember the fun times you had, I think. That's how I look back on it. I definitely romanticize it a little bit. I mean the firefights were the cool part; that's when your exhaustion is just gone. You could be running on an hour of sleep a night for weeks, and as soon as the first shots are fired, the adrenalin, it's just awesome. It's so hard to describe now. I'd be super-, hyperalert. I know everybody wants to hear about the combat, but what I want to tell people most about is just the stupid, stupid stuff; how it was just a major disappointment for me. I'm telling you all these horrible, stupid things about my experience, but I'm still really proud of it, and I feel really guilty about that pride because I don't feel like I deserve to be proud of it. I don't really feel like I went through anything too extreme; physically, I was pushed, but mentally I was never pushed to the breaking point or anything. When you read something like *With the Old Breed*, or I'm reading *The Guns of August* right now, or I also just finished *Storm of Steel*, by Ernst Jünger, and I just can't compare my experience with any of those experiences. I guess I kind of was looking for something like that.

20

Out of Sync

There are some experiences that don't translate very well; you just had to have been there. There is so much basic background that is needed before a person can get to the heart of the matter. Filling in those gaps is exhausting. The larger issues of the justice of war seem separate somehow from an individual's experience of being at war. What cause is worth what sacrifice? What ends justify what means? But a veteran usually does not want to narrate for that larger purpose of evaluation or to become an object lesson for some political agenda. It is his or her particular story that gets submerged beneath the double burdens of explanation and moral judgment. So we end this collection where it began: with that stubborn sense of misunderstanding among people who might wish to communicate.

WHY ARE WE SO out of sync with the civilian population we serve?

• • •

There's absolutely no frame of reference, so you have to go all the way down to the basics. And once you get to the basics, there's really nothing to talk about because to go from the basics to real experiences and real interaction takes too much time and oftentimes is futile; people don't want to listen that long.

• • •

She doesn't have any idea what I did; she doesn't have any idea of the sacrifices I made. She doesn't know that the morning my first daughter was born, I was in a firefight for my life. She doesn't know any of that stuff. As I talk to people day in and day out and they want to know what it's like or whatever, they have the same issues. They have no idea what it's like, so their questions are insensitive, uneducated, and essentially rude. I understand that they may not mean them that way. And maybe the most annoying person is the guy who wants to be in the military. He's maybe nineteen or twenty years old, and he's really respectful of what I've done, things like that. But he's still asking questions that make me want to punch him. I don't mean that in a really violent sense; it's just like, "Dude, really?"

• • •

I'm seeing that a lot with our wounded warriors. A lot of them are moving right back to San Antonio, and I'm asking them why. A lot of the severely wounded, the burned and amputees, are moving back to San Antonio because it's a military city and culture. The society accepts them more and doesn't call them "baby killers" and stuff. So they're moving back to San Antonio because they feel like they're safer here psychologically, if not for any other reason. So you learn real quick the ways to say certain things and do certain things. Your views, you just don't speak them at all because of the way you're viewed. People look at me and say, "You're a lot different than I thought you were. When I learned you were in the military, I did not like you. But now I feel much better around you. . . . It's just so interesting talking to you. Can we have coffee some time?" No kidding.

• • •

It really angers me because it's interfering with my life. Like, I don't have time to be scared . . . and I have to make time for it because otherwise it's just gonna continue to interfere with my life. It's hard because if you're at war, I guess on some level you're like, well, it's okay to be scared or be going through this process because other people can understand that we could all die in a second, whereas here in suburbia nobody has that sense. So I feel, again, acutely aware of that. And I guess I'm very self-conscious, and I can't stand that either, being very aware that people don't understand what I'm going through right now. So I'm still trying to figure it out.

GLOSSARY

249 or M249: a squad automatic weapon

50-cal: 50-caliber gun

ACU: Army combat uniform

AK-4: assault rifle

APO: Army Post Office

ANA: Afghan National Army

ANP: Afghan National Police

AO: area of operations

AQI: Al Qaeda in Iraq

BDA: battle damage assessment

C-130: military transport aircraft

C-4: plastic explosive

CAB: combat action badge

CE: Civil Engineering

CENTCOM: Central Command

CHU: containerized housing unit

CIB: combat infantry man badge

CLC: Concerned Local Citizens

CO: commanding officer

Comm: Communication

COP: combat outpost

COS: contingency operating site

CPA: Coalition Provisional Authority

C-RAM: counter rocket, artillery, and mortar

DO: director of operations

DoD: Department of Defense

E-4: In the Army this enlisted rank is also referred to as corporal

E-9: In the Air Force this enlisted rank is also referred to as chief master sergeant

EFP: explosively formed penetrator

EOD: Explosive Ordnance Disposal

ER: emergency room

FOB: forward operating base

Full Bird: a full colonel, as opposed to a lieutenant colonel, so named because of the distinctive eagle insignia on the uniform

Higher: short for higher command or senior officers

GRE: Graduate Record Exam

Green Zone: Area in both Baghdad and Kabul where Provisional Authority is housed

green zone: Agricultural zone along the banks of a river in Afghanistan

HET: Human (Intelligence) Exploitation Team

HK: Heckler and Koch handgun

HMMWV: high mobility multipurpose wheeled vehicle, commonly referred to as a Humvee

ICOM: Integrated Communications

ICU: Intensive Care Unit

ID: Infantry Division

IDF: indirect fire

IED: improvised explosive device

IRAM: improvised rocket-assisted munition

IV: intravenous (tube)

KBR: Kellogg Brown & Root

M1113: HMMWV variant

M-4: assault rifle

M-16: assault rifle

MATV: mine-resistant ambush-protected vehicle

MEU: Marine Expeditionary Unit

MOS: Military Occupation Specialty

MP: Military Police

MRE: meal ready to eat

MRI: magnetic resonance imaging

MSR: Main Supply Route

MULTI CAM: Camouflage designed to be used in multiple, or a wide range of, conditions

NCO: noncommissioned officer

OCD: obsessive-compulsive disorder

PFT: physical fitness test

PT: physical training

PX: Postal Exchange

PTSD: post-traumatic stress disorder

QRF: Quick Reaction Force

R&R: rest and relaxation

RG33: mine-resistant light-armored vehicle

RPG: rocket-propelled grenade

RTO: radiotelephone operator

S-3: battalion operations and training officer

SAW: squad automatic weapon

Scud: long-range surface-to-surface guided missile

SEAL: Sea, Air, and Land teams of the U.S. Navy

Stryker Brigade Combat Team: Infantry unit that uses a Stryker armored vehicle

SUV: sport utility vehicle

TCN: Third-Country National

TOC: Tactical Operations Center

UAVC: unmanned aerial vehicle with a camera

V-BEID: vehicle-borne improvised explosive device

VFW: Veterans of Foreign Wars service organization

XO: executive officer

Milton Keynes UK
Ingram Content Group UK Ltd.
UKHW031532120324
439084UK00014B/286